Mass-Elite Representation Gap in Old and New Democracies

NEW COMPARATIVE POLITICS

Series Editor   Michael Laver, New York University

Editorial Board   Ken Benoit, Trinity College, Dublin
Gary Cox, Stanford University
Simon Hix, London School of Economics
John Huber, Columbia University
Herbert Kitschelt, Duke University
G. Bingham Powell, University of Rochester
Kaare Strøm, University of California, San Diego
George Tsebelis, University of Michigan
Leonard Wantchekon, Princeton University

The New Comparative Politics series brings together cutting-edge work on social conflict, political economy, and institutional development. Whatever its substantive focus, each book in the series builds on solid theoretical foundations; uses rigorous empirical analysis; and deals with timely, politically relevant questions.

Mass-Elite Representation Gap in Old and New Democracies

Critical Junctures and Elite Agency

Edited by Jaemin Shim

University of Michigan Press
Ann Arbor

For questions or permissions, please contact um.press.perms@umich.edu

Published in the United States of America by the
University of Michigan Press
Manufactured in the United States of America
Printed on acid-free paper
First published August 2024

A CIP catalog record for this book is available from the British Library.

Library of Congress Cataloging-in-Publication Data

Names: Shim, Jaemin, 1983– editor. https://orcid.org/0000-0002-8401-
    4447 | Michigan Publishing (University of Michigan), publisher.
Title: Mass-elite representation gap in old and new democracies : critical junctures and
    elite agency / Edited by Jaemin Shim.
Description: Ann Arbor [Michigan] : University of Michigan Press, 2024. |
    Series: New comparative politics | Includes bibliographical references and index.
Identifiers: LCCN 2024008389 (print) | LCCN 2024008390 (ebook) |
    ISBN 9780472076949 (hardcover) | ISBN 9780472056941 (paperback) |
    ISBN 9780472904587 (ebook other)
Subjects: LCSH: Representative government and representation. | Democracy. |
    Elite (Social sciences)—Political aspects. | Political participation.
Classification: LCC JF1051 .M325   2024 (print) | LCC JF1051 (ebook) |
    DDC 321.8—dc23/eng/20240322
LC record available at https://lccn.loc.gov/2024008389
LC ebook record available at https://lccn.loc.gov/2024008390

DOI: https://doi.org/10.3998/mpub.12776814

The University of Michigan Press's open access publishing program is made possible thanks to additional funding from the University of Michigan Office of the Provost and the generous support of contributing libraries.

Contents

Part III. Critical Junctures and Mass–Elite Discrepancy: Religious and Foreign Policy Issues

Conclusion

Digital materials related to this title can be found on the Fulcrum platform via the following citable URL: https://doi.org/10.3998/mpub.12776814

Preface and Acknowledgments

Are noticeable policy preference gaps between the public and their representatives observed in democracies worldwide? Do the gaps vary in content, structure, and timing? How should their varieties be construed? How do parliamentary representatives contribute to the formation and persistence of such gaps? These are fundamental issues in the field of comparative democratic representation, and their importance has grown in the contemporary era as the consequences of representation deficiency become evident in politics, including declining voter turnout, democratic backsliding, and the rise of populism.

Informed by global examples and meta-analyses, this book maps out varieties in mass-elite representation gaps. It also proposes a novel approach to studying these gaps globally. Building on historical institutionalism, the book investigates the origins of different mass-elite gaps with due attention to surrounding contexts and identifies relevant events and political actors. In doing so, it moves beyond earlier studies that focused predominantly on gap size and zoomed in on context-free variables for explanation. The book places parliamentary elites at the forefront of our understanding of the representation gaps and, as such, should be of interest to scholars of democratic representation, as well as elite theory. The contributors to this volume examine distinct mass-elite gaps in multiple world regions, highlighting how a country's historical context, cleavage structure, and elite agency interact to create specific representation gaps. I hope the readers will find the contents stimulating and refreshing, and that the volume, as a collective endeavor, contributes to opening new lines of inquiry and analysis.

The volume has come a long way, representing the culmination of an individual project that began in 2016. Following the completion of my PhD dissertation on welfare politics in South Korea, Japan, and Taiwan, I embarked on a new project during my first post-doc position at the University of Tokyo, focusing on the mass-elite preference gap in the same three East Asian democracies. However, in the same year, witnessing Brexit and the rise of populist political leaders, I recognized the global relevance of the topic and decided to expand the project from an individual endeavor to a collaborative one. My second post-doc position at the German Institute for Global and Area Studies (GIGA) played a crucial role in realizing the project's newfound global ambition. The institute's cross-regional setting, global orientation, and the presence of numerous scholars working on various issues related to democracy provided me with much-needed encouragement and confidence.

Under the auspices of the Fritz Thyssen Foundation, I had the opportunity to host a conference at GIGA in 2018, bringing together scholars who shared a common interest in the project. Through this conference, I recognized the importance of adopting a global approach and officially named the project Global Mass-Elite Discrepancy (GMED). The project benefited immensely from a follow-up joint session workshop with the European Consortium for Political Research (ECPR) in 2019. The participants of the workshop engaged in fruitful discussions and exchanged ideas and opinions regarding representation gaps observed in both new and established democracies. Drawing on the papers presented and the discussions held during the workshop, the theoretical framework of the volume was born. It is comprehensive and adaptable enough to encompass mass-elite gaps worldwide over time while still substantively meaningful and concrete enough to grasp the particularities of mass-elite gap emerging (and sustaining) processes in different contexts.

Looking back, the GMED project was a highly ambitious project for me and, at the same time, a steppingstone to stand alone. As a junior scholar fresh out of my PhD project, taking on the leadership of a collaborative project with a global scope presented a clear challenge. I encountered numerous trials and errors and faced uncertainties about the possibility of producing something substantial and meaningful. In the end, in cooperation with fantastic GMED team colleagues, I could produce this volume and two spin-off studies on measurement strategies (one journal special issue guest-edited with Sergiu Gherghina, and one research article coauthored with Mahmoud Farag). I would like to thank the GMED team members for their originality, hard work, and patience in meeting the high demands of this project.

Beyond the contributors of the chapters, I had the opportunity to meet and engage in discussions with many panelists and discussants at various conferences and workshops. I would like to express my gratitude to all of them, including those at the EPSA conference in Milan, the "Convergence versus Divergence of Mass-Elite Political Cleavages" conference in Hamburg, and the ECPR joint session workshop in Mons. Their valuable input helped me develop, clarify, and refine the project. Furthermore, I received excellent questions and feedback during various talks at numerous institutions: for example, the University of Tokyo, Waseda University, University of Amsterdam, Glasgow University, the University of Nottingham, GIGA Hamburg, Heidelberg University, City University of Hong Kong, and others. I would like to extend special thanks to Saskia Ruth, Philip Manow, Anja Senz, Willy Jou, Sijeong Lim, Masahisa Endo, Airo Hino, Don S Lee, Fernando Casal Bertoa, Thomas Richter, David Kuehn, Sinan Chu, Jasper Lindquist, Ivo Plsek, Gregory Noble, Diego Fossati, and Mike Medeiros for their contributions. In addition to conferences and talks, I have received encouragement, editorial support, and constructive criticism from many friends and colleagues throughout the years I have worked on this volume. I would like to express my special thanks to Elena Korshenko, Patrick Koellner, Hobart Kropp, Christopher Ahn, and Benoit Guerin for their invaluable advice and close readings.

At the University of Michigan Press, I wish to thank the editors, Elizabeth Demers and Christopher Dreyer, and the editorial board, who were enthusiastic and supportive of the project from the start. Also, special thanks are due to Haley Winkle, Kevin Rennells, and Danielle Coty-Fattal for their efficient steering of the manuscript through the various stages of production. During the peer review and vetting process, I received valuable comments and suggestions from five anonymous readers. Their insights were perceptive and greatly contributed to the improvement and updating of the chapters. In the current academic climate, major university presses have become increasingly skeptical of edited volumes. However, I firmly believe that bringing together research conducted in different contexts can lead to important theoretical insights and findings. This volume stands as a testament to that belief. Without the case knowledge provided by the contributors, who covered various world regions and utilized the best possible sources, I would not have been able to connect the dots and uncover portable mechanisms and causal processes. Their contributions were essential to the completion of this project.

For the financial support that sustained this project, I am grateful to the Fritz Thyssen Foundation (Grant Number: Az.40.16.0.029PO), the Japan Society for the Promotion of Science (Grant Number: 16F16308), and the German Institute for Global and Area Studies. Relatedly, special thanks go to Patrick Koellner and Kenneth McElwain, who wholeheartedly supported me in securing the necessary grants.

CHAPTER I

Global Mass-Elite Discrepancy

An Introduction

Jaemin Shim

Congruence in policy preferences between voters and parliamentary representatives has long been thought a vital quality of representative democracy (Dahl 1971; Pitkin 1967; Schmitt and Thomassen 1999). Functioning democracy does not mean an immediate response to every expression of public opinion (Dahl 1956), but it is nevertheless fairly uncontested that any discrepancy should not persist in the long run (Pitkin 1967). In light of this, a worrying pattern in both old and new democracies[1] has become noticeable in the past decades. One of the clearest examples is the 2016 UK referendum on European Union membership. In contrast to the "Brexit" result (52–48 percent in favor), pre-referendum surveys showed that more than 80 percent of Westminster legislators preferred to remain in the EU. A similarly stark mass–elite preference gap can be found in the Nordic countries over European integration (Borre 2000; Mattila and Raunio 2012). On the other side of the Atlantic, the case of United States shows a conspicuous gap between elites, who prefer the country taking an active role in world affairs, and less-enthusiastic voters (Page and Barabas 2000; Page and Bouton 2008).

New democracies are not immune to the divergence between masses and elites either. For instance, the major politicized division between elected politicians in Taiwan has revolved around foreign policy issues in relation to Mainland China, with one side promoting independence and the other demanding reunification. However, the stances of the polarized elites have not mirrored the vast majority of the public, who have clearly preferred the status quo for more than two decades (Election Study Centre 2021). Poland is another clear example of preference mismatch where an overwhelming majority of the public supports EU membership (CBOS 2020) in contrast to Poland's Eurosceptic government. A case in point is the contrasting viewpoints regarding the EU's demand to roll back the latest judicial reforms: Poland's Constitutional Tribunal ruled that the EU treaties are incompatible with Poland's domestic constitution, although more than 70 percent of the public supports the EU's intervention in the country's judicial reform issue (Reuters 2021). Incongruence is observed in sociocultural issues as well. Tunisia after its democratic transition shows a deepening of the religious-secular division over the role of religion in politics at the mass level, in contrast to political elites who have increasingly moderated this division (Farag 2020).

These are not just exceptional and episodic examples, but a symptom of a substantial representation gap in key national-level political dimensions that is salient and observed for numerous electoral cycles. This long-term mass–elite policy preference discrepancy should not be regarded as a less-than-ideal description of democracy but as a phenomenon with real effect. For instance, a wealth of empirical research has repeatedly demonstrated that higher degrees of mass–elite incongruence lead to undesirable outcomes. Specifically, lower ideological proximity to elites makes the public less satisfied with democracy (Ezrow and Xezonakis 2011) and even reduces subjective well-being (Curini et al. 2015). A larger representation gap also lowers the public's support for the political regime (Muller 1970) and its trust in the government (Miller 1974). Furthermore, it has been noted that representation deficits facilitate populism (Kriesi 2014) and such deficits indeed have provided fertile soil for the growth of populism—be it the right-wing ethno-nationalist kind or the left-wing redistributive kind—in both new and old democracies alike.

1.1. Three Key Approaches

Considering the negative consequences that mass–elite discrepancy can bring, it is imperative to deepen our understanding of the mass–elite discrepancy itself. For this goal, the present volume conducts a comparative analysis of the mass–elite preference discrepancy (henceforth, MED) globally.[2] The volume builds on the representative democracy literature and examines the relationship between the elite and the masses who possess and can provide a democratic mandate, respectively—elected politicians and eligible voters. The present volume is an attempt to examine various manifestations of

MED and investigate the potential causes behind them. Among others, the following three points make up the central pillars of our collective efforts and effectively distinguish this volume from the extant scholarship.

1.1.1. Global Approach

Most of the existing empirical studies on MED have so far focused on established Western democracies, and particularly on Western European countries in the last decade (see chapter 2), despite the fact that mass–elite discrepancies exist across world regions. As a result, there is a clear supply-need mismatching in the literature: the extant mass–elite congruence literature has generated numerous insights about Western European countries but too few insights about cases where the mass-elite congruence research could actually have the biggest impact. As a matter of fact, research shows that democracies beyond Western Europe are faring worse in terms of multiple indicators that measure representation performance (Shim and Farag 2022). In addition to the obvious empirical gap that needs to be filled, what is more important is that—by confining its geographical boundaries to a particular region—the literature has thus far not been able to fully leverage the variation in the content, structure, and timing of mass–elite discrepancies, which becomes clear at the global level.

Upon careful examination, one can notice that representation gaps observed around the world vary in multiple ways. For instance, a mass–elite discrepancy is highly salient in the foreign relations policy area in the UK and Japan, but not in the sociocultural policy area—as in, for example, issues of religion in Tunisia. Even within the same (foreign relations) policy area, the nature of the discrepancy varies substantially between the UK and Japan—the former revolves around the EU integration issue while the latter centers on whether the country should rearm itself by changing a relevant article in the constitution. Moreover, the empirical reality shows that there has been sufficient structural variation—whether or not the mass or elites are divided—depending on the policy issue and the country. For example, the Indonesian case shows a deepening of religious divisions at the level of the masses, but not between elites. In contrast, in Western Europe, the masses tend to be divided on EU integration, which is, historically, a much less divisive issue among the elites. Last but not least, the timing of the representation gap's appearance and origin varies from one country to another depending on the policy area in question. Studies show that discrepancies vis-à-vis EU integration existed for more than two decades in the UK prior to Brexit, while the stance toward the EU started to clearly diverge between elites and the masses only after the mid-2010s in Bulgaria. In view of this disciplinary blind spot, the volume explicitly maps out variations in content, structure, and timing of mass–elite discrepancies with examples drawn from multiple regions. Going further, the volume offers a theoretical framework to explain the observed variations.

1.1.2. Historical Institutionalism Approach

With few exceptions, students of MED have largely neglected historical factors in explaining mass–elite incongruence (see chapter 4). This is surprising because it has been noted that the political dimensions along which a representation gap occurs reflect the particular legacies and trajectories of a country (Kitschelt et al. 1999). For example, the three major MED-bearing political dimensions in Western Europe—big vs. small government, libertarian vs. authoritarian values, and pro- vs. anti-EU integration (see chapter 2 for the details of each)—directly mirror the historical junctures of the development of political cleavages over the past century. Taking this into consideration, this volume draws on the historical institutionalism approach (Pierson 2004; Thelen 2004) to explain MED at the global level. It explicitly recognizes the socially, culturally, and internationally embedded nature of party politics and underscores that legacies of early choices can help us to explain temporally distant outcomes of interest. For a global-level approach including multiple countries (like the present volume), one needs to be even more sensitive to heterogenous contexts. Moreover, as will be made clear in the theoretical chapters, the historical approach will be particularly pertinent in explaining the different content, structure, and timing of a gap.

"Critical junctures" take a central place in historical institutionalism. They are defined as the moments in which increased uncertainty allows political agency to play a decisive causal role in setting a persistent path (Capoccia 2016). The volume posits that these periods are pivotal to MED because the timing of a discrepancy is directly connected to milestone events defining a critical juncture. However, what qualifies as a critical juncture can only be defined vis-à-vis a country's specific contexts at a particular time. In this respect, the volume demonstrates that these moments can go beyond conventionally recognized moments derived from Western European experiences in the twentieth century. Examples include decolonialization, foreign occupation, and civil war. Likewise, what qualifies as a key salient political dimension for a country can vary substantially. At the global level, political dimensions manifest in myriad forms; many of these are rather unfamiliar from the conventional Western European viewpoint, such as independence vs. unification in Taiwan, normal nation vs. peace state in Japan, and pro-EU vs. pro-Russia in Bulgaria. Similar to defining a critical juncture, the question of which key political dimensions to examine for a mass–elite discrepancy cannot be decided in an ahistorical manner. Being mindful of this, the empirical chapters in this volume devote a sufficient space to fleshing out what defines a critical juncture and what constitutes key political dimension(s) for the analyzed country during the period of observation.

1.1.3. Elite Agency Approach

By paying attention to the historical contexts of MED, the authors in the volume demonstrate when a specific critical juncture led to MED while others did not. However, critical junctures by themselves do not determine whether there will be a MED, let alone its specific structure and timing. Although critical moments of history push key stakeholders to revisit the status quo, in the end, specific decisions by political elites result in the MED we observe. Decisions can be either an action or inaction on the elite side and the motivation behind the decision can be either policy- or election-driven. The elite are defined as minorities possessing excessive capability to influence social reproduction owing to their position or reputation (Higley and Lengyel 2000). With respect to a country's key political dimensions, political elites directly elected at the national level elections are the most important group shaping MED. In other words, the volume views political elites as the central force determining both MED's existence and varieties. On elites' roles, the party politics scholarship has demonstrated the ability of elected political elites to influence political cleavages by restructuring relations within the party system or combining issue dimensions (Enyedi 2005; Deegan-Krause 2006). Likewise, elite theorists note that the actions of political elites are crucial in determining political outcomes and have increasingly zoomed in on what they do instead of who they are (Best and Higley 2018). Echoing the increasing role of elites during critical juncture times, students of elite theories have long argued that elites are particularly likely to be influential in transitioning societies (Higley and Burton 1989).

Changes or inertia on the mass side are, by all means, important in understanding MED; it is the other side of the same coin constituting MED. However, the primary interest of the volume lies in democratic representation by political elites. Therefore, it does not analyze why or how mass-level preference change happens or not. Whatever the reasons are for shifts in mass-level preferences, what is important and requires explanation is why elites fail to reflect such changed views, often for substantial periods of time. In this respect, the volume demonstrates that deliberate elite decisions during critical junctures affect the mass–elite preference mismatch observed in later periods. To make this point clear, all empirical analyses in this volume pay particular attention to the choices elites have taken or shunned, and the manner in which their choices generated incongruence with the masses as an outcome. At the same time, to establish that critical choices were a result of elite agency instead of some deterministic force, numerous chapters include counterfactuals from other comparable countries or periods.

1.2. Key Contributions

All in all, the book makes theoretical, empirical, and conceptual contributions. First, the volume makes a theoretical contribution by providing a globally applicable theoretical framework that explains why we observe a particular variety of salient mass–elite discrepancy at a particular period. Specifically, it demonstrates how a country's historical context, cleavage structure, and elite agency interact to cause a representation gap. By drawing its key analytical concepts from historical institutionalism, the theory adds historical factors to the analytical toolkit of existing scholarship, which largely views existing mass–elite policy preference discrepancies as something detached from a country's key historical juncture.

Second, despite the relevance of this topic around the globe, the existing literature on the mass–elite representation gap has predominantly focused on developed Anglo-European democracies, while newly democratized states have received little academic attention so far. Drawing evidence from democracies in North Africa, East Asia, Southeast Asia, South America, and Europe, the book, as a collective effort, fills this lacuna in the literature and makes an empirical contribution. Moreover, the theoretically and empirically rich analyses offered in the volume are informed by a large-scale meta-analysis of the mass-elite representation gap literature from 1960 to 2020. Specifically, 111 samples were systematically drawn from an established search engine and were employed throughout the edited volume to explicitly point out the current gaps in the existing literature—as well as to highlight the added value of our own analyses.

Third, the existing literature has largely confined its analytical focus to the "size of a gap," that is, it has aimed at measuring and explaining the degree of policy preference discrepancy between the masses and elites. As a result, the variations in "content, structure, and timing of a gap," obvious in global-level comparison, have hitherto gone unnoticed. By mapping out all three aspects of mass–elite discrepancy that vary across countries, the tightly integrated chapters in the volume will enrich our conceptual understanding of the phenomenon.

1.3. Plan of the Book

The book consists of 10 chapters divided into three substantive parts that offer a balance between conceptual (part I), theoretical (part II), and empirical (part III) contributions. All three policy areas where MED most frequently appears—socioeconomic, sociocultural, and foreign relations—are included in this volume (see chapter 2 for details). To be true to the global approach this volume claims, countries from six world regions—East Asia, Southeast Asia, North Africa, Western Europe, Eastern Europe, and South America—are covered across multiple empirical analyses. As is often noted as a goal for cross-regional comparisons (Koellner 2018, 14), the common theme running through this volume is our desire to uncover portable mechanisms and causal processes but with due attention to the potential impact of contextual settings.

The first part of the book, "Varieties of Mass–Elite Discrepancy: Global and EU-Level Conceptualization," is devoted to the conceptual expansion of our understanding of mass–elite discrepancy. The two chapters in this section point out that important qualitative differences in MED contents have been overshadowed in the extant literature.

In chapter 2, Jaemin Shim utilizes comprehensive meta-analysis results and shows that there has been an explosive growth in publications concerning MED in the past decade, which is largely driven by works covering Western Europe. Relatedly, the key policy domains or issue areas where MED has been identified reflect the party politics trajectories of Western Europe. He then demonstrates that, once we take a global approach, the contents of policy areas and issues where MED are observed broaden substantially and some directly mirror the different domestic and international environments within which party competition occurs. The chapter also notes that expanding our focus to various world regions allows us to capture important hitherto underexplored variations in the structure and timing of MED. Global-level variations in specific mass–elite gap content, structure, and timing uncovered in this chapter serve as the key point of focus in the subsequent theoretical and empirical chapters.

Chapter 3 echoes the key concern of the previous chapter: the importance of recognizing and investigating multiple political dimensions in which the mass–elite discrepancy emerges. However, the chapter goes a step further by demonstrating the necessity of dividing an existing aggregate-level political dimension further into subdimensions for a comprehensive understanding of MED. Specifically, Andrea Pareschi, Gianfranco Baldini, and Matteo Giglioli delve into one political dimension that is now widely recognized as prominent across the EU countries: the issue of EU integration. They argue that the EU integration (foreign policy issue) merits consideration as an autonomous political dimension alongside the big vs. small government (socioeconomic issue) and libertarian vs. authoritarian (sociocultural issue) political dimensions. Moreover, leveraging mass and elite survey data conducted in 10 EU countries in 2016, the three authors demonstrate that EU integration issues can be disaggregated into subdimensions in three policy domains—economy, immigration, and international security issues—each showing variously sized mass–elite representation gaps.

In part II, "Theorizing Causes behind Mass–Elite Discrepancy in Old and New Democracies," two chapters theorize causes behind mass–elite discrepancies grounded in two key analytical pillars of the volume—critical junctures and elite agency. In both chapters, the theorizations draw from new and old democracies around the globe but, at the same time, use Western Europe as the point of reference to develop the key arguments.

Grounded in the previous meta-analysis, chapter 4, by Jaemin Shim, starts by providing a systematic review of causal factors that have turned out to be significant in explaining MED. It reveals that research so far has neglected historical factors behind MED despite the fact that the political dimensions where MED appear are intrinsically historical. Bearing this in mind, the chapter draws its key insights from historical institutionalism to generate a theoretical framework with which different MED contents, structures, and timings can be explained. In generating the framework, the chapter first focuses on the political cleavage literature and, at the same time, adapts it to a wider international context. Subsequently, the chapter develops a novel theoretical framework positing that salient MED observed in numerous global examples are a result of elites' deliberate actions or inaction during a critical juncture period. What happens during the critical juncture casts a long shadow, since the political dynamics crystallized during this time tend to be path dependent due to three mechanisms: elites' opponent marginalization, self-selection, and socialization.

Directly building on the previous chapter, Simon Bornschier in chapter

5 further theorizes the idea that behavior of political elites during a critical juncture can affect mass–elite congruence. Specifically, he distills the conditions under which elites' agency increases and demonstrates how high levels of elite agency can affect MED. By comparing numerous democracies in East Asia, Africa, and South America to Western European democracies, the author argues that elites tend to have more leeway in politicizing or depoliticizing political dimensions when (1) multiple cleavages cross-cut each other, (2) mobilization from below is weak, (3) repressive capacity is stronger, or (4) there exist frequent authoritarian turns. Elites beyond Western European democracies tend to have higher degrees of discretion since the last three conditions are more prevalent outside of Western Europe. In the empirical part of the chapter, Bornschier conducts a set of paired comparisons of South American democracies during critical junctures of the early twentieth century. Leveraging varying degrees of a mass–elite policy preference gap on socioeconomic issues across South American democracies, the chapter demonstrates that elite-level decisions were crucial in representing mass-level demand.

Part III, "Critical Junctures and Mass–Elite Discrepancy: Religious and Foreign Policy Issues," includes full-fledged empirical analyses of new democracies in North Africa, Eastern Europe, East Asia, and Southeast Asia. Every chapter in this section aims to achieve two goals—one descriptive and one explanatory. In order to achieve the former, each chapter first specifies the contexts of party competition and key political dimensions in the studied region and maps out the state of the mass–elite discrepancy in a salient political dimension of national importance. As for the latter, each chapter connects the observed discrepancy to critical juncture(s) pertinent to the political dimension of interest. Specifically, chapter authors demonstrate how elites' politicizing or depoliticizing of particular issues resulted in a particular form of MED at a particular time, as well as why their actions or inactions cast a long shadow on the way the mass public is represented. Although the chapters in part III follow the same overarching theoretical framework of the volume, the first two chapters focus on the religious-secular political dimension while the last two chapters focus on the foreign policy political dimension. By diversifying the geographical regions, periods, and policy areas, part III is designed to maximize the external validity of the theoretical framework put forward in part II.

As for the research design and method, all four empirical chapters follow an identical format; each describes the mass–elite discrepancy in a quantitative manner and qualitatively traces that gap to elite-level politicization or depoliticization at a specific critical juncture. Since qualitative tracing from the observed MED to a related critical juncture requires detailed knowledge of the analyzed country and sources in the original language, contributors in this volume were chosen from among political scientists with regional expertise. Finally, to measure the state of a discrepancy, multiple data sources are utilized, including mass and elite surveys, public speeches, roll call votes, and bill sponsorship.

Chapter 6 is one of the first attempts to explicitly examine the mass–elite representation gap within a new democracy in the North African region: Tunisia. In this chapter, Mahmoud Farag first outlines the political context there and explains the historical significance of religious–secular divisions between left- and right-leaning political actors. Following this, by combining the results from three hitherto underexplored elite-level datasets in the country—election manifestos, bill sponsorship, and roll-call votes—he demonstrates that clear religious–secular divisions have been lacking among political elites. Contrasting this with the survey results pointing to a more divided mass, the author argues that the discrepancy can be attributed to religious elites' decision to downplay the religious–secular political dimension through concessions made to secular elites during the revolution of 2010–11. The author explains that this was due to the uncertain postrevolutionary political landscape in Tunisia, during which key political actors pursued political stability by moderating their ideological differences. Through socialization between governing elites, the salient religious-secular division at the mass level has been continuously silenced by political elites in the governing coalition. As a result, the mass–elite discrepancy has subsequently persisted.

Similar to the Tunisian case, Andreas Ufen in chapter 7 focuses on the religious–secular political dimension in Indonesia, a hitherto underexplored democracy in the mass–elite representation literature. After fleshing out the country's political contexts, he provides the latest quantitative and qualitative evidence that demonstrates that political elites there do not reflect mass preferences, which have become increasingly divided over religious issues. To account for this discrepancy, Ufen traces its origin to the period of redemocratization between the late 1990s and the early 2000s, during which political elites intentionally downplayed the religious cleavage and, at the same time, cartelized politics. Ever since, the mass-level division in the religious-secular dimension has been muted by party elites as the elite-level co-optation has reinforced itself along with the increasing commercialization of party politics. By comparing this to the initial democratization period when the mass religious–secular divide was reflected by elites, the author demonstrates the significance of elite agency during critical junctures.

In chapter 8, Kenneth McElwain focuses on a foreign policy mass–elite discrepancy that has been understudied in the literature to date, namely the constitutional revision issue in Japan. He begins by outlining Japanese political contexts and explains major political dimensions during the postwar period. Specifically, McElwain explains how amending Article 9 of the constitution—which bans Japan from possessing the means for waging war—has been a long-standing source of political division between the left and right, often known as the "normal nation" versus "peace state" political cleavage. The author employs recent survey data to demonstrate that, compared to the masses, political elites are more pro-revision in general and, at the same time, more polarized between progressive and conservative parties. McElwain then traces the origin of this discrepancy to Japan's second critical juncture in the early 1990s, when a window of opportunity opened and elites made the decision to politicize the normal nation–peace state dimension by starting to increase its saliency. The MED became pronounced in the mid-2010s when the elites in favor of revision secured the necessary seats and began multiple political initiatives to change the constitution. In explaining the persistence of MED, McElwain argues that elites have failed to persuade the masses to become more supportive of constitutional revision due to their inconsistent messaging and lack of credibility on the issue in question. He tests the second point with a survey experiment.

Petar Bankov and Sergiu Gherghina in chapter 9 cover the mass–elite discrepancy on the EU integration issue in Bulgaria. Despite the same EU focus, they differ from chapter 3 in that Bulgaria is a country where the pro-EU integration issue takes a rather different form than in Western Europe, because it encompasses views on relations with Russia. First, the authors detail the historical and geopolitical contexts behind the Euro-Atlantic vs. Russia political dimension in Bulgaria. Then, based on elite-level public speeches and Eurobarometer surveys between 2013 and 2017, they provide evidence that political elites are more skeptical in general and are divided over EU integration—which clearly diverges from the more pro-EU tendencies of the Bulgarian masses. Bankov and Gherghina then trace the origin of this division between elites to the critical juncture of the mid-2010s; namely, the Ukraine crisis of 2013–14 and the migration crisis of 2015. Utilizing various pieces of qualitative evidence, the two authors demonstrate how both the left- and right-leaning political forces in Bulgaria have utilized the EU integration issue to further their position in domestic politics and, as a result, have become more polarized than the masses themselves.

In part 4, "Conclusion," Stephen Whitefield and Robert Rohrschneider summarize the key findings of the volume and locate the volume's contributions in the context of existing literatures related to mass-elite representation gap and political cleavage. The authors also discuss the study's relevance for understanding the phenomenon of mass–elite discrepancy. Finally, the authors outline four avenues of future research that can build on this volume.

Notes

1. The volume regards old democracies as those countries whose transition to a democratic political regime occurred prior to World War II.

2. The term "mass–elite discrepancy" will be used interchangeably with "mass–elite (opinion) incongruence," "mass–elite (representation) gap," and "mass–elite (preference) mismatch" throughout this volume. Similarly, there are several other terms used interchangeably in the chapters: (1) "political dimension" and political cleavage, and (2) "legislators," Members of Parliament (MPs), elected politicians, and lawmakers.

References

Andeweg, R. B. 2011. "Approaching Perfect Policy Congruence: Measurement, Development, and Relevance for Political Representation." In *How Democracy Works*, edited by M. Rosema, B. Denters, and K. Aarts. Amsterdam: Pallas.

Bankov, P., and S. Gherghina. 2020. "Post-Accession Congruence in Bulgaria and Romania: Measuring Mass-Elite Congruence of Opinions on European Integration through Mixed Methods." *European Political Science* 19 (4): 562–72.

Best, H., and J. Higley. 2018. Introduction to *The Palgrave Handbook of Political Elites*, edited by Heinrich Best and John Higley, 1–6. London: Palgrave Macmillan.

Borre, O. 2000. "Critical Issues and Political Alienation in Denmark." *Scandinavian Political Studies* 23 (4): 285–309.

Capoccia, G. 2016. "Critical Junctures." In *The Oxford Handbook of Historical Institutionalism*, edited by Orfeo Fioretos, Tulia G. Falleti, and Adam Sheingate, 89–112. Oxford: Oxford University Press.

CBOS (Centrum Badania Opinii Spolecznej). 2020. Support for and Opposition to Poland's Members of the EU. See https://cbos.pl/PL/home/home.php

Costello, R., J. Thomassen, and M. Rosema. 2012. "European Parliament Elections and Political Representation: Policy Congruence between Voters and Parties." *West European Politics* 35 (6): 1226–48.

Curini, L., W. Jou, and V. Memoli. 2015. *Why Policy Representation Matters: The Consequences of Ideological Proximity between Citizens and Their Governments*. London: Routledge.

Dahl, R. A. 1956. *A Preface to Democratic Theory*. Chicago: University of Chicago Press.

Dahl, R. A. 1971. *Polyarchy*. New Haven: Yale University Press.

Deegan-Krause, Kevin. 2006. *Elected Affinities: Democracy and Party Competition in Slovakia and the Czech Republic*. Stanford: Stanford University Press.

Election Study Center. 2021. "Changes in the Unification-Independence stances of Taiwanese as Tracked in Surveys." National Chengchi University.

Enyedi, Z. 2005. "The Role of Agency in Cleavage Formation." *European Journal of Political Research* 44 (5): 697–720.

Ezrow, L., M. Tavits, and J. Homola. 2014. "Voter Polarization, Strength of Partisanship, and Support for Extremist Parties." *Comparative Political Studies* 47 (11): 1558–83.

Ezrow, L., and G. Xezonakis. 2011. "Citizen Satisfaction with Democracy and Parties' Policy Offerings." *Comparative Political Studies* 44 (9): 1152–78.

Farag, M. 2020. "Mass-Elite Differences in New Democracies: Tunisia as a Case Study (2010–2016)." *European Political Science* 19 (4): 550–61.

Higley, John, and Michael Burton. 1989. "The Elite Variable in Democratic Transitions and Breakdowns." *American Sociological Review* 54 (1): 17–32.

Higley, J., and G. Lengyel. 2000. "Elite Configurations after State Socialism." In *Elites after State Socialism*, edited by John Higley and György Lengyel, 1–21. Lanham, MD: Rowman and Littlefield.

Kitschelt, H., Z. Mansfeldova, R. Markowski, and G. Toka. 1999. *Post-Communist Party Systems: Competition, Representation, and Inter-party Cooperation.* Cambridge: Cambridge University Press.

Kriesi, H. 2014. "The Populist Challenge." *West European Politics* 37 (2): 361–78.

Mattila, M., and T. Raunio. 2012. "Drifting Further Apart: National Parties and Their Electorates on the EU Dimension." *West European Politics* 35 (3): 589–606.

Miller, A. H. 1974. "Political Issues and Trust in Government: 1964–1970." *American Political Science Review* 68 (3): 951–72.

Muller, E. N. 1970. "The Representation of Citizens by Political Authorities: Consequences for Regime Support." *American Political Science Review* 64 (4): 1149–66.

Page, B. I., and J. Barabas. 2000. "Foreign Policy Gaps between Citizens and Leaders." *International Studies Quarterly* 44 (3): 339–64.

Page, B. I., and M. M. Bouton. 2008. *The Foreign Policy Disconnect: What Americans Want from Our Leaders but Don't Get.* Chicago: University of Chicago Press.

Pierson, P. 2004. *Politics in Time.* Princeton: Princeton University Press.

Pitkin, H. F. 1967. *The Concept of Representation.* Berkeley: University of California Press.

Reuters. 2021. "Most Poles Says Government Should Give Ground in EU Rule-of-Law Row—Survey." October 26. https://www.reuters.com/world/europe/most-po les-says-govt-should-give-ground-eu-rule-of-law-row-survey-2021-10-26/

Schmitt, H., and J. Thomassen. 1999. *Political Representation and Legitimacy in the European Union.* Oxford: Oxford University Press.

Shim, J., and M. Farag. 2022. "Blind Spots in the Study of Political Representation: Actors and Political Dimensions." Paper presented at the 2022 Annual Meeting of the Swiss Political Science Association.

Thelen, K. 2004. *How Institutions Evolve.* Cambridge: Cambridge University Press.

Thomassen, J. J., and S. A. H. Denters. 2010. *How Democracy Works: Political Representation and Policy Congruence in Modern Societies: Essays in Honour of Jacques Thomassen.* Amsterdam: Amsterdam University Press.

PART I

Varieties of Mass–Elite Discrepancy

Global and EU-Level Conceptualization

CHAPTER 2

Fifty Shades of Mass–Elite Discrepancy

Varieties of Political Dimensions and Discrepancy Forms

Jaemin Shim

The study of the mass–elite representation gap can be approached from multiple directions. As in the present volume, potential causes behind the representation gap can be examined. Alternatively, impacts of mass–elite discrepancies can be investigated in relation to important democratic qualities such as voter turnout, political trust, or the rise of populism. More fundamentally, one can raise normative questions about the oft-assumed negativity of the representation gap itself, such as, Can't the gap be beneficial if it is in the long-term public interest, or if it safeguards the protection of minority groups? Irrespective of the specific direction one takes, for comparable research, it is imperative to have a clear definition of and approach to the "representation gap" itself. In other words, what is meant by the "gap" and who exactly is being compared when deriving an observed gap require clarification.

Existing research comparing the policy preference match between masses and elites is directly related to the mass–elite discrepancy literature in party politics. Although specific labels vary from one work to another—for example, "issue representation" (Luna and Zechmeister 2005), "opinion congruence" (Mattila and Raunio 2006), "policy representation" (Miller et al. 1999), "issue congruence" (Powell 2004), and "policy congruence" (Enyedi, Pedrazzani, and Segatti 2020)—each examines the degree to which elites and the masses match in terms of the broad left–right ideological spectrum or their specific policy positions/priorities.

Beyond this common purpose, the ways in which the existing scholarship conducts research diverge quite substantially. For instance, how masses and elites are defined, compared, and measured varies from one study to another, which has important implications for whether and to what extent a mass–elite discrepancy exists in specific countries at particular times (Shim and Gherghina 2020).

First, following the most common way to measure mass-elite discrepancy in the existing scholarship (Shim and Gherghina 2020), the volume regards "a gap" as the average positional differences between masses and elites. The primary analytical goal of this edited volume lies in explaining various mass–elite preference gaps appearing in key political dimension(s). Therefore, the representation gap is compared at the national level based on preference differences occurring at the same time point. In light of this, this volume differs from studies whose mass–elite preference comparisons are conducted in one (or several) regions within a country, for example, Kuklinski (1978), and from studies, often known as "responsiveness literature," whose key focus lies on investigating how elites shift their position over time and to what degree this matches shifts in the electorate, for example, Wlezien (1995). Furthermore, this volume approaches the mass–elite discrepancy theme from the perspective of representative democracy; therefore, the primary comparison is between voters and parliamentary representatives. In other words, elites who do not seek electoral mandates (e.g., economic or media elites) and the public without the right to give a mandate (e.g., underaged citizens or short-term foreign residents) are not included as the main point of analysis. Besides, insofar as eligible voters are concerned, no special attention is given to any particular group. In this sense, this book diverges from studies focusing on the representation performances of elites in relation to specific mass-level social groups such as immigrants, low-income groups, and women, for example, Bartels (2016) and Reher (2018).

Having defined the scope of this edited volume within the MED scholarship, the primary goal of this chapter is to identify key trends in the related literature and to point out diverse patterns of mass–elite representation gaps around the world. To make the scholarship review process more systematic, I conducted a meta-analysis of empirical works[1] that compare the preferences of masses and elites at the national level. In an attempt to choose well-qualified and widely read empirical contributions to the MED literature, I used the keyword search function from the Web of Science citation database (for details of the selection process and the full list, see appendix). Eventually, 111 empirical works were selected. To my knowledge, this is the most comprehensive list of the MED theme as covered in journal articles and book chapters published between 1960 and 2020. Each selected piece has been coded across multiple aspects in order to map out patterns related to numerous parts in this chapter and in chapter 4.

Grounded in the meta-analysis results, the subsequent section identifies geographic and temporal trends in the existing literature and then demonstrates three key policy areas wherein mass–elite discrepancies are frequently found. Next, the chapter demonstrates that more diverse types of gap contents can be identified in terms of both policy areas and related issues if we step beyond the literature's conventional geographic boundaries. The chapter concludes by underscoring the historical nature of mass–elite representation gaps and sets the stage for the subsequent theoretical chapters by noting that gaps are mostly asymmetric—when elites divide and the masses do not, or vice versa—and observed at various time points.

2.1. Key Political Dimensions for Mass–Elite Discrepancy

2.1.1. General Trends in the Literature

The meta-analysis results shown in figure 2.1 divide the publication periods into three—before 2000, 2000–2009, and 2010–20—and the results clearly point to the increasing saliency of the mass–elite discrepancy theme. Specifically, the number of published articles and book chapters moved from 22 (1960–99) to 15 (2000–2009), and then to 74 (2010–20). To put this increasing trend into perspective, the publication explosion in the mass–elite representation gap literature after 2010 is twice that of the average increase recorded in the political science field (Shim and Farag 2022).

The second point of focus of the meta-analysis is the geographical coverage of published works. When it comes to the empirical approach to the mass–elite congruence theme, the general consensus dates it back to the early 1960s when McClosky, Hoffman, and O'Hara (1960) and Miller and Stokes (1963) published their seminal works comparing US voters and legislators. However, from the 1970s onward, other developed Western nations came into the spotlight within the MED literature. This can be exemplified by key empirical works covering either single or multiple countries, for example, Converse and Pierce (1986) on France; Holmberg (1989, 1997) on Sweden and Scandinavia; Thomassen and Schmitt (1997) on the Netherlands; Barnes (1971) on Italy; McAllister (1991) on Australia; and Dalton (1985) on Western Europe. Only around the turn of the millennium did the literature began to move beyond the Anglo-European regions to cover

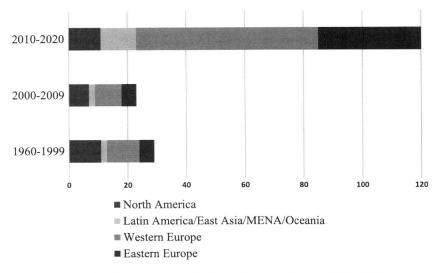

Fig. 2.1. Geographic Coverage of the Published Works by Period (1960–2020)
Note: The total number of papers goes beyond 100 because some papers contain more than one region.

democracies in Central and Eastern Europe, East Asia, South America, and North America, for example, Kitschelt et al. (1999) on Central and Eastern Europe; Jou et al. (2017) on Japan; Luna and Zechmeister (2005) on South America; Fossati et al. (2020) on Indonesia; and Farag (2020) on Tunisia. In tandem with the investigation of hitherto underexplored regions, another noteworthy trend in the literature is the increasing presence of global-level analyses that compare mass–elite discrepancies of numerous old and new democracies across multiple regions based on the same dataset, for example, Powell (2013), Dalton et al. (2011), and Hoffmann-Lange (2019).

The geographical distinctions in figure 2.1 clearly capture the literature's geographical focus over time. Specifically, these distinctions demonstrate that roughly 80 percent of the works are confined to Western European and North American countries before 2010. While geographical diversity has increased for works published since 2010, with a noticeable increase in Eastern European countries, democracies beyond the old Western democracies continue to be grossly overlooked despite the size of their populations and economies (Shim and Farag 2022). Another noticeable pattern in figure 2.1 is that, even between established democracies, the literature has become highly centered on Western Europe. It is clear that the dramatic increase in the publication numbers for MED scholarship since 2010 is largely driven by those works covering Western European countries. Western European countries have increased their publication share over time and, in the past decade, had roughly five times more publication coverage compared to North American countries; and the trend is not solely led by Western Europe–based scholars publishing more studies about their home region. Prior to 2010, the share of authors based in North American institutions who included Western European countries in their analyses was merely 16 percent, while that figure jumped to 46 percent between 2010 and 2020.

2.1.2. The Key Focus of MED Research and the Three Main Political Dimensions Based on Western Europe

What specifically does the existing scholarship analyze when examining mass–elite congruence? The existing scholarship on mass-elite congruence is composed of two major research strands. One strand examines the broad ideological spectrum differences, such as "left or right," that are often used to summarize general policy stances, shape party competition, and determine the voting choices of the electorate. Such a difference is often described as a "super issue" that is representative of the major ideological and politicized conflicts present within the political system (Gabel and Huber 2000). The meta-analysis shows that 45 percent of the scholarship includes this strand as the focus of the mass–elite gap.

The second major research strand, meanwhile, investigates the mass–elite preference gap on specific policy issues. Contrary to prior criticisms that the existing research focuses mostly on the first strand (e.g., Lefkofridi and Horvath 2012), the policy-specific approach is the more common form of investigation, making up 79 percent of the works included in the meta-analysis, with 55 percent of the scholarship examining policy issues alone and an additional 24 percent looking at the broad ideological spectrum and policy issues simultaneously. The extant research has compared mass–elite preferences on a wide range of policy issues known to be important in the country of interest at the time of analysis. On the one hand, 27 percent of the studies compared the preference gap based on a list of issues without noting similarities/dissimilarities between them or making any attempt to bundle them. On the other hand, the rest—73 percent—nested the specific issues being compared within upper-level concepts; for instance, issues such as smoking bans in bars or the adoption of children by same-sex couples are labeled as "sociocultural" or "libertarian vs. authoritarian" issues. The process of nesting specific issues within broader concepts is based on either

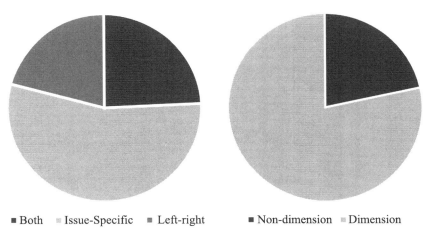

■ Both   ■ Issue-Specific   ■ Left-right   ■ Non-dimension   ■ Dimension

Fig. 2.2. Focus of MED Research: Issue/Ideology (*left*) and Issue Dimension (*right*)

employing a systematic inductive method such as factor analysis/canonical discriminant analysis (e.g., Farag 2020; Bornschier 2020; Fossati et al. 2020) or by deductively referring to the existing conventional distinctions in the literature.

Here, in figure 2.2, I refer to a study employing the grouping of policy issues by upper-level concepts as taking a "dimension approach." In view of the fact that the first research strand concerning left and right is intrinsically an upper-level aggregation of politics, it can be said that students conducting empirical research on the mass–elite discrepancy mostly take the dimensional approach.

Of all policy issue dimensions, which ones are particularly well addressed in the existing literature? The meta-analysis clearly points to three major policy areas: socioeconomic, sociocultural, and foreign relations. Table 2.1 encapsulates different types of political dimensions included in each policy area and shows which sets of issues have been subsumed. Because "political dimension" is an upper-level concept, how it specifically manifests in the real world in particular issues varies greatly across time and countries. Although space limitations prevent me from doing full justice to the issue diversity noted in the literature, I include the most frequently appearing issues in table 2.1.

First, in the socioeconomic policy area, the primary political dimension is characterized as state vs. market conflict (also known as "big vs. small government" or "public vs. private"). The divide hinges on the role of government in the economic sphere: one side emphasizes the idea of small government, with low taxation, small deficits, privatization, and minimal welfare provision, while the other side advocates for the opposite. In the existing MED literature, this dimension is specifically tapped into, for instance, through asking questions regarding the necessity of higher taxes, the transfer of income to the poor, more family support for the middle class, and the privatization of health care. In the Western European setting, this political dimension has been known to correlate highly with the left–right distinction, with the left arguing for a larger government role and the right for a lesser government role (Freire and Belchior 2013; Schmitt and Thomassen 1999).

Second, with regard to the sociocultural policy area, the key related political dimensions are often noted as conflicts between libertarianism and authoritarianism, materialism and postmaterialism, or individualism and collectivism. Oftentimes collectively bundled as the Green-Alternative-Libertarian (GAL) vs. Traditional-Authoritarian-Nationalist (TAN) conflict (Hooghe et al. 2002), such issues largely center on identities and ways of life concerning, for instance, law and order, environmental protection, minority equality, and multiculturalism. Studies typically capture this dimension through questions related to abortion rights, marijuana legalization, same-sex marriage, the necessity of alternative energy, affirmative action for women, and harsher sentences for criminals. The emerging consensus in the party politics literature has held that this dimension frequently cuts across the socioeconomic one (e.g., Bornschier 2010). Moreover, it is increasingly recognized as a political dimension defining the overarching left-right political distinction along with the socioeconomic one (Kitschelt 1994; Meyer and Wagner 2020).

The third policy area concerns foreign relations, which can be defined as "the management of relationships and dealings between countries." The empirical works that address the third policy area included in the meta-analysis largely point out the tension between global integration and national autonomy. Since the research is largely conducted within the European context concerning the issue of European Union (EU) expansion, the relevant dimensions are often specifically noted as pro-European integration vs. anti-European integration or Europhile vs. Eurosceptic. This "EU dimension" features strains between weakening national sovereignty and cultural identity, on the one hand, and increasing immigration and international economic exchange, on the other. Resembling the center-periphery dimension that emerged during Europe's national revolution period (Lipset and Rokkan 1967),[2] it can be said that the EU dimension concerns the supranational revolution unfolding since the European integration process began after World War II. Specific issues designed to capture this dimension include the varying degrees of ideal integration levels in multiple policy fields exemplified by the adoption of the euro, a single EU army, migration and border controls, and common EU-level taxes and social security. As can be guessed from the nature of these issues, some elements of the EU dimension are either socioeconomic or sociocultural. Nevertheless, the EU dimension can be distinguished from the previous two dimensions based on the fact that it is lower-level political entity having tension with an upper-level political entity that lies at the core, similar to the center-periphery conflict noted by Lipset and Rokkan (1967).

As for the empirical distinctiveness of this dimension, a number of studies have pointed out that foreign relations issues tend to cut across both the socioeconomic and sociocultural issues (McElroy and Benoit 2012; Thomassen and Schmitt 1997; Carrieri 2020). The fact that numerous works included in the meta-analysis approach this dimension simultaneously along with the socioeconomic and sociocultural dimensions attests to its autonomy (e.g., Walczak and van der Brug 2013; McEvoy 2012). In the chapter that follows, by situating EU integration issues in a historical context, Andrea Pareschi, Baldini, and Giglioli expound upon why the dimension merits an independent status. Furthermore, the chapter makes a conceptual contribution by dividing the EU integration dimension into six sub-dimensions within three policy areas—immigration, economy, and security—and demonstrates how specific sub-dimensions differently affect the overall EU dimension's mass–elite discrepancy in different European countries.

Within the three most analyzed policy areas, in which area can we see a substantial degree of mass–elite discrepancy? Authoritatively defining whether there is a substantial discrepancy or not is impossible since "discrepancy" is a continuous concept and there is not a conventionally accepted threshold from which the substantiality of a discrepancy can be judged. To make matters worse, as noted lately by Shim and Gherghina (2020), studies measuring the mass–elite gap diverge on whether they (1) examine absolute or relative difference, (2) compare preference distribution or mean, and (3) employ uni- or multiscale survey questions. Nevertheless, for ease of comparison, I define "a substantial level of discrepancy" as occurring if a study reports more than a 15 percent difference in the central values for multiscale measurements (e.g., a 0.15 gap between elites and masses on a 0 to 1 scale range for the abortion issue) or for a uni-scale measurement (e.g., a 15 percent gap between elites and masses on a question asking, "Do you agree that your country should leave the European Union?"). For studies comparing the total distribution in multiscales—that is, the degree to which policy preference dispersion overlaps between the masses and elite—the threshold is set at 60 percent (below this level means "a substantial level of discrep-

Table 2.1. Mass–Elite Discrepancy Policy Areas, Political Dimensions, and Issue Examples Based on Western Europe

Policy Areas	Political Dimensions	Issues
Socioeconomic	Big vs. Small government Public vs. Private State vs. Market	Larger tax necessity; Income transfer to the poor; Free childcare; Privatizing health care; Prioritizing government deficit; Building more day-care centers; Six-hour working day; Increase public sector size; Government should guarantee good standard of living; State should be the main education provider; Public servant unionization; Stronger banking sector regulation; Progressive income tax; Nationwide minimum wage
Sociocultural	Multiculturalism vs. Nationalism Materialism vs. Postmaterialism Libertarianism vs. Authoritarianism Individualism vs. Collectivism GAL vs. TAN	Affirmative action for women or racial/ethnic minorities; Accepting immigrants; Marijuana legalization; Abortion/contraception access; Same-sex marriage legalization; Capital punishment; War on terror/gang crimes; Forbidding torture; Keeping nuclear plants; Stronger measures to protect environment; Parental consent for abortion; More power to police; Firearm permits; Smoking ban in pubs and bars; Detaining terrorism suspects without charge; Experiments on animals; Plastic waste disposal in landfills; Censorship of movies
Foreign relations	Pro- vs. Anti-European integration Europhile vs. Eurosceptic	EU integration too far or push further; EU border control/freedom of movement; Common EU-level tax or social security schemes; Common EU army; EU-level refugee/asylum seeker increase; Euro adoption; Deciding EU treaties with referendum; Satisfaction with EU democracy level; More EU aid to Third World

ancy"). Finally, for those measuring the relative difference between masses and elites, a 0.6 positive correlation is taken as the threshold.[3]

In light of the aforementioned thresholds, the results show that foreign relations are the policy area where a substantial degree of discrepancy is most frequently observed (27 studies), followed by the sociocultural area (26 studies), and then the socioeconomic area (19 studies). In addition to these three policy areas, I examined to what extent there is a mass–elite gap

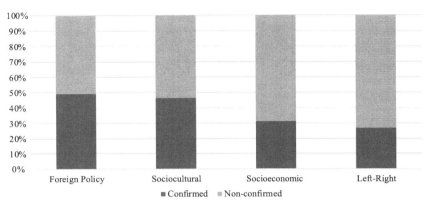

Fig. 2.3. Proportion of Studies with Confirmed Mass–Elite Discrepancy

in the left–right dimension, applying the same thresholds. Echoing existing research demonstrating that the discrepancy tends to be lower in the ideological spectrum dimension than for policy issues (Rosset and Stecker 2019), only 14 studies exhibited a substantial discrepancy, lower than any of the three policy areas. Bearing in mind that a high number can be simply a by-product of a specific area being examined more, I factored in the total number of studies addressing each policy area. This did not alter the order of discrepancy-observing frequencies: 49 percent for foreign relations issues (27/55), 46 percent for sociocultural issues (26/56), 31 percent for socioeconomic isses (19/61), and 27 percent for the left–right dimension (14/52).

2.2. Beyond Western Europe: The Diversity of Mass–Elite Discrepancy in Contents

As figure 2.1 makes clear, most of the existing empirical studies have focused on established Anglo-European democracies, often even limited to Western Europe, despite the fact that mass–elite discrepancies exist—and often to a greater extent—in other world regions (Shim and Farag 2022). In view of the literature's regional overconcentration, it is not surprising that the key political dimensions in all three policy domains of mass–elite discrepancy reflect the critical junctures of political developments in developed Western democracies. For instance, the state vs. market political dimension within socioeconomic policy area traces its origin back to early twentieth-century Europe when the masses gained the franchise and class conflicts came to the fore as a result of the industrial and communist revolutions (Lipset and Rokkan 1967). In the case of the sociocultural policy domain, the key political dimension of GAL vs. TAN is directly linked to the mobilization of new social movements on gender and racial equality, antiwar sentiment, and environmental protection in the West in the 1970s and 1980s (Kitschelt 1994). Similarly, the pro- and anti-EU integration political dimension within the foreign relations policy area reflects the foremost significant integration trend within the European context, that is, the regional integration of sovereign states under the banner of the European Union. As will be detailed in chapter 3, the regional integration trend accelerated with the signing of the Maastricht Treaty in 1992 and continued apace with the introduction of other national sovereignty-weakening measures, including the adoption of the euro and continent-wide freedom of movement. This process drove a wedge between the transformation's winners and losers (Kriesi 1998) and the conflict became clear in the mid-2010s during the sovereign debt and migration crises. In addition to its connection to the unique critical juncture, each of the three political dimensions can be characterized by the rise of social democratic parties, green parties, and populist right parties, respectively (De Vries and Hobolt 2020).

If a political cleavage is defined as a "lasting and salient political division,"[4] all three of the aforementioned political dimensions qualify as a political cleavage in the Western European context, since each political dimension features high levels of national-level saliency and the existence of a lasting political division on at least one level (mass or elite).[5] Beyond developed Western democracies, students of party politics have paid scant attention to lasting political dividing lines. For instance, analyses of party politics in new democracies often point out the large numbers of swing voters, high levels of electoral volatility, frequent mergers and splits between parties, incoherent ideological dividing lines, and personalistic and clientelistic party-voter linkages (e.g., Mair 1997; Tworzecki 2003; Katz and Crotty 2005). Echoing this, it has been said that the dimensional approach to politics has no bearing in the Third World until mass parties enter the political scene (Sartori 2005). However, a low level of party system institutionalization does not necessarily indicate that a country lacks lasting, nationwide political divisions. Two decades have passed since students of party politics have pointed out that it is too early to apply the term "political cleavage" to third-wave democracies, (e.g., Mainwaring 1999; Kitschelt et al. 1999), yet a large number of non-Western democracies have already passed Huntington's two turnover test.

For many non-Western democracies, of course, the process of democratic deepening is quite distinct. For instance, unlike Western European democracies, which moved step-by-step from national integration to industrialization and finally to the democratization process, two or even three processes have often been intermingled and may even be happening at the same time in numerous non-Western democracies (Randall 2003). Relatedly, the new social movements of the 1960s and 1970s have been largely absent in non-Western democracies, while many countries coped with dynamics not common in Western European democracies, such as decolonization, civil wars, and frequent democratic backsliding and redemocratization. Notwithstanding the differences in the trajectory of political development, numerous empirical works have evinced that lasting political division appears around the world.

For instance, like the primary political dimensions in Western Europe, the left–right divide over the role of the market has been an important dividing line in South America (Seligson 2007; Wiesehomeier and Doyle 2012). In other cases, primary political dimensions often appear in a form dissimilar to Western European countries. For instance, an established global-level survey, the Comparative Study of Electoral Systems (CSES), has been measuring "alternative dimensions to left–right." Examples since its 1996 survey include pro-periphery (Hong Kong) vs. pro-center (Beijing) for Hong Kong, pro-Slavic vs. pro-Latvia for Latvia, pro-Russia vs. anti-Russia for Estonia, liberalism vs. conservatism in Mexico and Poland, and pro-Montenegrin vs. pro-Serbian in Montenegro. Moreover, instead of treating political dimensions in the non-Western world as residual or exceptional, the latest works have explicitly incorporated them in their global-level analyses. For example, a global survey of political cleavages conducted by Gethin, Martínez-Toledano, and Piketty (2021) covers voting patterns from 50 old and new democracies over the past six decades. Similarly, based on their political dimension database, Shim and Farag (2023) demonstrate that many of the lasting political dimensions documented beyond advanced Western democracies are amenable to the spatial understanding of political competition and can be verified with reliable quantitative data.

All considered, when a mass–elite policy preference gap is observed in a non-Western setting, it is imperative not to regard it as merely a symptom of inchoate and unstructured political competition. The gap frequently occurs in key political dimensions that have lasted numerous electoral cycles. These political dimensions, from the perspective of established Western democracies, might appear in different forms and might be created through unconventional paths. Nonetheless, they are frequently a lasting political division and deserve serious empirical scrutiny. Based on the findings of the existing empirical works included in this volume and prominent examples from the meta-analysis, table 2.2 maps out key political dimensions over multiple policy areas in which mass–elite discrepancies are found in non-Western European countries.

Starting from the policy area where the mass–elite discrepancy is most

Table 2.2. Mass–Elite Discrepancy Policy Areas, Political Dimensions, Issue Examples beyond Western Europe

Policy Areas	Political Dimensions	Issues
Socioeconomic	State vs. Market (South America)	Private or public ownership; Privatization beneficial; Nationalization of petroleum and gas; More taxes for more welfare; Controlling service/product prices; Setting wages; Competition good or bad; More job creation at the expense of rise in prices; Government expenditure on unemployment insurance
Sociocultural	Religious vs. Secular (Tunisia, Indonesia, Eastern Europe)	Influence of Islamic sharia law (for enacting laws in general, marriage and divorce matters in particular); Preferring a religious political party over a nonreligious one; Religious people holding public positions; Banks charging interest; Role of Islam in politics Church attendance; School prayer; Subsidizing religious schools; Teaching religion in state-funded schools
Foreign relations	Peace state vs. Normal nation (Japan)	Amend Article 9 so that army can possess offensive military capabilities; Expand military personnel and budget; Enhance collective defense
	Global intervention vs. Isolation (US)	Actively involved or should stay out of world affairs; Favor US troop use if North Korea/Arab forces/China invade South Korea/Israel/Taiwan
	Pro-EU vs. Pro-Russia (Bulgaria)	Attachment to EU and Russia
Democratic regime	Democratic vs. Authoritarian (Tunisia, South America)	Suitability of democracy for the country; Democracy better form of government; Preference on army rule

frequently observed in the existing literature—foreign relations—it is clear that mass-elite discrepancies appearing in the political dimensions outside Western Europe manifest quite differently from the pro- versus anti-EU integration dimension. In Japan, for instance, the key political dimension revolves around the peace state versus normal nation dimension based on the potential revision of Article 9 of the constitution (a peace constitution that currently forbids war, whose origin can be traced to the postwar era). Left-leaning political actors advocate for keeping the constitution as it is, while right-leaning actors attempt to revise Article 9 and restore Japan to the status of a "normal nation" (for further background details on this dimension, see chapter 8). Unrelated to any of the critical junctures in Western Europe, the very existence of this gap-bearing dimension can be linked to external forces, since the US imposed the peace constitution during the postwar Occupation period. Similarly, in the neighboring East Asian democracy of Taiwan, the primary political dimension where a mass–elite gap is observed revolves around the diplomatic stance toward the People's Republic of China. Namely, the right believes that Taiwan and China should unify, while the left advocates for Taiwan as a sovereign country that therefore should seek greater international recognition. The very existence of this political dimension can be attributed to external force since it would have not existed without the Chinese Nationalist Party (KMT) fleeing mainland China in the late 1940s after its defeat by the Communist Party.

As for the US, the key foreign relations discrepancy can be summed up as global interventionist vs. isolationist—which centers on whether the country should play the role of "world policeman." This, of course, reflects the unique power-projecting capabilities of the US in the postwar period. In contrast to the European examples, this political dimension has nothing to do with the integration of the US with a bigger political entity in the context of globalization. This is made clear from the types of questions included to capture this dimension, for example, whether the US should take an "active part" or should "stay out" of world affairs; its military involvement in Afghanistan or in the Vietnam War; the expansion of antiballistic missile programs. Even when it comes to the European integration dimension, different variations of the political dimension exist once we step outside Western Europe. As detailed in chapter 9, in Bulgaria, since the mass–elite gap on the EU integration dimension involves another larger force, "Russia," Bulgaria's foreign relations dimension exhibits the pro-EU vs. pro-Russia form. Akin to the East Asian and American cases, this rather unconventional political dimension can be understood in light of the country's historical legacies and geopolitical contexts.

Zooming in on the policy area with the second most frequent mass–elite discrepancy—sociocultural policy area—the key political dimension most frequently observed beyond Western European countries is the religion versus secularism debate. This dimension mainly concerns the role of religion in politics in Muslim-majority democracies such as Tunisia and Indonesia (for further background details on this dimension, see chapters 6 and 7). Specifically, it relates to issues like (1) the degree to which the laws should be in line with Islamic sharia law; (2) preferences for a religious political party over a nonreligious party; and (3) preferences about religious people holding public positions in the state. This political dimension highly resembles the church vs. state dimension in Western Europe, which precedes the current preoccupation with liberal and libertarian concerns (Kriesi et al. 2008). Although not as evident as it is in Tunisia or Indonesia, the mass–elite gap is also found along the religious dimension in some Eastern European countries between postcommunist secular parties and anticommunist religious parties (Kitschelt et al. 1999).

In the socioeconomic area, evidence gathered from the existing literature demonstrates that the primary political dimension where the mass–elite gap is observed in non-Western European contexts resembles the Western Europe case: it appears in the state vs. market dimension. This dimension is particularly pronounced in South American countries whose sequence of party development echoes Western Europe's, as specified in Lipset and Rokkan's seminal work (1967). For other regions, surprisingly, the state vs. market dimension mostly does not even qualify as a "primary political dimension." For instance, in numerous democracies in the East Asian, Eastern European, and Middle East and North Africa regions, elite-level comparisons between left and right-leaning parties exhibit no recognizable differences in the role of government vis-à-vis the market (Fossati et al. 2020; Farag 2020; Shim 2020; Zielinski 2002). This is not surprising since numerous new democracies followed a substantially different trajectory of political development than did Western Europe and often lack the necessary preconditions for class-based politics. A case in point is East Asia. At the supply level, communist/socialist parties were heavily suppressed in many countries due to Cold War geopolitical concerns during authoritarian regime periods (Deyo 1987). At the same time, the right-leaning, party-led developmental state model in East Asian countries features high levels of state intervention in the economy (Deyo 1987), which counters the expectation of the conventional right in the state vs. market political dimension. At the mass level, postwar growth with equity in numerous East Asian countries narrowed the economic gap between the haves and have-nots (Peng and Wong 2010); in addition, widespread clientelistic party-voter linkages cross-cut different income groups (Scheiner 2006) and, as a result, neutralized potential class conflicts.

In addition to the diversity of political dimensions, the range of policy areas where salient mass–elite gaps are frequently observed expands when we step beyond Western Europe. For instance, the area of democratic regimes constitutes a highly important axis of conflict for many new democracies (Moreno 2019). The most frequently noted political dimension is the democracy vs. authoritarianism dimension, and the gap between elites and masses is measured through, for instance, comparing answers on the suitability of democracy for the country in question, or answers about the level of confidence one puts in government, parliament, and party. Unsurprisingly, this political dimension becomes highly salient in new democracies that have transitioned from an authoritarian regime. A case in point is the third-wave democracies, many of which transitioned from communism, a one-party dominant party system, or a military regime, for example, Russia, Chile, South Korea, Serbia, and Ukraine. The examples of the mass–elite gap in Tunisia (Farag 2020) and South America (Luna and Zechmeister 2005) show that this dimension retains its importance for democracies even in the twenty-first century; furthermore, new evidence demonstrating that the democratic-authoritarian divide has reemerged in Turkey as a result of recent democratic backsliding (Selçuk and Hekimci 2020) indicates that this dimension will continue to be widely relevant across world regions.

The democracy vs. authoritarian dimension is naturally less relevant for established democracies in Western Europe. Therefore, studies examining the mass–elite gap in the democratic regime policy area investigate the way in which a regime operates (e.g., Von Schoultz and Wass 2016; Mendez-Lago and Martinez 2002; André and Andeweg 2018). Among others, frequently appearing studies include those comparing mass–elite preference with respect to elites' ideal representation priority (e.g., should legislators prioritize social group, local constituency, or citizen?), representation style (e.g., should legislators act as trustee, delegate, or partisan?), or representation role (e.g., should legislators play the role of welfare officer, policy specialist, or generalist?).

2.3. A Global Approach to MED Analysis

2.3.1. Historical Contexts of Diverse MED Political Dimensions around the Globe

As noted earlier with Western European examples, three major MED-bearing political dimensions can be linked to specific historical junctures in the twentieth century. Similarly, in understanding key political dimensions in other democracies, historical contexts should be taken seriously in determining which political dimension will rise to the surface and become politicized. The historical trajectory of party politics development differs quite substantially between Western Europe and the rest. Drawing from the experiences of Western Europe, for example, mass enfranchisement or new social movements, the process of the formation of key political dimensions reflects a domestic-level, bottom-up political process. In contrast, in the non-Western context, many key political dimensions reflect an international-level, top-down political process. For instance, around the period of democratization, many new democracies around the globe were dealing with recent legacies of colonization by old democracies or had to cope with the effects of the Cold War. In other words, numerous new democracies lacked system autonomy (Randall 2003). That is, the very content of party politics is more likely to be shaped by international elites such as foreign governments. On the one hand, multiparty politics was often imposed on new democracies by old democracies in the immediate postindependence period, which reflects their colonial legacies. On the other hand, old democracies played a crucial geopolitical role in creating the key political dimensions that new democracies live with today. Examples of how outside influences shape key political dimensions were presented earlier in the case of foreign relations in East Asian countries.

Beyond the East Asian examples, Cold War legacies have cast a long shadow in numerous Eastern European democracies. In Ukraine, overlapping with the East vs. West divide, there is a clear political division between pro- and anti-Russia views at the domestic politics level (Zimmerman 1998). Similarly, empirical evidence suggests that the pro-Russia vs. anti-Russia division is the most discernable political difference in Lithuania (Ramonaitė 2020). In Bulgaria, despite the lack of a sizeable Russian-speaking minority, the EU integration political dimension includes another large force in the idea of "Russia," which manifests in a division between pro-EU vs. pro-Russia attitudes. The Middle East is no exception to this pattern. In Israel, a key political divide between the left and the right concerns the relationship with the Palestinians, and takes the form of dovish engagement vs. hawkish engagement (Arian and Shamir 2008). Although this division was firmly crystallized after the Six-Day War in 1967, the seeds of conflict were sown in the early twentieth century by external forces such as the Balfour Declaration of the British Empire in 1917. Other Middle Eastern countries today also present examples of how the influence of external forces can shape potential conflicts at the domestic politics level. For instance, the rivalry between Shia-majority Iran and Sunni-majority Saudi Arabia has manifested itself in past decades in the form of proxy wars in neighboring states, which has the potential to leave strong imprints on the corresponding countries' domestic politics during democratic transitions and beyond.

2.3.2. Beyond MED Contents: Diversity in MED Structure and Timing

I have so far evinced various policy areas and political dimensions where mass–elite gaps appear. Furthermore, I have also underscored that salient discrepancy-bearing political dimensions are historically rooted both in new and old democracies alike. Finally, in addition to the gap contents, I want to stress that there is global-level diversity in the structure and timing of mass elite-gaps.

As for the structure of gaps, theoretically, four types can be distinguished based on whether masses or elites, or both, are divided.[6] The meta-analysis shows that three types of mass–elite gap structures can be empirically identified from the studies that have identified a "significant gap" and, at the same time, include information on preference distribution. There was no example with a significant representation gap when both masses and elites were divided. On the contrary, 10 percent of studies exhibiting a significant preference gap show that masses and elites are not divided. For instance, extensive longitudinal evidence drawn from both mass and elite surveys on America's ideal role in the international setting—internationalism vs. isolationism—reflects this pattern (Page and Barabas 2000; Page and Bouton 2008). Both masses and elites had visibly higher proportions of the population with an international orientation (as opposed to those preferring the isolationist approach), but elites were substantially more internationally oriented than the public. For other cases, the representation gap structure is asymmetric: 57 percent of studies demonstrating a substantial gap showed that only masses are divided, while 33 percent of studies identifying a significant gap indicated that only elites are divided.

The timing of a gap can be captured by the period during which the gap of interest was observed; and the meta-analysis results demonstrate that the identified period of mass–elite discrepancies by empirical studies varies significantly. Measurements were based on the median year of an observed gap time and the gap-observed period spanned over six decades: 1950s (3 percent), 1970s (9 percent), 1980s (16 percent), 1990s (15 percent), 2000s (34 percent), and 2010s (22 percent). However, when it comes to the historical origin of an observed gap, there was no single study in the meta-analysis that explicitly traced the historical origin of an observed gap as part of the main analysis. When information related to historical origin is included, it is mentioned in passing in the case description or discussion section. This volume sees this as a major shortcoming in the literature since it has long been known that political dimensions in which a representation gap occurs reflect particular legacies and historical trajectories of a country (Kitschelt et al. 1999).

Mapping out and analyzing the structure and timing of a mass–elite discrepancy merits academic scrutiny because both have clear implications for democratic regimes and representation performance. For instance, regarding two specific asymmetric structures of the mass–elite gap, Kitschelt et al. (1999) distinguish between a "polarizing trustee relationship" and a "moderating trustee relationship." Namely, the former indicates the cases where elites overstate differences among voters while the latter points to examples where elites defy voters' radicalism and consciously converge on a narrow common policy space. From the viewpoint of democratic representation, both types of relationships are problematic. On the one hand, polarizing trustees indicate that the representative elites are wasting their precious political capital on issues for which the public does not recognize the merit of alternative directions. On the other hand, moderating trustees suggest a lack of clear alternatives among politicians on issues where people's views diverge or there is a lack of public-level appreciation for the necessity of moderation.

As for the importance of understanding mass–elite discrepancy timing, we can draw insights from Paul Pierson's remark (2004, 55) that "if two events or particular processes occur at the same historical moment, the results may be very different from when they are temporally separated." For instance, the timing of mass–elite discrepancy can be crucial if it leads to the rise of an antiregime party in a precarious democratic regime and, as a result, backslides into an authoritarian regime.

Bearing in mind the significance of analyzing mass–elite discrepancy structure and timing, this volume is explicitly focused on related variations.

Table 2.3. Global Examples of Mass–Elite Gap Types

	Mass **(Not divided)**	**Mass** **(Divided)**
Elite (Not divided)	Pro- vs. Anti-European integration in Spain (2010s)	Pro- vs. Anti-European integration in France, Germany, and Greece (2010s) Religion vs. Secularism in Tunisia (2010s) and Indonesia (2000–2010s) State vs. Market in Peru, Colombia, and Venezuela (late twentieth century)
Elite (Divided)	Peace state vs. Normal nation in Japan (2010s) Pro-Europe vs. Pro-Russia in Bulgaria (2010s)	

Note: Time periods in the parentheses indicate the mass–elite gap empirically identified by the authors of this volume.

As summarized in table 2.3, the countries analyzed in the subsequent chapters exhibit nationally salient mass–elite representation gaps varying in content, structure, and observed period. By tracing the historical origin of each gap, the volume endeavors to further our understanding of these hitherto underexplored qualities of the representation gap.

2.4. Conclusion

The chapter began by clarifying how the volume is positioned within the democratic representation scholarship—as a national level comparison of voter–parliamentary elite preferences on key political dimensions. Subsequently, grounded in a meta-analysis of 111 related empirical works, I have shown that the literature has seen an explosive growth in publications in the past decade, largely driven by studies covering Western European countries. A natural corollary to this regional overconcentration in the scholarship is that three major political dimensions with prominent mass–elite gaps—big vs. small government, authoritarianism vs. libertarianism, and pro vs. anti-European integration—reflect the historical trajectories of the development of party politics in Western Europe.

This chapter makes a conceptual contribution by demonstrating that, once we approach the mass–elite gap using a wide range of global examples, discrepancy-exhibiting political dimensions expand substantially, and many of them are rooted in historical experiences different from Western Europe's experience. Moreover, drawing on meta-analysis patterns, the chapter brings attention to the global variation in mass–elite gap content, structure, and timing, and consequently enriches our conceptual understanding of mass–elite discrepancy. It demonstrates that asymmetrical representation gaps—wherein only masses or elites are divided—are widely observed. Moreover, the timing of observed representation gaps vary significantly. Yet, to the best of my knowledge, no existing work has accounted for different structures and timing in mass–elite discrepancies across different world regions. Based on two core analytical concepts—elite agency and critical junctures—the subsequent theory chapters in this volume attempt to achieve this goal.

Appendix

2.1: Search Process for Meta-Analysis

1. Search process: I selected empirical works based on an established science search engine, Web of Science, on January 31, 2021. Specifics of the search process are as follows:

    A. I used four relevant key terms: "issue congruence"; "opinion congruence"; "issue representation"; and "policy representation." The publication format includes book chapters and articles and the search parameters included all time periods—but were confined to English-language academic works in political science.
    B. I listed the search results in order of "relevance" and then manually winnowed out empirical works concerning mass-elite representation gap measurement. This resulted in 87 samples.
    C. The samples were further reduced by removing those empirical works comparing the mass-elite representation gap on (1) specific region(s) within a nation, (2) specific group(s) of voters instead of all eligible voters, or (3) the degree of preference change shift over time. This filtering process resulted in 71 samples.
    D. Based on 71 samples, I employed the snowballing method from the reference lists and obtained 40 more empirical works fitting the criteria set in this volume.

Limitations: (1) key terms-based selection was reliant on "web-built search algorithms" and narrowing down empirical works to those published in English inevitably excludes important parts of the mass-elite congruence literature that does not include any of the four keywords or is written in languages other than English, or both; (2) manually winnowing out relevant empirical works and the subsequent application of the snowballing method might have introduced potential bias.

2.2: Full List of Meta-Analysis Samples

Table A2.1. Meta-Analysis Samples and Related Information

Nos.	Authors	Year	Publication	Study Title	Published Format
1	Dalton, Russell J.	2014	*Citizen Politics: Public Opinion and Political Parties in Advanced Industrial Democracies*	Political Representation	Book chapter
2	Klingemann, Hans-Dieter Volkens, Andrea Bara, Judith L. Budge, Ian McDonald, Michael D.	2006	*Mapping Policy Preferences II*	A Common Space or Electoral Communication? Comparing Party and Voter Placements on a Left-Right Continuum in Western Europe and CEE	Book chapter
3	Jou, Willy Endo, Masahisa Takenaka, Yoshihiko	2017	*Asian Survey*	An Appraisal of Japan's Right Turn	Article
4	Andeweg, Rudy	2011	*How Democracy Works: Political Representation and Policy Congruence in Modern Societies*	Approaching Perfect Policy Congruence	Book chapter
5	Pellegata, Alessandro	2016	*International Political Science Review*	Assessing the Complex Relationship between Government Alternation and Ideological Congruence	Article
6	Granberg, Donald Holmberg, Sören	1996	*European Journal of Political Research*	Attitude Constraint and Stability among Elite and Mass in Sweden	Article
7	Schoultz, Asa Wass, Hanna	2016	*Parliamentary Affairs*	Beating Issue Agreement: Congruence in the Representational Preferences of Candidates and Voters	Article
8	Mattila, Mikko Raunio, Tapio	2006	*European Union Politics*	Cautious Voters–Supportive Parties: Opinion Congruence between Voters and Parties on the EU Dimension	Article
9	Leimgruber, Philipp Hangartner, Dominik Leemann, Lucas	2010	*Swiss Political Science Review*	Comparing Candidates and Citizens in the Ideological Space	Article

Nos.	Authors	Year	Publication	Study Title	Published Format
10	Miller, Warren Stokes, Donald	1963	*American Political Science Review*	Constituency Influence in Congress	Article
11	Borre, Ole	2000	*Scandinavian Political Studies*	Critical Issues and Political Alienation in Denmark	Article
12	Fiorina, Morris Levendusky, Matthew	2006	*Red and Blue Nations*	Disconnected: The Political Class versus the People	Book chapter
13	Blais, André Bodet, Marc André	2006	*Comparative Political Studies*	Does Proportional Representation Foster Closer Congruence between Citizens and Policy Makers?	Article
14	Mattila, Mikko Raunio, Tapio	2012	*West European Politics*	Drifting Further Apart: National Parties and Their Electorates on the EU Dimension	Article
15	Esaiasson, Peter Holmberg, Sören	1996	*Representation from Above: Members of Parliament and Representative Democracy in Sweden*	Thinking Alike	Book chapter
16	Esaiasson, Peter Holmberg, Sören	1996	*Representation from Above: Members of Parliament and Representative Democracy in Sweden*	Dynamic Representation from Above	Book chapter
17	Rogers, Steven	2017	*American Political Science Review*	Electoral Accountability for State Legislative Roll Calls and Ideological Representation	Article
18	Hooghe, Liesbet	2003	*European Union Politics*	Europe Divided? Elites vs. Public Opinion on European Integration	Article
19	Costello, Rory Thomassen, Jacques Rosema, Martin	2012	*Western European Politics*	European Parliament Elections and Political Representation	Article
20	Lewis, Daniel Jacobmeiser, Matthew	2017	*State Politics and Policy Quarterly*	Evaluating Policy Representation with Dynamic MRP Estimates	Article

Nos.	Authors	Year	Publication	Study Title	Published Format
21	Reher, Stefanie	2015	*European Journal of Political Research*	Explaining Cross-National Variation in the Relationship between Priority Congruence and Satisfaction with Democracy	Article
22	Belchior, Ana Maria	2012	*Comparative Political Studies*	Explaining Left-Right Party Congruence across European Party Systems: A Test of Micro-, Meso-, and Macro-Level Models	Article
23	Thomassen, Jacques van Ham, Carolien	2014	*Western European Politics*	Failing Political Representation or a Change in Kind?	Article
24	Page, Benjamin	2000	*International Studies Quarterly*	Foreign Policy Gaps between Citizens and Leaders	Article
25	Traber, Denise Giger, Nathalie Häusermann, Silja	2017	*Western European Politics*	How Economic Crises Affect Political Representation: Declining Party–Voter Congruence in Tmes of Constrained Government	Article
26	Rohrschneider, Robert Whitefield, Stephen	2012	*The Strain of Representation: How Parties Represent Diverse Voters in Western and Eastern Europe*	Ideological Congruence	Book chapter
27	Golder, Matt Stramski, Jacek	2010	*American Journal of Political Science*	Ideological Congruence and Electoral Institutions	Article
28	Klingemann, Hans-Dieter Gancheva, Darina Wessels, Bernhard	2017	*Parties, Governments and Elites*	Ideological Congruence: Choice, Visibility, and Clarity	Book chapter
29	Freire, Andre Belchior, Ana Maria	2013	*Journal of Legislative Studies*	Ideological Representation in Portugal	Article
30	Walgrave, Stefaan Lefevere, Jonas	2013	*Journal of Elections, Public Opinion, and Parties*	Ideology, Saliency, and Complexity: Determinants of Policy Issue Congruence between Voters and Parties	Article

Nos.	Authors	Year	Publication	Study Title	Published Format
31	Rohrschneider, Robert Whitefield, Stephen	2012	*West European Politics*	Institutional Context and Representational Strain in Party-Voter Agreement in Western and Eastern Europe	Article
32	Burden, Barry	2005	*State Politics and Policy Quarterly*	Institutions and Policy Representation in the States	Article
33	Belchior, Ana Maria Freire, André	2012	*International Political Science Review*	Is Party Type Relevant to an Explanation of Policy Congruence? Catchall versus Ideological Parties in the Portuguese Case	Article
34	Rohrschneider, Robert	2015	*German Politics*	Is There a Regional Cleavage in Germany's Party System?	Article
35	McClosky, Herbert Hoffman, Paul O'Hara, Rosemary	1960	*American Political Science Review*	Issue Conflict and Consensus among Party Leaders and Followers	Article
36	Thomassen, Jacques Schmitt, Hermann	1999	*Political Representation and Legitimacy in the European Union*	Issue Congruence	Book chapter
37	Belchior, Ana Maria	2010	*Journal of Legislative Studies*	Issue Congruence among European Political Parties	Article
38	Lefkofridi, Zoe Horvath, Ken	2012	*Representation*	Migration Issues and Representation in European Liberal Democracies	Article
39	Stecker, Christian Tausendpfund, Markus	2016	*European Journal of Political Research*	Multidimensional Government-Citizen Congruence and Satisfaction with Democracy	Article
40	Budge, Ian Klingemann, Hans-Dieter	2001	*Mapping Policy Preferences from Texts: Statistical Solutions for Manifesto Analysts*	Parties, Citizens, and Representation	Book chapter

41

Nos.	Authors	Year	Publication	Study Title	Published Format
41	McAllister, Ian	1991	*Canadian Journal of Political Science*	Party Elites, Voters and Political Attitudes: Testing Three Explanations for Mass-Elite Differences	Article
42	Widfeldt, Anders	1995	*Citizens and the State*	Party Membership and Party Representativeness	Book chapter
43	Dalton, Russell J.	2017	*Party Politics*	Party Representation across Multiple Issue Dimensions	Article
44	Zipp, John	1983	*American Political Science Review*	Perceived Representativeness and Voting: An Assessment of the Impact of Choices vs. Echoes	Article
45	Carroll, Royce Kubo, Hiroki	2018	*Public Choice*	Polarization and Ideological Congruence between Parties and Supporters in Europe	Article
46	Önnudóttir, Eva	2014	*Western European Politics*	Policy Congruence and Style of Representation: Party Voters and Political Parties	Article
47	Montjoy, Robert Shaffer, William Weber, Ronald	1980	*American Politics Quarterly*	Policy Preferences of Party Elites and Masses	Article
48	Thomassen, Jacques Schmitt, Hermann	1997	*European Journal of Political Research*	Policy Representation	Article
49	Dalton, Russell J.	1985	*Comparative Political Studies*	Political Parties and Political Representation	Article
50	Luna, Juan Zechmeister, Elizabeth	2005	*Comparative Political Studies*	Political Representation in Latin America: Congruence in Nine Countries	Article
51	Mendez-Lago, Monica Martinez, Antonia	2002	*Journal of Legislative Studies*	Political Representation in Spain: An Empirical Analysis of the Perception of Citizens and MPs	Article

Nos.	Authors	Year	Publication	Study Title	Published Format
52	Cohen, Jeffrey	1997	*Presidential Responsiveness and Public Policy-Making*	Presidential Responsiveness and Policy Formulation	Book chapter
53	Monroe, Alan	1998	*Public Opinion Quarterly*	Public Opinion and Public Policy	Article
54	Karyotis, Georgios Rüdig, Wolfgang Judge, David	2014	*South European Society and Politics*	Representation and Austerity Politics: Attitudes of Greek Voters and Elites Compared	Article
55	Powell, Bingham	2013	*Perspectives on Politics*	Representation in Context: Election Laws and Ideological Congruence Between Citizens and Governments	Article
56	Walczak, Agnieszka van der Brug, Wouter	2012	*European Union Politics*	Representation in the European Parliament	Article
57	Rohrschneider, Robert Miles, Matthew	2015	*Environmental Politics*	Representation through Parties? Environmental Attitudes and Party Stances in Europe in 2013	Article
58	Van Esch, Femke Joosen, Rik van Zuydam, Sabine	2016	*Politics and Governance*	Responsive to the People? Comparing the European Cognitive Maps of Dutch Political Leaders and Their Followers	Article
59	Giger, Nathalie Lefkofridi, Zoe	2014	*Swiss Political Science Review*	Salience-Based Congruence between Parties and Their Voters	Article
60	Wratil, Christopher	2018	*American Journal of Political Science*	Territorial Representation and the Opinion-Policy Linkage	Article
61	Thomassen, Jacques	2012	*Representation*	The Blind Corner of Political Representation	Article

Nos.	Authors	Year	Publication	Study Title	Published Format
62	Valen, Henry	2007	*European Journal of Political Research*	The Conditional Party Mandate: A Model for the Study of Mass and Elite Opinion Patterns	Article
63	Brandenburg, Heinz Johns, Robert	2014	*Political Studies*	The Declining Representativeness of the British Party System, and Why It Matters	Article
64	Dalton, Russell J. Farrell, David M. McAllister, Ian	2011	*How Democracy Works: Political Representation and Policy Congruence in Modern Societies*	The Dynamics of Political Representation	Book chapter
65	Reher, Stefanie	2014	*Electoral Studies*	The Effect of Congruence in Policy Priorities on Electoral Participation	Article
66	Reher, Stefanie	2016	*Journal of Elections, Public Opinion, and Parties*	The Effect of Congruence in Policy Priorities on Satisfaction with Democracy	Article
67	Müller, Wolfgang Jenny, Marcelo Ecker, Alejandro	2012	*The Europe of Elites*	The Elites-Masses Gap in European Integration	Book chapter
68	Power, Bingham	2009	*Comparative Political Studies*	The Ideological Congruence Controversy	Article
69	Castello, Rory	2017	*Irish Political Studies*	The Ideological Space in Irish Politics: Comparing Voters and Parties	Article
70	André, Audrey Depauw, Sam	2017	*Political Behaviour*	The Quality of Representation and Satisfaction with Democracy: The Consequences of Citizen-Elite Policy and Process Congruence	Article
71	McEvoy, Caroline	2012	*Representation*	Unequal Representation in the EU	Article
72	Spoon, Jae-Jae Klüver, Heike	2015	*European Journal of Political Research*	Voter Polarization and Party Rsponsiveness	Article

Nos.	Authors	Year	Publication	Study Title	Published Format
73	Ezrow, Lawrence Tavits, Margit Homola, Jonathan	2014	*Comparative Political Studies*	Voter Polarization, Strength of Partisanship and Support for Extremist Parties	Article
74	Dolny, Branislav Babos, Palov	2015	*West European Politics*	Voter-Representative Congruence in Europe: A Loss of Institutional Influence	Article
75	Klüver, Heike Spoon, Jae-Jae	2014	*British Journal of Political Science*	Who Responds? Voters, Parties, and Issue Attention	Article
76	Rasmussen, Anne Reher, Stephanie	2019	*Comparative Political Studies*	Civil Society Engagement and Policy Representation in Europe	Article
77	Bornschier, Simon	2020	*European Political Science*	Combining Deductive and Inductive Elements to Measure Party System Responsiveness in Challenging Contexts: An Approach with Evidence from Latin America	Article
78	van Ditmars, Mathilde M. de Lange, Sarah L.	2019	*Acta Politica*	Differential Representation? The Gaps between Mainstream and Niche Party Representatives and Their Voters in the Netherlands	Article
79	Romeijn, Jeroen	2020	*Party Politics*	Do Political Parties Listen to The(ir) Public? Public Opinion–Party Linkage on Specific Policy Issues	Article
80	Shalaby, Marwa Aydogan, Abdullah	2020	*Parliamentary Affairs*	Elite-Citizen Linkages and Issue Congruency under Competitive Authoritarianism	Article

Nos.	Authors	Year	Publication	Study Title	Published Format
81	Rosset, Jan Stecker, Christian	2019	*European Political Science Review*	How Well Are Citizens Represented by Their Governments? Issue Congruence and Inequality in Europe	Article
82	Navarrete, Rosa M.	2020	*Journal of Elections, Public Opinion, and Parties*	Ideological Proximity and Voter Turnout in Multi-Level Systems: Evidence from Spain	Article
83	Fossati, Diego Aspinall, Edward Muhtadi, Burhanuddin Warburton, Eve	2020	*Electoral Studies*	Ideological Representation in Clientelistic Democracies: The Indonesian Case	Article
84	Tromborg, Mathias	2019	*Political Studies*	Issue Salience and Candidate Position Taking in Parliamentary Parties	Article
85	Farag, Mahmoud	2020	*European Political Science*	Mass-Elite Differences in New Democracies: Tunisia as a Case Study (2010–2016)	Article
86	Goldberg, Andreas C. Van Elsas, Erika J. De Vreese, Claes H	2020	*Journal of European Public Policy*	Mismatch? Comparing Elite and Citizen Polarisation on EU Issues across Four Countries	Article
87	Bakker, Ryan Jolly, Seth Polk, Jonathan	2020	*Journal of European Public Policy*	Multidimensional Incongruence, Political Disaffection, and Support for Anti-establishment Parties	Article
88	Bankov, Petar Gherghina, Sergiu	2020	*European Political Science*	Post-accession Congruence in Bulgaria and Romania: Measuring Mass-Elite Congruence of Opinions on European Integration through Mixed Methods	Article

Nos.	Authors	Year	Publication	Study Title	Published Format
89	Stadelmann, David Portmann, Marco Eichenberger, Reiner	2019	*British Journal of Political Science*	Preference Representation and the Influence of Political Parties in Majoritarian vs. Proportional Systems: An Empirical Test	Article
90	Hooghe, Marc Dassonneville, Ruth Oser, Jennifer	2019	*Political Studies*	Public Opinion, Turnout and Social Policy: A Comparative Analysis of Policy Congruence in European Liberal Democracies	Article
91	Werner, Annika	2020	*British Journal of Politics and International Relations*	Representation in Western Europe: Connecting Party-Voter Congruence and Party Goals	Article
92	Vrânceanu, Alina	2019	*Party Politics*	The Impact of Contextual Factors on Party Responsiveness regarding Immigration Issues	Article
93	Rasmussen, Anne Reher, Stefanie Toshkov, Dimiter	2019	*European Journal of Political Research*	The Opinion-Policy Nexus in Europe and the Role of Political Institutions	Article
94	Graham, Matthew H. Orr, Lilla V.	2020	*Electoral Studies*	What Would Delegates Do? When and How the Delegate Paradox Affects Estimates of Ideological Congruence	Article
95	Page, Benjamin I. Bouton, Marshall M.	2008	*The Foreign Policy Disconnect: What Americans Want from Our Leaders but Don't Get*	A Disconnect between Policy Makers and the Public?	Book chapter
96	Moury, Catherine De Sousa, Luis	2011	*Portuguese Journal of Social Science*	Comparing Deputies' and Voters' Support for Europe: The Case of Portugal	Article
97	Backstrom, Charles H.	1977	*American Politics Quarterly*	Congress and the Public: How Representative Is the One of the Other?	Article

Nos.	Authors	Year	Publication	Study Title	Published Format
98	Powell, Lynda W.	1982	*Journal of Politics*	Issue Representation in Congress	Article
99	Achen, Christopher H.	1978	*American Journal of Political Science*	Measuring Representation	Article
100	Kitschelt, Herbert Mansfeldova, Zdenka Markowski, Radoslaw Toka, Gabor	1999	*Post-Communist Party Systems: Competition, Representation, and Inter-party Cooperation*	Political Representation	Book chapter
101	Holmberg, Sören	1989	*Scandinavian Political Studies*	Political Representation in Sweden	Article
102	Giger, Nathalie Lefkofridi, Zoe	2016	*Political Representation: Roles, Representatives and the Represented*	Alignment of Objectives between Parties and Their Electors: The Role of Personal Issue Salience in Political Representation	Book chapter
103	Vogel, Lars Göncz, Borbála	2018	*National Political Elites, European Integration and the Eurozone Crisis*	European Integration in the View of Political Elites and Citizens—An Increasing Gap?	Book chapter
104	Enyedi, Zsolt Pedrazzani, Andrea Segatti, Paolo	2020	*Parliamentary Candidates between Voters and Parties: A Comparative Perspective*	Policy Representation in Europe	Book chapter
105	Holmberg, Soren	2000	*Beyond Westminster and Congress: The Nordic Experience*	Issue Agreement, beyond Westminster and Congress	Book chapter
106	Converse, Philip Pierce, Roy	1986	*Political Representation in France*	Policy Attitudes of Mass and Elite	Book chapter
107	Holmberg, Soren	1999	*Policy Representation in Western Democracies*	Collective Policy Congruence Compared	Book chapter
108	Wessels, Bernhard	1999	*Policy Representation in Western Democracies*	System Characteristics Matter: Empirical Evidence from Ten Representation Studies	Book chapter
109	Hoffmann-Lange, Ursula	2019	*Elites and People: Challenges to Democracy*	The Development of Political Legitimacy among MPs and Citizens in Old and Young Democracies	Book chapter

Table A2.1—*Continued*

Nos.	Authors	Year	Publication	Study Title	Published Format
110	Andre, Audrey Depauw, Sam Andeweg, Rudy	2017	*Mind the Gap: Political Participation and Representation in Belgium*	Public and Politicians' Preferences on Priorities in Political Representation	Book chapter
111	McElwain, Kenneth	2020	*European Political Science*	When Candidates Are More Polarised Than Voters: Constitutional Revision in Japan	Article

Notes

1. Here empirical works are defined as works comparing preferences of masses and elites on the basis of quantitative datasets.

2. The central-periphery dimension has not disappeared even in today's developed Western world, as manifested by secessionist movements in Quebec, Scotland, and Catalonia; empirical research covering these regions demonstrates the existence of the third political dimension in addition to the socioeconomic and sociocultural divide (Medeiros et al. 2015; Wheatley et al. 2014).

3. All these thresholds are informed by the approximate mean value of the identified gap from studies employing the same type of measurement.

4. This definition deviates from Bartolini and Mair's (2007) strict conceptualization of political cleavage, which is viewed as long-lasting political division where each side has encompassing interests, normative or attitudinal outlooks, and a strong organizational base. It resembles a more relaxed definition of political cleavage by Rae and Taylor (1970), which defines political cleavage as the criteria dividing groups with important political differences based on ascriptive/trait (e.g., race or caste), attitudes/opinions (e.g., preference or ideology), or behavior/act (e.g., voting).

5. From this viewpoint, EU integration could not be qualified as "a political cleavage" until 1992 since both elites and masses held largely the same pro-integration view (Carrubba 2001)

6. Here, I refer to masses or elites as "divided" if the distribution of opposing policy preferences falls into the benchmark range set in this volume: 40–60 percent. For example, across countries, the proportion for or against abortion among elites can be 70:30 (country A), 50:50 (country B), 60:40 (country C), 45:55 (country D), and 20:80 (country E). Based on the set benchmark, countries B, C, and D are "divided" while A and E are "not divided."

References

André, A., S. DePauw, and R. B. Andeweg. 2018. "Public and Politicians' Preferences on Priorities in Political Representation." In *Mind the Gap: Political Participation and Representation in Belgium*, edited by Chris Deschouwer, 51–73. Colchester, UK: ECPR Press.

Arian, A., and M. Shamir. 2008. "A Decade Later, the World Had Changed, the Cleavage Structure Remained: Israel 1996–2006." *Party Politics* 14 (6): 685–705.

Aydogan, A., and J. B. Slapin. 2015. "Left–Right Reversed: Parties and Ideology in Modern Turkey." *Party Politics* 21 (4): 615–25.

Barnes, S. H. 1971. "Left, Right, and the Italian Voter." *Comparative Political Studies* 4 (2): 157–75.

Bartels, L. M. 2016. "Economic Inequality and Political Representation." In *Unequal Democracy: The Political Economy of the New Gilded Age*, by Larry Bartels, 233–68. Princeton: Princeton University Press.

Bartolini, S., and P. Mair. 2007. *Identity, Competition and Electoral Availability: The Stabilisation of European Electorates 1885–1985*. Colchester, UK: ECPR Press.

Bornschier, S. 2010. *Cleavage Politics and the Populist Right: The New Cultural Conflict in Western Europe*. Philadelphia: Temple University Press.

Bornschier, S. 2016. "Historical Polarization and Representation in South American Party Systems, 1900–1990." *British Journal of Political Science* 49 (1): 1–27.

Bornschier, S. 2020. "Combining Deductive and Inductive Elements to Measure Party System Responsiveness in Challenging Contexts: An Approach with Evidence from Latin America." *European Political Science* 19 (4): 540–49.

Carrieri, L. 2020. *The Impact of European Integration on West European Politics: Committed Pro-Europeans Strike Back*. Palgrave Macmillan Cham.

Carrubba, C. J. 2001. "The Electoral Connection in European Union Politics." *Journal of Politics* 63 (1): 141–58.

Comparative Study of Electoral Systems. 1996–2021. Module 1–5 Codebook. https://cses.org/

Converse, P. E., and R. Pierce. 1986. *Political Representation in France*. Cambridge: Harvard University Press.

Dalton, R. J. 1985. "Political Parties and Political Representation: Party Supporters and Party Elites in Nine Nations." *Comparative Political Studies* 18 (3): 267–99.

Dalton, R. J., D. M. Farrell, and I. McAllister. 2011. *Political Parties and Democratic Linkage: How Parties Organize Democracy*. Oxford: Oxford University Press.

Dalton, R. J., D. M. Farrell, and I. McAllister. 2012. "The Dynamics of Political Representation." In *How Democracy Works: Political Representation and Party Congruence in Modern Societies*, edited by Martin Rosema, Bas Denters, and Kees Aarts, 21–38. Amsterdam: Amsterdam University Press.

Deegan-Krause, K., and Z. Enyedi. 2010. "Agency and the Structure of Party Competition: Alignment, Stability and the Role of Political Elites." *West European Politics* 33 (3): 686–710.

De Vries, C. E., and S. B. Hobolt. 2020. *Political Entrepreneurs: The Role of Challenger Parties in Europe*. Princeton: Princeton University Press.

Deyo, F. C., ed. 1987. *The Political Economy of the New Asian Industrialism*. Ithaca: Cornell University Press.

Downs, A. 1957. "An Economic Theory of Political Action in a Democracy." *Journal of Political Economy* 65 (2): 135–50.

Enyedi, Z., A. Pedrazzani, and P. Segatti. 2020. "Policy Representation in Europe." In *Parliamentary Candidates between Voters and Parties*, edited by L. De Winter, R. Karlsen, and H. Schmitt, 164–95. London: Routledge.

Farag, M. 2020. "Mass-Elite Differences in New Democracies: Tunisia as a Case Study (2010–2016)." *European Political Science* 19 (4): 550–61.

Fossati, D., E. Aspinall, B. Muhtadi, and E. Warburton. 2020. "Ideological Representation in Clientelistic Democracies: The Indonesian Case." *Electoral Studies* 63. https://doi.org/10.1016/j.electstud.2019.102111

Freire, A., and A. Belchior. 2013. "Ideological Representation in Portugal: MPs'–Electors' Linkages in Terms of Left–Right Placement and Substantive Meaning." *Journal of Legislative Studies* 19 (1): 1–21.

Gabel, M. J., and J. D. Huber. 2000. "Putting Parties in Their Place: Inferring Party Left-Right Ideological Positions from Party Manifestos Data." *American Journal of Political Science* 44 (1): 94–103.

Gethin, A., C. Martínez-Toledano, and T. Piketty, eds. 2021. *Political Cleavages and Social Inequalities: A Study of Fifty Democracies, 1948–2020*. Cambridge: Harvard University Press.

Gijsberts, M., and P. Nieuwbeerta. 2000. "Class Cleavages in Party Preferences in the New Democracies in Eastern Europe: A Comparison with Western Democracies." *European Societies* 2 (4): 397–430.

Grauvogel, J., A. A. Licht, and C. von Soest. 2017. "Sanctions and Signals: How International Sanction Threats Trigger Domestic Protest in Targeted Regimes." *International Studies Quarterly* 61 (1): 86–97.

Hillen, S., and N. D. Steiner. 2020. "The Consequences of Supply Gaps in Two-Dimensional Policy Spaces for Voter Turnout and Political Support: The Case of Economically Left-Wing and Culturally Right-Wing Citizens in Western Europe." *European Journal of Political Research* 59 (2): 331–53.

Hoffmann-Lange, U. 2019. "The Development of Political Legitimacy among MPs and Citizens in Old and Young Democracies." In *Elites and People: Challenges to Democracy*, edited by Fredrik Engelstad, Trygve Gulbrandsen, Marte Mangset, and Marie Teigen, 35–59. Bingley, UK: Emerald Publishing.

Holmberg, S. 1989. "Political Representation in Sweden." *Scandinavian Political Studies* 12 (1): 1–36.

Holmberg, S. 1997. "Dynamic Opinion Representation." *Scandinavian Political Studies* 20 (3): 265–83.

Hooghe, L., and G. Marks. 2004. "Does Identity or Economic Rationality Drive Public Opinion on European Integration?" *PS: Political Science & Politics* 37 (3): 415–20.

Hooghe, L., G. Marks, and C. J. Wilson. 2002. "Does Left/Right Structure Party Positions on European Integration?" *Comparative Political Studies* 35 (8): 965–89.

Jou, W. 2011. "Left–Right Orientations and Ideological Voting in New Democracies: A Case Study of Slovenia." *Europe-Asia Studies* 63 (1): 27–47.

Jou, W., M. Endo, and Y. Takenaka. 2017. "An Appraisal of Japan's 'Right Turn': Citizen-Government Congruence and Ideological Understanding." *Asian Survey* 57 (5): 910–32.

Karvonen, L., and S. Kuhnle, eds. 2003. *Party Systems and Voter Alignments Revisited*. London: Routledge.

Katz, R. S., and W. J. Crotty, eds. 2005. *Handbook of Party Politics*. London: Sage.

Kim, H., J. Y. Choi, and J. Cho. 2008. "Changing Cleavage Structure in New Democracies: An Empirical Analysis of Political Cleavages in Korea." *Electoral Studies* 27 (1): 136–50.

Kitschelt, H. 1994. *The Transformation of European Social Democracy*. Cambridge: Cambridge University Press.

Kitschelt, H., Z. Mansfeldova, R. Markowski, and G. Toka. 1999. *Post-Communist Party Systems: Competition, Representation, and Inter-Party Cooperation*. Cambridge: Cambridge University Press.

Kriesi, H. 1998. "The Transformation of Cleavage Politics: The 1997 Stein Rokkan Lecture." *European Journal of Political Research* 33 (2): 165–85.

Kriesi, H., E. Grande, R. Lachat, M. Dolezal, S. Bornschier, and T. Frey. 2008. *West European Politics in the Age of Globalization*. Cambridge: Cambridge University Press.

Kuklinski, J. H. 1978. "Representativeness and Elections: A Policy Analysis." *American Political Science Review* 72 (1): 165–77.

Lefkofridi, Z., and K. Horvath. 2012. "Migration Issues and Representation in European Liberal Democracies." *Representation* 48 (1): 29–46.

Lipset, S. M., and S. Rokkan, eds. 1967. *Party Systems and Voter Alignments: Cross-National Perspectives*. New York: Free Press.

Luna, J. P., and E. J. Zechmeister. 2005. "Political Representation in Latin America: A Study of Elite-Mass Congruence in Nine Countries." *Comparative Political Studies* 38 (4): 388–416.

Mainwaring, S. 1999. *Rethinking Party Systems in the Third Wave of Democratization: The Case of Brazil*. Stanford: Stanford University Press.

Mair, P. 1997. *Party System Change: Approaches and Interpretations*. Oxford: Clarendon Press.

Mair, P. 2007. "Left–Right Orientations." In *The Oxford Handbook of Political Behavior*, edited by Russell J. Dalton and Hans-Dieter Klingemann. Oxford: Oxford University Press.

Mattila, M., and T. Raunio. 2006. "Cautious Voters–Supportive Parties: Opinion Congruence between Voters and Parties on the EU Dimension." *European Union Politics* 7 (4): 427–49.

Medeiros, M., J. P. Gauvin, and C. Chhim. 2015. "Refining Vote Choice in an Ethno-Regionalist Context: Three-Dimensional Ideological Voting in Catalonia and Quebec." *Electoral Studies* 40: 14–22.

Méndez-Lago, M., and A. Martínez. 2002. "Political Representation in Spain: An Empirical Analysis of the Perception of Citizens and MPs." *Journal of Legislative Studies* 8 (1): 63–90.

McAllister, I. 1991. "Party Elites, Voters and Political Attitudes: Testing Three Explanations for Mass-Elite Differences." *Canadian Journal of Political Science/Revue canadienne de science politique* 24 (2): 237–68.

McClosky, H., P. J. Hoffmann, and R. O'Hara. 1960. "Issue Conflict and Consensus among Party Leaders and Followers." *American Political Science Review* 54 (2): 406–27.

McElroy, G., and K. Benoit. 2012. "Policy Positioning in the European Parliament." *European Union Politics* 13 (1): 150–67.

McEvoy, C. 2012. "Unequal Representation in the EU: A Multi-Level Analysis of Voter–Party Congruence in EP Elections." *Representation* 48 (1): 83–99.

Meyer, T. M., and M. Wagner. 2020. "Perceptions of Parties' Left-Right Positions: The Impact of Salience Strategies." *Party Politics* 26 (5): 664–74.

Miller, W. E., and D. E. Stokes. 1963. "Constituency Influence in Congress." *American Political Science Review* 57 (1): 45–56.

Miller, W. E., R. Pierce, J. Thomassen, R. Herrera, P. Esaisson, S. Holmberg, and B. Wessels. 1999. *Policy Representation in Western Democracies*. Oxford: Oxford University Press.

Moreno, A. 2019. *Political Cleavages: Issues, Parties, and the Consolidation of Democracy*. London: Routledge.

Page, B. I., and J. Barabas. 2000. "Foreign Policy Gaps between Citizens and Leaders." *International Studies Quarterly* 44 (3): 339–64.

Page, B. I., and M. M. Bouton. 2008. *The Foreign Policy Disconnect: What Americans Want from Our Leaders but Don't Get*. Chicago: University of Chicago Press.

Peng, I., and J. Wong. 2010. "East Asia." In *The Oxford Handbook of the Welfare State*, edited by F. G. Castles, S. Leibfried, J. Lewis, H. Obinger, and C. Pierson. Oxford: Oxford University Press.

Pierson, P. 2004. *Politics in Time*. Princeton: Princeton University Press.

Powell, G. B., Jr. 2004. "Political Representation in Comparative Politics." *Annual Review of Political Science* 7: 273–96.

Powell, G. B., Jr. 2013. "Representation in Context: Election Laws and Ideological Congruence between Citizens and Governments." *Perspectives on Politics* 11 (1): 9–21.

Rabinowitz, G., and S. E. Macdonald. 1989. "A Directional Theory of Issue Voting." *American Political Science Review* 83 (1): 93–121.

Rae, D. W., and M. Taylor. 1970. *The Analysis of Political Cleavages*. New Haven: Yale University Press.

Ramonaitė, A. 2020. "Mapping the Political Space in Lithuania: The Discrepancy between Party Elites and Party Supporters." *Journal of Baltic Studies* 51 (4): 477–96.

Randall, V. 2003. "Party Systems and Voter Alignments in the New Democracies of the Third World." In *Party Systems and Voter Alignments Revisited*, edited by Lauri Karvonen and Stein Kuhnle, 258–79. London: Routledge.

Reher, S. 2018. "Gender and Opinion–Policy Congruence in Europe." *European Political Science Review* 10 (4): 613–35.

Rohrschneider, R., and S. Whitefield. 2009. "Understanding Cleavages in Party Systems: Issue Position and Issue Salience in 13 Post-Communist Democracies." *Comparative Political Studies* 42 (2): 280–313.

Rosset, J., and C. Stecker. 2019. "How Well Are Citizens Represented by Their Governments? Issue Congruence and Inequality in Europe." *European Political Science Review* 11 (2): 145–60.

Sartori, G. 2005. *Parties and Party Systems: A Framework for Analysis*. Colchester, UK: ECPR Press.

Scheiner, E. 2006. *Democracy without Competition in Japan: Opposition Failure in a One-Party Dominant State*. Cambridge: Cambridge University Press.

Schmitt, H., and J. Thomassen. 1999. *Political Representation and Legitimacy in the European Union*. Oxford: Oxford University Press.

Schultz, C. 1996. "Polarization and Inefficient Policies." *Review of Economic Studies* 63 (2): 331–44.

Selçuk, O., and D. Hekimci. 2020. "The Rise of the Democracy–Authoritarianism Cleavage and Opposition Coordination in Turkey 2014–2019." *Democratization* 27 (8): 1496–1514.

Seligson, M. A. 2007. "The Rise of Populism and the Left in Latin America." *Journal of Democracy* 18 (3): 81–95.

Shim, J. 2020. "Left Is Right and Right Is Left? Partisan Difference on Social Welfare and Particularistic Benefits in South Korea, Japan, and Taiwan." *Journal of International and Comparative Social Policy* 36 (1): 25–41.

Shim, J., and M. Farag. 2022. "Blind Spots in the Study of Political Representation: Actors and Political Dimensions." Paper presented at the 2022 Annual Meeting of the Swiss Political Science Association.

Shim, J., and M. Farag. 2023. "Beyond Clientelism and Personalism: Political Divisions beyond Western Democracies." Paper presented at the 2023 Annual Meeting of the Swiss Political Science Association.

Shim, J., and S. Gherghina. 2020. "Measuring the Mass-Elite Preference Congruence: Findings from a Meta-Analysis and Introduction to the Symposium." *European Political Science* 19 (4): 509–27.

Thomassen, J., and H. Schmitt. 1997. "Policy Representation." *European Journal of Political Research* 32 (2): 165–84.

Tworzecki, H. 2003. *Learning to Choose: Electoral Politics in East-Central Europe*. Stanford: Stanford University Press.

Van Ditmars, M. M., and S. L. De Lange. 2019. "Differential Representation? The Gaps between Mainstream and Niche Party Representatives and Their Voters in The Netherlands." *Acta Politica* 54 (2): 295–314.

Von Schoultz, Å., and H. Wass. 2016. "Beating Issue Agreement: Congruence in the Representational Preferences of Candidates and Voters." *Parliamentary Affairs* 69 (1): 136–58.

Walczak, A., and W. Van der Brug. 2013. "Representation in the European Parliament: Factors Affecting the Attitude Congruence of Voters and Candidates in the EP Elections." *European Union Politics* 14 (1): 3–22.

Walker, C. 2016. "The Authoritarian Threat: The Hijacking of 'Soft Power.'" *Journal of Democracy* 27 (1): 49–63.

Wheatley, J., C. Carman, F. Mendez, and J. Mitchell. 2014. "The Dimensionality of the Scottish Political Space: Results from an Experiment on the 2011 Holyrood Elections." *Party Politics* 20 (6): 864–78.

Wiesehomeier, N., and D. Doyle. 2012. "Attitudes, Ideological Associations and the Left–Right Divide in Latin America." *Journal of Politics in Latin America* 4 (1): 3–33.

Wlezien, C. 1995. "The Public as Thermostat: Dynamics of Preferences for Spending." *American Journal of Political Science* 39 (4): 981–1000.

Zielinski, J. 2002. "Translating Social Cleavages into Party Systems: The Significance of New Democracies." *World Politics* 54 (2): 184–211.

Zimmerman, W. 1998. "Is Ukraine a Political Community?" *Communist and Post-Communist Studies* 31 (1): 43–55.

CHAPTER 3

European Integration and Its Different Guises across Europe

A Subdimensional Perspective on Mass–Elite Discrepancy

Andrea Pareschi, Gianfranco Baldini, and Matteo Giglioli

In contemporary Europe, European integration revolving around the EU has become a bone of contention among both political parties and national populations (Hooghe and Marks 2009; Vasilopoulou 2023). Virtually every member state—from the established western democracies to the "newer" eastern ones—now houses a distinctive pattern of contestation on the issue, both inside its party system and within its public opinion (Van der Eijk and Franklin 2004). From the viewpoint of global mass–elite discrepancies, the political dimensions of integration have potentially assumed "key" relevance in about 30 countries simultaneously.

Since its early stages, integration has configured itself as a project conceived by elites and a process led by elites. An insightful account detailing the rationale and the changing patterns of the relationship between political elites and European integration has described the latter as the "unplanned and imperfect Babylonian tower resulting from the accumulated construction work of several generations of European elites under changing conditions, following different standards and building plans" (Best, Lengyel, and Verzichelli 2012, 3). Yet Haas's (1958, 17) claim that, to interpret the process, it suffices "to single out and define the political elites in the participating countries . . . and assess changes in attitude on their part"—with mass opinion surveys being unnecessary—has become less tenable. Indeed, according to contemporary leading scholars, citizens' preferences now lie "at the heart of political, popular and academic debates regarding the present state and future of European integration" (Boomgaarden et al. 2011, 242). In other words, "*the unprecedented development in supranational governance in recent years has led to greater public contestation, yet at the same time the Union is more reliant on public support for its continued legitimacy than ever before*" (De Vries 2018, 5, emphasis in original).

While the European Economic Community era already featured a political impetus generating numerous landmarks with "high politics" reverberations, the Maastricht Treaty is regarded as a "watershed" moment. In terms of policy, it marked "the moment when divisions between European and domestic policy [began] to become increasingly blurred in the areas of political, economic, social, legal, environmental and foreign affairs" (Usherwood and Startin 2013, 3). In terms of politics, it provoked an "awakening" of sorts among national populations, who switched to more divided and less supportive views within months in 1991–92 (Eichenberg and Dalton 2007; Down and Wilson 2008). Ever since the ensuing referendums on the treaty yielded a narrow "No" in Denmark (50.7%) and a "*petit oui*" in France (51.0%), and even more so after the French (54.7%) and the Dutch (61.5%) rejected the European Constitution in 2005, concerns about mass–elite discrepancies in the support for a united Europe have repeatedly surfaced.

In the 1990s and 2000s, a phase of institutional activism led to the treaties of Amsterdam and Nice, the aborted constitution, and the Lisbon Treaty. Other recognizable milestones such as the 2004 enlargement— together with the venue offered by European Parliament elections every five years and the frequent occurrence of referendums (Oppermann 2018)— also provided opportunities for voices articulating criticism of integration. The past 15 years have further entrenched the European question, beyond specific countries and treaties, through several crises (Börzel and Risse 2018; Riddervold et al. 2021): the Eurozone crisis and problematic European response, disputes over migrant inflows, democratic backsliding, the COVID-19 pandemics, geopolitical turmoil well before the war in Ukraine and its dire economic consequences, wavering solidarity ties, and a broader crisis of legitimacy and governance. Meanwhile, as several Eurosceptic political forces have succeeded in European and national elections—some even entering government—the salience and divisiveness of Europe among elites and citizens have gradually strengthened.

According to the "constraining dissensus" paradigm (Hooghe and Marks 2009), more-divided and tepid public opinion acts as a restraining factor in this far less smooth stage of the integration process. Indeed, the alleged existence of mass–elite gulfs has been an ingredient in popular suspicion and in challenger parties' accusations against the mainstream, which is often presumed to have lost contact with ordinary citizens. Against this backdrop, the substantive preferences of masses and elites on EU matters and the actual extent of agreement[1] seem highly consequential, and not of merely normative interest. As a matter of fact, further transfers of sovereignty depend on decisions to be taken by weakly integrated political elites of individual EU member states that are split between intergovernmental and supranational approaches, subject to electoral constraints (Engelstad et al. 2019), and face relatively attentive public opinion.

However, not all member states experience the same process: on the contrary, in each country a different contest over Europe is taking place (Taggart 2006). Scholars have variously underscored how strongly "public responses to Europe are refracted through national institutions and patterns of discourse that reflect distinct historical trajectories" (Hooghe and Marks 2009, 14; Díez Medrano 2003; De Vries 2018), where the relevant factors include length of membership, country size, institutional "goodness-of-fit," and so on. Arguably, the differences in historical trajectories are compounded by the asymmetric nature of the contemporary crises. "European integration" as perceived by the British in relation to Brexit, for instance, presumably diverges from developments associated with the EU in countries bearing the brunt of migration inflows, or in countries on either side of the austerity rift.

This chapter studies the extent of mass–elite discrepancies in 10 member states in 2016, as measured using a general scale of support for European unification and six policy area-specific scales to gauge aspects of the economy, migration, and international security. Chosen because they relate to salient issues faced by European countries—the sovereign debt crisis; the migration crisis; and crises linked to Ukraine, Libya, and Syria, respectively—and because they plausibly represent distinct and cross-cutting aspects, these three policy areas are likely to have elicited stable preferences among both political elites and ordinary citizens. As we show, national "performances" of EU-related congruence visibly vary when preferences pertaining to different policy areas are considered, proving the policy area's autonomy.

Empirically, this study first uncovers prevalent patterns of association between general and domain-specific views among masses and elites, respectively. Very rarely do the two groups in the same country associate European integration with the same subdimensions, but across the board they converge in linking integration to authority over immigration policy. Second, mass–elite congruence strains occur for this subdimension as well as for authority over economic policy, although the substantive evaluation of discrepancies partly depends on the measurement used. Therefore, our findings uphold the value of a subdimensional perspective on EU issue congruence. Furthermore, by focusing on certain national cases whose levels of mass–elite discrepancy stand out, we seek explanatory power in country-specific circumstances. In so doing, we pave the way for reflections on the relevance of critical junctures and elite agency.

This chapter first shows how, within EU studies, clusters of works inspecting elite or mass stances, or both, have approached European integration as a key political dimension. Having identified the dimensionality of EU-related attitudes as a "blind spot" in studies appraising opinion congruence, we present our dataset in order to examine the strength of associations between general and specific scales, and to assess mass–elite discrepancies by country across such scales. We then inspect contextual evidence from exemplary cases in order to suggest institutional and discursive drivers of mass–elite congruence performances. In our conclusion, we recapitulate our findings; reflect on their implications, particularly with regard to elite agency, and suggest extant puzzles to be solved.

3.1. Political Elites, National Populations, and the European Integration Dimension

By and large, existing scholarship on political dimensions has identified three key dimensions: socioeconomic, sociocultural, and foreign relations (see chapter 2). From a global perspective, European integration apparently possesses a sui generis character with respect to these dimensions and the main political conflicts related to them. But even in the European context, where the EU issue has been treated as an autonomous dimension—grafted onto a political space defined by an overarching left-right dimension, though increasingly divided into "socioeconomic" and "sociocultural" components—its precise status vis-à-vis other political axes is neither stable nor uniform across member states.

We contend that, just as the usual interpretations of the threefold approach (to socioeconomic, sociocultural, and foreign relations issues) miss important global variation in mass–elite discrepancies (see chapter 2 for further details), in the European context a perspective on integration that pays attention to subdimensions may shed more light on representational strains than the hitherto dominant uni-dimensional approach. We draw on several influential clusters of research in EU studies to argue that (1) owing to its nature, the European dimension is indeed autonomous at both the elite and mass levels; (2) the EU-related preferences of the two levels cannot simply be inferred from each other; and (3) there are grounds for expecting discrepancies on at least some subdimensions of European integration.

First, the European Communities—as well as the EU itself—may be described as international regimes and organizations. Insofar as integration entails the international position of European countries, as well as their external sovereignty and its limitations, it represents an important part of foreign policy. However, the "level," "scope," and "inclusiveness" of EU decision-making (De Wilde and Zürn 2012) have increased so much that hardly any national policy domain is now devoid of a European-level governance aspect. Different political forces within member states seek to build linkages between the EU and different policy issues (Hoeglinger 2016), framing Europe as a matter of democracy, neoliberalism, identity, social protection, and so on (Pareschi 2023). And although Whitefield and Rohrschneider (2019) point to the formation of "integration families" within the mainstream left and right, numerous accounts portray mainstream parties as having sought to defuse the "maverick" issue of integration or embed it in traditional patterns of competition in order to thwart its unsettling potential (Mattila and Raunio 2006). By the same logic, "challenger" parties have been incentivized to instead push EU matters up the agenda (Rovny 2012; De Vries and Hobolt 2020). Clearly, European integration has become a force to be reckoned with in domestic policy and politics.

Hence, the burgeoning literature on the *politicization* of the EU (e.g., Hutter and Kriesi 2019) has highlighted trends of increased salience (despite clear variance across Europe), enhanced polarization of opinions and preferences, and expansion of actors and audiences debating the issue. But what about the degree of autonomy of EU-related preferences from the aforementioned socioeconomic and sociocultural divides? According to Hooghe and Marks (2018, 123), "in much of Europe the crises have reinforced a new transnational cleavage that has at its core a cultural conflict pitting libertarian, universalistic values against the defense of nationalism and particularism"; this is mobilized by radical right Traditional-authoritarian-nationalist (TAN) parties around the issues of immigration *and* Europe. Nevertheless, although the sociocultural aspects often give the impression of driving the EU dimension, the center-periphery tension between the EU and member states may well have a life of its own. Since this tension manifests in numerous policy fields, it is not surprising that researchers have sought to ascertain the place of the European integration dimension in complex issue spaces. Echoing this, various empirical analyses have attributed to European integration a space of its own (Van der Brug and Van Spanje 2009), at times pointing to three-dimensional issue spaces structured around the socioeconomic dimension, the sociocultural dimension, and the European integration dimension (Bakker, Jolly, and Polk 2012; Costello, Thomassen, and Rosema 2012).[2]

Additionally, the relative autonomy of the EU issue is buttressed by works stressing its increased importance as a driver of electoral behavior (*EU issue voting*). Indeed, EU-related preference leanings have reportedly come to affect vote choices in those elections and in national ones as well, attesting to a partial awakening of the "sleeping giant" described by Van der Eijk and Franklin (2004).

Our second argument is that mass and elite preferences cannot simply be inferred from each other. We must recall that works on *mass-based Euroscepticism* and *party-based Euroscepticism* have mostly gone their separate ways. A rich subfield anchored in surveys has investigated the drivers of public support and opposition to the EU,[3] uncovering a plethora of individual-level traits: sociotropic or individual utilitarianism, identity or culture, partisan cue-taking or satisfaction toward national democracy (see Hobolt and De Vries 2016). Parallel research on parties has been spurred by the North Carolina school, which was built on the Chapel Hill Expert Survey (CHES) and emphasizes ideological divisions encapsulated by cleavage theory; and by the Sussex school, which classifies parties through definitions and qualitative evaluations (Mudde 2011). Recent contributions have urged researchers to transcend this artificial divide (Vasilopoulou 2013) because "Euroscepticism is neither simply an elite phenomenon, which the population is manipulated into adopting every time the issue is put on the agenda, nor a straightforward bottom-up phenomenon, whereby the political parties reflect the preferences of their electorate" (Skinner 2013, 123).

Attempting to clarify the interplay of mass–elite opinion on European integration, some longitudinal studies have tested the (prevailing) direction of influence (*EU mass–elite linkages*). Carrubba (2001), controlling for reverse causation, has strikingly proved that parties adapted their manifestos to their voters' EU-related stances long before Maastricht; while Arnold et al. (2012) found that the average voter position strongly influences parties' positions on European integration. Nevertheless, equally sophisticated analyses have reached diverging conclusions that stress top-down mechanisms (Hellström 2008). Overall, processes of reciprocal elite-mass linkages—conditioned by third variables, for example, electoral contexts, party traits, characteristics of party systems—have constituted the habitual finding rather than the exception (Ray 2003; Steenbergen, Edwards, and De Vries 2007). Persistent ambiguity between top-down and bottom-up empirical accounts of representation on the European dimension further proves the extreme difficulty in inferring one level's stances from the other.

With respect to our third line of argument about discrepancies in the subdimensions of European integration, and in line with the discussion undertaken in chapter 2, growing concerns about the possible presence of mass–elite gaps in support for the EU have spawned direct assessments of preference discrepancies. The literature on *EU mass–elite congruence*, which dates back to the 1990s, continues in the present day to elicit interest and to prompt investigations (Devine and Ibenskas 2021; Pareschi, Baldini, and Giglioli 2023). In this respect, the available evidence points to a sufficiently recognizable mismatch in mass and elite preferences on the subject of European integration (Real-Dato 2017; Pareschi, Baldini, and Giglioli 2023). However, the enduring success of certain Eurosceptic forces leads us to wonder whether consequential mass–elite discrepancies may also arise on specific subdimensions within the general political dimension of European integration. The literature on EU issue congruence traditionally relies on the aforementioned general scale, and other works have considered equally general Eurobarometer questions about whether a country's EU membership is a good thing, or whether the country has benefited (e.g., Hooghe and Marks 2006). The subdimensions of EU-related views have long remained a blind spot for most clusters reviewed above,[4] not just for congruence studies. But when subdimensional perspectives have underpinned assessments of mass–elite discrepancies, a more nuanced picture is obtained.

In the 1990s, Thomassen and Schmitt (1997, 1999; Schmitt and Thomassen 2000) assessed EU mass–elite congruence on specific policy scales, dealing with (1) a common European currency, (2) the removal of national borders, and (3) the prioritization of a European employment program, as opposed to single market completion. Unlike along the general dimension, political elites—whether at the party or country level (see also Marsh and Wessels 1997)—consistently favored pro-integration policies much more than their voters did. Conversely, using a 1996 one-time survey of EU-15 elites sensu lato, Hooghe (2003) juxtaposed aggregate preferences among European elites and citizens regarding the "Europeanisation" of 13 policy areas, spotting different patterns elicited by different domains rather than a generalized pro-EU elite bias.

More recently, Müller, Jenny, and Ecker (2012) have employed elite and mass survey data gathered in 2007 to calculate discrepancies for five possible extensions of EU competences between the median voter, the median party in parliament, and the government for 15 EU member states. The voters, parliaments, and governments of all countries favored cohesion policy and a single foreign policy. With regard to common tax and social security systems, while the picture across Europe still leaned toward support, some countries displayed a three-way alignment on the anti-integration side, and in a few national cases alignment failed as the three positions spanned both sides. Based on the same survey data, combined to produce an index of the four mentioned policy areas, Sanders and Toka (2013) noted that discrepancies between average mass and elite positions appeared limited and specific to some countries. Such evidence sits uneasily with the conventional wisdom that simply depicts a "mass–elite gap" on European integration, and this mismatch warrants a subdimensional perspective.

3.2. Probing the Subdimensionality of European Integration and Mass–Elite Discrepancies

3.2.1. Examining the Autonomous Status of Six EU Subdimensions

Factoring the subdimensionality of the European issue into the evaluation of discrepancies is only the beginning: how the complex nexus is best understood is not obvious. Regular surveys contain separate questions revolving around the EU and European integration: attachment to Europe, satisfaction with EU democracy, trust in its institutions, and so on. Other efforts to disentangle different facets of "Europeanness" have singled out an emotive component, a cognitive-evaluative component, and a projective-conative component (Best, Lengyel, and Verzichelli 2012; Best 2012). Yet other attempts have built on Eastonian categories to distinguish between diffuse and specific support and to extricate attitudes toward distinct EU-level targets: community, regime, policies, authorities (Krouwel and Abts 2007; Boomgaarden et al. 2011). However, "it may not be entirely realistic to suggest that people are cognitively able to distinguish between all [these] different aspects of the European integration process" (De Vries 2018, 43). Disentangling preferences for specific EU policies—or the Europeanization of specific domains—provides other entry points.

This chapter leverages questions identically posed to elected political elites and ordinary citizens of 10 European countries in 2016, in the framework of the EUEngage project. Spanning cognitive and conative standpoints (Best 2012), these questions offer a suitable basis for a subdimensional perspective on mass–elite discrepancies. They make use of appropriate wording, neither so technical as to risk "manufacturing" opinions nor so simplistic as to be unpalatable to elites.[5] The traditional EU unification item allows comparison with previous studies and comes close to representing a general dimension. Six additional domain-specific scales inquire into the preferred balance between the nation-state and the EU level in relation to salient matters faced by member states during the past few years, which should provide access points to the EU even for individuals with weak political cognition. The scales are all morphologically identical, with a range of 0–10, and enable interviewees to fine-tune their responses while permitting multiple statistical approaches to mass–elite comparison.

All questions were posed to 21,820 citizens and 696 Members of Parliament (MPs)/Members of the European Parliament (MEPs) across 10 countries: Czechia, France, Germany, Greece, Italy, the Netherlands, Poland, Portugal, Spain, and the United Kingdom. The countries represent a reasonably diverse subset of the 28 member states in terms of size, region, length of membership, intensity of integration, varieties of capitalism, and welfare regimes. As for the status of MPs and MEPs, in line with the positional method of elite identification (Hoffmann-Lange 2018), "there can be little doubt that elected members of parliament in representative democracies are part of the political elite," given their "important role in shaping fundamental policy decisions [and] deciding about the institutional order of the polity" (Best and Vogel 2018, 339).

While cross-national surveys have been increasingly employed as a tool for studying political elites over the past decades (Semenova 2018), with special attention devoted to the political elites of EU member states and to the representative linkage with citizens (Rodríguez-Teruel and Daloz 2018), it is also true that transnational elite surveys are costly and rare (Müller, Jenny, and Ecker 2012). In fact, not even the European Election Studies include an elite study of every European election (the latest was in 2009). Therefore, EUEngage represents a virtually unrivaled source of data identically gathered among elites and masses, on both general and specific EU-related attitudes, in multiple European countries concurrently. Its mass-level fieldwork occurred between mid-June and mid-July 2016, whereas elite-level data collection took place between April and October. Further information is provided in the appendix (for more detailed reports, see EUEngage 2017a, 2017b).

Table 3.1 displays the content and wording of the survey items. Two questions concern economic governance (budgetary decision-making powers and pooling of resources). Three concern the governance of migration (which level should decide on migrant quotas per year, cover costs of asylum, and take responsibility for hosting immigrants). Finally, one question concerns security threats in the troubled vicinities of Europe. Given the novel character of these survey items, it cannot be proved ex ante that

Table 3.1. EUEngage Survey Questions and Their Related Subdimensions

Policy Area	Subdimensions	Item wording
Unif	*General European integration*	In your opinion, has the unification of the EU gone too far (0) or should it be taken further (10)?
Econ1	*Authority over economic policy*	Giving the European Union more authority over Member States' economic and budgetary policies (0) vs. Retaining full powers for economic decision-making in each Member State (10)
Econ2	*Pooling of economic resources*	Each country should rely on its own resources to fix its economic problems (0) vs. The European Union's countries should pool resources to fix economic problems (10)
Imm1	*Authority over immigration policy*	[COUNTRY] should decide for itself how many immigrants to accept each year (0) vs. The European Union should decide how many immigrants should be accepted by each Member State each year (10)
Imm2	*Costs of providing asylum*	The costs of providing asylum should be shared among all the European Union's Member States (0) vs. Each country should bear the costs depending on how many asylum seekers it receives (10)
Imm3	*Responsibility for hosting migrants*	The country immigrants arrive in should be responsible for hosting them (0) vs. All the European Union's Member States should be responsible for the hosting of immigrants (10)
Sec1	*Response to security threats*	Each Member State should decide on its own when responding to major security threats (0) vs. EU Member States should have a common response to major security threats (10)

they crosscut each other. Yet, insofar as respondents adopt problem-oriented rather than ideology-oriented views of European integration, in principle the domains correspond to autonomous preferences as to what integration should cover. Think, for instance, of a Polish citizen wishing for a united EU response to Russian threats, but wary of common approaches to either the economy or migration.

This section begins by probing whether general and domain-specific preferences constitute a consistent bundle in elites' and citizens' minds or whether the domain-specific preferences are autonomous. After uncovering evidence that supports the latter scenario, we probe which scales have tighter linkages with the more abstract dimension, how the elite-level and mass-level pictures of association relate, and which patterns appear across countries. Then, we focus directly on the mass–elite discrepancy. For each country and along each scale, we compute two congruence indicators: the difference between the mass-level and the elite-level average score, and the difference between the pro-integration proportions of masses and elites. Each quantitative indicator is then complemented with a binary judgment, stating whether national elites and masses stand on the same side.

In regard to the first step, we follow previous literature in employing the Pearson correlation coefficient between two dimensional scales as a measure of their respective independence or superimposition (see Schmitt and Thomassen [2000] and Van der Eijk and Franklin [2004] on the relationship between left–right and the European axis).[6] Hence, the lower the correlation coefficient linking each domain-specific scale to the general scale, the higher the former's autonomy from the latter.

Two tables report the strength and statistical significance of correlation coefficients between each domain-specific scale and the general scale. Table 3.2 displays correlations among the national samples of political elites; table 3.3 exhibits the corresponding mass-level correlations. For each country's row, the highest correlation coefficient is in ***bold italic***, the second-highest is in **bold**. All correlation coefficients, with one exception, take the expected sign, confirming positive relationships between favoring European integration and supporting the European governance of pressing crises. Nevertheless, the strength of Pearson's r is often moderate or weak: out of the total 66 coefficients, only 22 coefficients in table 3.2, and as few as 3 in table 3.3, reach the 0.50 threshold. In fact, all domain-specific scales are more strongly associated with the general scale among elites, which also holds true for a majority of subdimensions in each country except Czechia and France. Accordingly, we hardly detect any bundle of attitudes bound by high correlations: only the Polish, Dutch, and British elites, and to some extent the British population, closely resemble this picture.

More thought-provoking are the respective elite-level and mass-level patterns of association. Among elites, all aggregate correlation coefficients range between 0.42 and 0.54—attesting to comparable linkages with the general dimension—with authority over economic policy, authority over immigration policy, and response to security threats exceeding 0.50. In particular, the question of budgetary authority displays the highest Pearson's r in half the countries. Among populations, where aggregate correlations range between 0.17 and 0.43, differences in the strength of ties are more discernible and consistent. Unmistakably, the question concerning the pooling of economic resources and authority over immigration policy displays the highest or second-highest correlation coefficient in each of eight countries. Conversely,

Table 3.2. Elite-Level Correlations of the Six Domain-Specific Scales with the EU Unification Item, by Country

	Eco1	Eco2	Imm1	Imm2	Imm3	Sec1
Czech Republic	*0.46****	0.31*	**0.36****	0.14	0.24	0.34*
France	*0.41***	0.13	0.39**	*0.50****	0.29	0.33*
Germany	*0.47****	0.32*	**0.46****	0.24	0.38**	0.43**
Greece	*0.52****	0.05	0.30*	0.01	0.11	**0.36****
Italy	*0.55****	0.38***	**0.52****	0.30*	0.34**	0.45***
Netherlands	0.43	*0.77****	0.59*	0.48	0.43	**0.70****
Poland	*0.73****	0.53***	0.61***	0.62***	**0.68****	0.60***
Portugal	0.22	*0.39****	0.36**	0.03	0.25*	**0.44****
Spain	0.30*	*0.49****	0.44***	0.12	0.41***	**0.56****
United Kingdom	0.46**	0.50***	0.62***	*0.67****	**0.66****	0.65***
Overall	**0.52****	0.45***	*0.54****	0.42***	0.47***	**0.52****

Note: Cells with **bold italic** and **bold** respectively indicate survey items with the highest and the second-highest correlation coefficients within a country.

* $p < 0.05$; ** $p < 0.01$; *** $p < 0.001$.

Table 3.3. Mass-Level Correlations of the Six Domain-Specific Scales with the EU Unification Item, by Country

	Eco1	Eco2	Imm1	Imm2	Imm3	Sec1
Czech Republic	0.34***	0.33***	*0.37****	0.23***	0.23***	**0.36****
France	0.32***	**0.40****	*0.46****	0.15***	0.30***	0.31***
Germany	0.28***	**0.41****	*0.41****	0.11***	0.26***	0.37***
Greece	0.26***	**0.32****	*0.30****	−0.01	0.08***	0.27***
Italy	0.30***	0.36***	**0.38****	0.08***	0.15***	*0.39****
Netherlands	0.41***	**0.48****	*0.51****	0.03	0.29***	0.31***
Poland	0.23***	**0.40****	0.32***	0.18***	0.34***	*0.42****
Portugal	0.16***	*0.31****	**0.31****	0.07***	0.19***	0.24***
Spain	0.23***	**0.32****	0.26***	0.07**	0.19***	*0.33****
United Kingdom	0.41***	**0.54****	*0.63****	0.23***	0.44***	0.31***
Overall	0.33***	*0.43****	**0.42****	0.17***	0.29***	0.36***

Note: Cells with **bold italic** and **bold** respectively indicate survey items with the highest and the second-highest correlation coefficients within a country.

* $p < 0.05$; ** $p < 0.01$; *** $p < 0.001$.

preferences about the costs of providing asylum—and, to some extent, about responsibility for hosting migrants—are very weakly connected with European integration. Hence, comprehensive examination of the tables notably reveals the general dimension to be similarly related, by both political elites and ordinary citizens, to *Authority over immigration policy.*

Remarkably, only in one country is the highest-ranking correlation the same for citizens and elites: Spain, where they also converge in their second-highest correlation. Otherwise, no country displays corresponding patterns of linkages at the two levels. Our indirect test therefore appears to deny the presence of dominant country-specific discourses linking the EU to contemporary crises. In sum, the landscape emerging from the correlations analysis is not a clear-cut one where countries are marked by internal mass–elite convergence and external rifts are single-handedly determined by the crises being faced. In a sense, our result parallels a recent analysis that pointed out that structural factors, asymmetrically affecting different countries, "did not result in country-specific patterns with higher polarization in countries more affected by the respective developments" (Goldberg, Van Elsas, and De Vreese 2020, 324).

3.2.2. State of Mass–Elite Discrepancies on EU Integration: General Dimension and Subdimensions

The fundamental part of the story concerns actual mass–elite preference discrepancies in the 10 countries.[7] Table 3.4 and table 3.5 display issue congruence by country for general European integration. The first two columns of table 3.4 highlight mass-level and elite-level average scores on the 0–10 continuum, the third column displays their difference, and the fourth column reports a qualitative judgment based on whether they fall on the same side of the midpoint (5). The four columns of table 3.5 follow the same logic: they result from mass-level and elite-level proportions on the pro-integration side of the scale;[8] and the qualitative evaluation is based on alignment above or below the majority threshold (50.0%).[9] As illustrated across seven graphs (figs. 3.1a–3.1g), we then graph the majority-based measurement along the seven scales that stem from the general dimension of European integration and its subdimensions. The data displayed prompt several reflections about the degrees of discrepancy along different subdimensions and between different countries.

A first question regards the presence of an overall pro-EU elite bias in the 10 countries, across scales and measures. As tables 3.4 and 3.5 show, the majority-based indicators closely mirror the means-based ones, essentially yielding analogous conclusions. Indeed, quantitative differences in both means and proportions reveal a negative sign, and thus a pro-EU elite bias, for seven to nine national cases along each question.[10] In addition to the direction of the mass–elite discrepancy, the proportions of pro-EU elites and pro-EU masses in 10 countries clearly indicate that masses are more divided over EU integra-

Table 3.4. General European Integration: Means-Based Discrepancies

	Mass mean	Elite mean	Δ in means	Aligned means?
Czechia	3.82	4.91	–1.09**	anti-EU alignment
France	4.48	6.58	–2.10***	pro-EU elite bias
Germany	5.11	6.91	–1.80***	pro-EU alignment
Greece	5.25	7.34	–2.09***	pro-EU alignment
Italy	6.62	7.47	–0.85*	pro-EU alignment
Netherlands	4.17	3.33	0.84	anti-EU alignment
Poland	5.81	6.23	–0.42	pro-EU alignment
Portugal	5.70	5.99	–0.29	pro-EU alignment
Spain	6.37	7.90	–1.53***	pro-EU alignment
United Kingdom	3.54	3.44	0.10	anti-EU alignment

$^*p < 0.05$; $^{**}p < 0.01$; $^{***}p < 0.001$.

Table 3.5. General European Integration: Majority-Based Discrepancies

	Pro-EU mass %	Pro-EU elite %	Δ in %	Aligned majorities?
Czechia	35.6%	49.1%	–13.5	anti-EU alignment
France	45.1%	73.3%	–28.2	pro-EU elite bias
Germany	53.2%	71.3%	–18.1	pro-EU alignment
Greece	54.2%	84.0%	–29.8	pro-EU alignment
Italy	73.3%	78.4%	–5.1	pro-EU alignment
Netherlands	42.2%	30.0%	12.2	anti-EU alignment
Poland	62.3%	69.2%	–6.9	pro-EU alignment
Portugal	61.7%	67.6%	–5.9	pro-EU alignment
Spain	71.4%	90.5%	–19.1	pro-EU alignment
United Kingdom	33.9%	32.9%	1.0	anti-EU alignment

tion issues. Calculating the arithmetic mean from 10 countries, 65 percent of elites are pro-EU whereas the equivalent number for the masses is only 53 percent. Insofar as the general EU dimension is concerned, both the direction and distribution of the mass–elite discrepancy highly resonate with the previous findings noted in the meta-analysis results (see chapter 2).

A second relevant theme is whether the pictures of mass–elite congruence emerging from the six subdimensions substantially diverge from the panorama observed on the general dimension. Our discrepancy analysis further vindicates the claim that the former matter in their own right, considering that preferences on economics, migration, and international security governance can alter judgments concerning the representational "performances" of different countries. Even France, whose mass–elite discrepancy on general European integration is dramatic, reveals differentiated degrees of strain. For other member states, discrepancies in a specific domain become

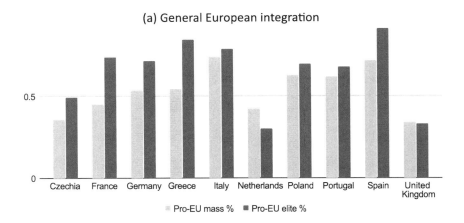

(a) General European integration

Pro-EU mass %   Pro-EU elite %

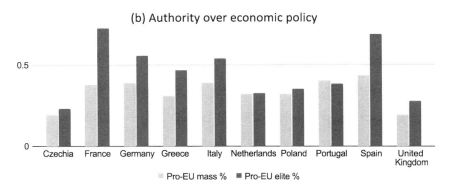

(b) Authority over economic policy

Pro-EU mass %   Pro-EU elite %

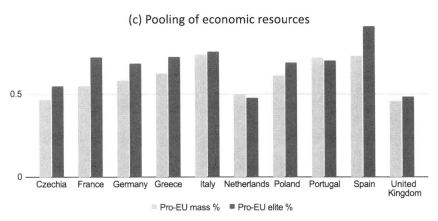

(c) Pooling of economic resources

Pro-EU mass %   Pro-EU elite %

Fig. 3.1. Mass-Level and Elite-Level Proportions on the Pro-Integration Side for General European Integration (*a*) and the Related Six Subdimensions (*b-g*)

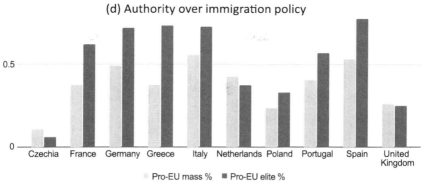

(d) Authority over immigration policy

Pro-EU mass %　Pro-EU elite %

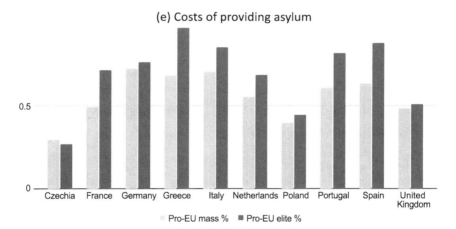

(e) Costs of providing asylum

Pro-EU mass %　Pro-EU elite %

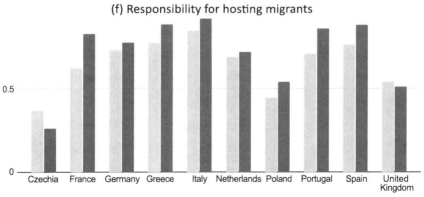

(f) Responsibility for hosting migrants

Pro-EU mass %　Pro-EU elite %

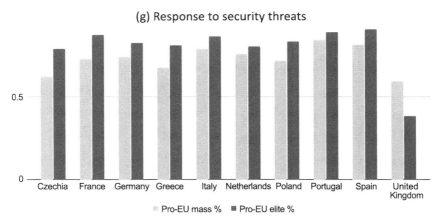

Fig. 3.1—*Continued*

evident beyond general congruence, for example, the considerable anti-EU bias of British elites with regard to international security. A few remarkable cases are singled out for discussion in the next section.

Third, the actual degrees of discrepancy clearly differ across subdimensions. On general European integration, four countries—France, Greece, Germany, and Spain—are characterized by wide and highly significant mass–elite gaps, even though only in France does the majority of the population take an anti-integration stance. Overall, four of the six questions elicit comparable or higher levels of mass–elite congruence. In contrast, questions about authority over economic policy and immigration policy reveal where representational strains are widespread: four member states even display a qualitative pro-EU elite "bias," notably including France and Germany along both scales, while the dichotomous "alignment" characterizing other countries comes with heavy quantitative gaps.

Finally, we briefly dwell on the relationship between mass–elite alignment and substantive positions. On the four questions where discrepancies are limited, roughly two-thirds of the countries exhibit mass–elite alignment on the pro-integration side, with the minority—the UK, Czechia, Poland, and the Netherlands—often expressing anti-integration alignment instead. The two scales that concern authority over economic and migration policies, rather than transnational solidarity, show a different pattern, inasmuch as almost no national population supports the Europeanization of such decision-making. Thus, the prevalent situation is anti-EU alignment, while the national elites embracing a pan-European perspective do so at their own risk.[11]

3.3. Glaring vs. Modest, Expected vs. Unforeseen Discrepancies: Exemplary National Cases

Since this chapter analyzes data at the country level, we deem it best to relate this data to contextual considerations about the circumstances in which the surveys took place in mid-2016. First, the following figure 3.2 outlines the broad classification of the 10 countries based on their degrees of mass–elite discrepancy across the board, the number of scales revealing binary misalignment and their attendant quantitative gaps, and the correlations between such scales and the general dimension at the mass and elite levels. For a few noteworthy cases, in table 3.6, we summarize potentially relevant factors, including the presence of populist and Eurosceptic parties, the structural impact of the economic and migration crises, and more contingent events especially linked to the election cycle.

In view of our data, a sizeable congruence—especially for those subdimensions more strongly associated with the general dimension—is shown by the Netherlands and Czechia, together with Poland and Portugal. Conversely, France constitutes the unrivaled example of an equally sizeable and generalized lack of mass–elite congruence. Halfway between the two poles, the Mediterranean countries of Italy and Spain are joined by the rather

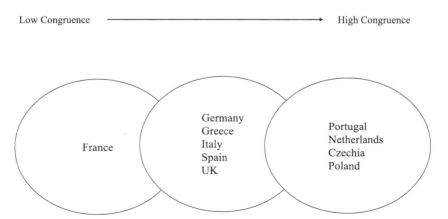

Fig. 3.2. Sets of Countries by Overall Degree of Mass–Elite Congruence

peculiar British case, whereas the representational strains associated with Germany and Greece are somewhat more pronounced. In the remainder of this section, we focus on selected cases by reason of their extreme, typical, or uncommon character.

3.3.1. Countries with Low-Level Mass–Elite Discrepancy

Marked by the lowest opinion discrepancies, the Netherlands, Czechia, and Poland only experience problematic congruence along one scale each. In the first two countries, EU mass–elite incongruence surfaces for the pooling of economic resources: for the Netherlands, the discrepancy is particularly small but the association between the scale and the general dimension is comparatively strong, while a slightly wider mismatch and lower correlation with the general dimension characterize the related evidence on Czechia. Poland, whose own mass–elite discrepancy occurs in relation to responsibility for hosting migrants, is located midway for both respects. Notably, mass–elite alignment on the anti-integration side is not infrequent among the three countries as far as other scales are concerned.

Long-term political culture dynamics may have been at work in the Netherlands and Czechia, countries with very different integration histories but where traditional versions of political and economic liberalism have strong historical roots. This free-market orientation has produced caution toward economic integration that predates the contemporary crises—as exemplified by Czechia's decision not to adopt the euro, or the Netherlands' recurrent qualms about regulations impacting its multinationals. Hence, presumably, the lukewarm stances and uncertain mass–elite alignment on the pooling of economic resources. The immigration issue—where the Dutch masses and elites, who favor Europeanization along two subdimensions, actually differ from their consistently anti-integrationist Czech counterparts—also taps into longer-term trends, that is, the predicament of the Dutch integration model and the developing anti-immigrant consensus in Eastern Europe. For that matter, in both countries, populist challenger parties did not appear in sync with the global financial or migration crises: in the Netherlands, because the Pim Fortuyn/Geert Wilders breakthrough occurred well before; in Czechia, because the country did not meaningfully suffer from either crisis, so that its populist forces (Andrej Babiš's Action of Dissatisfied Citizens, ANO; Tomio Okamura's Freedom and Direct Democracy, SPD) have typically emphasized domestic corruption.

In the case of Poland, more contingent dynamics may have been in play alongside the aforementioned anti-immigrant consensus. The survey field-work coincided with a critical moment in EU relations with Poland, as the European Commission issued "Rule of Law" recommendations targeting the policies pursued by the newly elected Prawo i Sprawiedliwość (Law and Justice) government with respect to judicial independence and the control of mass media. The crisis certainly served to heighten the salience and con-tentiousness of European matters in Polish public opinion. Significantly, the clash was framed in domestic political discourse as illustrative of a widening rift in core values between new member states and the old European core, and was portrayed as succumbing to a "socially liberal, cosmopolitan" drift (Szczerbiak 2016). Immigration, and the perception of Western integration models of culturally heterogeneous populations as politically and ideologi-cally bankrupt, served as an obvious flashpoint. However, the Polish govern-ment matched such broad claims with tactically adroit and discriminating maneuvers in its dealings with Brussels (Szczerbiak 2016). Hence, the dis-crepancy in relation to *Responsibility for hosting migrants*, coupled with anti-integration alignment on other scales gauging the subdimension of immi-gration, may have entailed an overshooting of confrontational rhetoric for domestic consumption.

3.3.2. Countries with High-Level Mass–Elite Discrepancy

For its part, France displays true mass–elite gulfs, resulting in qualitative assessments of "pro-EU elite bias" not just on general European integration—the only country in this respect—but also on authority over economic gov-ernance and immigration policy, both decently associated with the abstract dimension. On the other four questions, the country exhibits dichotomous "alignment," but means-based and majority-based differences are remark-able and significant. At the country level, different indicators had already singled out France as a discrepancy-ridden case in recent times (Dolný and Baboš 2015; Real-Dato 2017): Does this point to country-specific factors?

The reasons may lie in the stability ensured by the French variant of semi-presidentialism. Via near-simultaneous presidential and parliamentary elections and the president's preeminence, the political system is substan-tially insulated from public unrest and permanent electoral campaigning over a five-year term. In mid-2016, France was entering the last year of the unprecedentedly unpopular François Hollande presidency, amid a cli-mate of intense dissatisfaction and perceived loss of status especially vis-à-vis Germany. In the run-up to the 2017 elections, the challenge of the Front

National and public contestation of the EU would be met by political elites through ambivalent stances voiced by almost all presidential candidates, and through "repositioning" attempts harnessed by Emmanuel Macron's La République en Marche. Presumably the two-rounds majoritarian electoral system, which prevents the Front National from gaining significant parliamentary representation, also plays a part in leading to pronounced country-level discrepancies on EU matters.

3.3.3. Countries with Medium-Level Mass–Elite Discrepancy

Despite proving to be closer to glaring discrepancies than to modest ones, Germany represents in our perspective a "typical" case among the surveyed countries, inasmuch as it represents the prevalent cross-national trends of correlation and (in)congruence across general European integration and its subdimensions. Indeed, the German population mostly relates European integration to the pooling of economic resources and authority over immigration policy, which also displays the highest elite-level correlation together with budgetary authority and international security. Opinion gaps are wide precisely on the two scales linked to decision-making authority, resulting in dichotomous mass–elite misalignment, but are negligible elsewhere. Alignment on the general dimension results from widespread elite favor toward integration (71.3%) compared with a much less enthusiastic public opinion (53.2%).

This mixed picture matches expectations raised by the national context in 2015–17, when Germany was behaving as a "reluctant hegemon" enjoying stable domestic politics, epitomized by Angela Merkel's eleventh year as chancellor. Yet Merkel's opening of Germany's borders to Syrian asylum-seekers in 2015, preceded by the outbreak of the Pegida movement and soon followed by the striking news of sexual assaults in different towns on New Year's Eve, was heavily targeted on the political right. In the general election held one year after the EUEngage survey, the vote for Alternative für Deutschland—which inflexibly criticized the management of both Eurozone governance and migrant inflows—rose to 12.6 percent, with the party entering the Bundestag for the first time with 94 seats. It is not entirely clear why mass anti-integration stances are specifically expressed on the questions linked to decision-making, but the roots of related mass–elite discrepancy are clearer: Germany has "a public opinion that has supported the present distribution of power but that would come under strain if there were renewed turbulence in the eurozone or renewed migration flows" (Bulmer and Paterson 2018, 118).

Table 3.6. EU Issue Congruence: Exemplary Cases and Possible Explanatory Factors

		Main critical policy area	Strong populist or Eurosceptic parties, or both, by 2016?	Structural factors (economic and migration crises, national institutions)	Contingent factors (plus timing of closest elections)
High congruence	**Netherlands**	Economy	Populist and Eurosceptic parties since early 2000s (Pim Fortuyn, then PVV; also SP)	Serious impact of economic crisis, medium impact of migration crisis	Parliamentary elections 2017
	Czechia	Economy	Mainly populist (ANO main party since 2011), also Eurosceptic (SPD, KSČM)	Limited impact of both economic and migration crises	Parliamentary elections 2017
	Poland	Immigration	Populist and Eurosceptic (Kukiz'15, but especially PiS)	Limited impact of both economic and migration crises	EU Rule of Law recommendations in spring 2016; presidential and parliamentary elections 2015
	Germany	Economy, Immigration	Die Linke, but especially AfD, rising since 2015 and turning from mainly antibailout to anti-immigrant	Medium impact of economic crisis, serious impact of migration crisis	Parliamentary elections 2017
Low congruence	**France**	General, Economy, Immigration	FN as early and successful populist and Eurosceptic party	Serious impact of economic crisis, medium impact of migration crisis; semi-presidentialism, majoritarian electoral system	Unpopularity of President Hollande; presidential and parliamentary elections 2017

Note: The acronyms in table 3.6 refer to the following parties: AfD = Alternative for Germany; ANO = Action of Dissatisfied Citizens; FN = National Front; KSČM = Communist Party of Bohemia and Moravia; PVV = Party for Freedom; PiS = Law and Justice; SP = Socialist Party; SPD = Freedom and Direct Democracy.

The UK represents a remarkable and less legible intermediate case, not least because in June 2016—right in the middle of the EUEngage fieldwork—the country unexpectedly voted to leave the EU in the Brexit referendum, which offered the prime instance of a real-world preference gap between masses and political elites. Yet, contrary to conventional wisdom, on the general European dimension Britain turns out to exhibit perfect congruence. What is more, mass–elite differences are limited and nonsignificant across all questions but one. Britain additionally displays two almost unique factors. First, its political elites are shown to favor the Europeanization of international security much less than the population. Second, on issues such as the pooling of economic resources, the costs of providing asylum and responsibility for hosting migrants, British elites *and* citizens split into roughly equal halves.

It is difficult to relate the opinion gap concerning security threats to standpoints expressed during the heated referendum campaign, as "Britain's world role, including the foreign and defense implications, played out in [its] margins" (Daddow 2018, 208). British distinctiveness among the 10 countries does not stem from the mass level. All national populations invoke the European umbrella, possibly spurred by wariness of military interventions abroad; and despite the fallout from Afghanistan and Iraq, the average British citizen is, if anything, less keen than her European counterparts. In contrast, only 38.4 percent of British elites favor common responses,[12] the second-lowest figure being 78.7 percent among Czech elites. This may depend on a lingering seduction exerted by former imperial status, or on enduring elite attachment to the "special relationship" with the US.

3.4. Conclusions

Across European political systems, the EU issue has elicited increased contestation between (and within) parties and among national populations. Concerns revolving around preference gaps between masses and political elites—who are reputed to favor European integration more than ordinary citizens do—have accumulated over the decades in line with the "constraining dissensus" paradigm. After recapitulating how different clusters of literature have examined the European dimension in national politics, paving the way for studies of EU mass–elite congruence, we have noted the scarce attention paid to the subdimensionality of related attitudes. Analyzing elite and mass survey data gathered in 2016 in 10 countries, this chapter has assessed mass–elite discrepancies not just on integration in general but also for six questions gauging "Europeanisation" in domains closely connected with contemporary crises: economic governance, migrations, and international security.

By inspecting the strength of associations between the abstract dimension and the domain-specific scales, we have proved that subdimensions are largely autonomous: correlations are weaker among masses but rarely high among elites either. Moreover, the correlations characterizing individual countries do not easily map onto how severely they were struck by the different crises. Rather, transnational patterns emerge. Almost everywhere, citizens' views on European integration are primarily linked with preferences on the pooling of economic resources and authority over yearly migrant quotas. Despite greater cross-country variability, political elites similarly associate the European dimension with authority over immigration policy, but also with authority over economic policy and responses to international threats.

Moving to congruence assessments along the seven scales, we have compared citizens' and elites' average positions and their respective proportions on the pro-integration side; we have also categorized "alignment" or "bias" dichotomously, depending on whether the two groups stood on the same side. First, mixed pictures of (in)congruence distinguish every country beyond the general dimension, further proving the relevance of the subdimensional evaluation of discrepancies. Second, on each subdimension, the elites of most member states favor integration more than their citizens, yet in dichotomous terms a majority of countries show mass–elite "alignment." On the general scale, for instance, eight countries display a pro-EU elite bias, statistically significant in six, but in as many as nine, binary "alignment" obtains. Third, two questions signal acute representational strain, that is, authority over economic policy and authority over immigration policy.

Concerning national cases, we have singled France out by reason of its notable discrepancies across the board, tentatively attributing them to domestic institutional factors. At the opposite pole, three countries—the Netherlands, Poland, and Czechia—boast considerable congruence, exhibiting strain on only one question each. We have presented Germany as a typical, intermediate case that exemplifies the predominant cross-national patterns of correlation and congruence, and we have discussed its discrepancies in connection with the 2017 general election. Lastly, the peculiar British case displays near-perfect quantitative congruence across the board, except on international security: yet, while masses and elites clearly oppose the Europeanization of decision-making authority, on matters involving EU solidarity both groups are divided fairly evenly.

Based on this consideration and our findings, we call for further efforts to clarify the relationship between EU issue congruence and the impact of the European dimension within member states' domestic politics. For some national cases, we have traced the picture of mass–elite (in)congruence back to the political context during the survey fieldwork, but other countries elude our attempts to pinpoint such a connection. We must then wonder whether country-level appraisals of congruence only tell part of the tale— that is, whether the consequential dynamics taking place must be examined through complementary approaches. The fundamental underpinnings of this puzzle are theoretical, and are closely related to two building blocks at the heart of global analysis of mass–elite discrepancy: critical junctures and elite agency.

To be sure, recent research within EU studies has noted both the relevance of political entrepreneurs in translating the European dimension into actual political struggle and the windows of opportunity offered by critical junctures. Britain is a case in point in both respects: despite the unveiled absence of mass–elite discrepancy on the abstract dimension, the issue has produced very tangible political change after being made salient along the lines of a Leave/Remain divide in the 2016 referendum, as a result of a certain sequence of events no less than of elite strategies working through issue emphasis, issue blurring, and differential framing. Our study has gone some way toward suggesting how these factors may play out, yet much remains to be elucidated. For instance, our inspection of subdimensional correlations has found scarce traces of either tight bundles of EU-related attitudes or shared national understandings single-handedly determined by critical circumstances. Hence, our perspective hints at opportunities for political actors to turn the tables on the European dimension by altering its linkages to various policy domains and, consequently, the impact of certain mass–elite discrepancies on the equilibria of domestic politics. In this volume, Petar Bankov and Sergiu Gherghina's mass–elite comparison on the EU dimension in the Bulgarian case (chapter 9) demonstrates how political elites took advantage of EU issues for domestic political purposes during the migrant and Ukraine crisis. For a more systematic understanding of how elites contribute to varying levels of mass–elite discrepancies during critical junctures, the subsequent two chapters together provide a theoretical framework drawing from examples of both old and new democracies.

Appendix: The EUEngage Mass and Elite Surveys

The mass and elite surveys providing the empirical evidence inspected within our chapter took place in the framework of the transnational research project EUEngage (2015–18), which specifically focused on the interplay between EU governance and public reactions at the national level. As part of the EUEngage research endeavor, two consecutive waves of surveys were carried out between 2016 and 2018 among samples of national populations (Work Package 6) and among elected political elites, that is, incumbent MPs and MEPs (Work Package 1). The 10 EU member states mentioned in the chapter were covered: Czechia, France, Germany, Greece, Italy, the Netherlands, Poland, Portugal, Spain, and the United Kingdom (which would go on to formally exit the EU in January 2020).

The dataset we employ represents the outcome of Wave 1 of the EUEngage surveys, which was launched and completed in 2016. In this regard, basic information is summarized in table A3.1. At the mass level, the fieldwork period began in mid-June and lasted until mid-July, with slight variations between individual countries. Setting out to reach a target of 2,200 adult citizens among the resident population of each country, the mass survey ultimately achieved 23,804 completed questionnaires, from which a "final sample" of 21,820 respondents was drawn. The sample size per coun-

Table A3.1. General Information about the EUEngage Wave 1 Fieldwork and Samples

Country	Fieldwork (adult population sample)	Period of completion (political elites)	N (adult population sample)[a]	N (political elites)[b]
United Kingdom	June 14–July 12	April 29–October 27	2,256	59
Czechia	June 16–July 16	May 18–September 6	2,164	77
France	June 16–July 12	June 15–October 20	2,222	72
Germany	June 17–July 7	May 23–October 4	2,169	60
Greece	June 17–July 20	May 10–September 29	2,130	61
Italy	June 16–July 18	April 21–August 8	2,207	93
Netherlands	June 16–July 15	May 12–October 26	2,226	21
Poland	June 16–July 15	May 24–September 7	2,140	84
Portugal	June 16–July 19	May 11–October 8	2,155	87
Spain	June 16–July 19	June 4–October 14	2,151	82
Overall	June 14–July 20	April 21–October 27	21,820	696

a We would opt to use the whole pool of valid responses (23,804), including the "reserve sample" (1,760) as well as the "final sample" (21,820), in order to maximize the number of observations, especially for smaller parties. However, this is not possible since weights were prepared for citizens included in the "final sample" only.

b We include incomplete elite questionnaires in our analyses, and thus in the numbers reported in this column.

try ranged from a minimum of 2,130 citizens (Greece) to a maximum of 2,256 citizens (United Kingdom). As for the elite survey, data collection was carried out between April and October (depending on the country, it began between April and June and ended between September and October). All in all, 696 elected legislators took the survey, even though only 514 interviews were fully completed. Except for the Netherlands (21 respondents), in each surveyed country the survey managed to gather at least 59 responses (United Kingdom), reaching a maximum of 93 (Italy).

More detailed information on the characteristics of the mass survey, such as response targets, sampling procedures, fieldwork, weighting, and data cleaning, may be found in a technical report issued by EUEngage researchers (EUEngage 2017a). The survey had been crafted with the express purpose of generating data that could be analyzed on a country-by-country basis. Questionnaire scripting and web hosting were centralized. In all the 10 countries, respondents belonging to the general population were approached through online panels. To ensure the representative character of the sample to be selected, quota targets were imposed for each country on demographic traits such as gender (male or female), age (five cohorts), and region (country-specific entities based on NUTS2 classification).

It must also be noted that the nonprobabilistic sampling procedure might engender a certain self-selection bias, related to participation in the panel in general and in the survey in particular. Furthermore, online panels may overrepresent or underrepresent certain segments of the population, including strata that are more civically engaged and politically committed than the average citizen. As a way to redress any imbalance caused by the sampling procedures, thus maximizing the representativeness of the sample, a sophisticated, multipurpose array of sets of weights was conceived. Notably, to reflect the peculiar traits associated with internet users, education was added to the original quota targets as a fourth weighting variable. Capping of weights and an iterative rim weighting procedure completed the picture.

Coming to the elite survey, dedicated information and a preliminary descriptive overview are contained in an interim report also published by EUEngage researchers (EUEngage 2017b). Following on the heels of distinguished predecessors like the IntUne project, they consciously sought to attenuate the methodological pitfalls that notoriously arise upon surveying political elites (Rodríguez-Teruel and Daloz 2018). The questionnaire was purposefully designed so as to preserve compatibility and opportunities for comparison with the mass survey items and with past surveys as well. Four thematic blocs touching upon EU matters subsumed the content of the survey: general attitudes toward European integration, the economic crisis, the migration crisis, and the security crisis.

Parliamentary elites, belonging either to national parliaments or to the European Parliament, were selected using their party affiliation and party size as quota targets. The fieldwork took place primarily by means of computer-assisted web interviews (CAWI): MPs and MEPs were contacted through their institutional e-mail address or telephone number and invited to complete the questionnaire online, receiving a unique web link to access it. At their explicit request, some elected legislators were instead surveyed through computer-assisted telephone interviews (CATI) or computer-assisted personal interviews (CAPI).

Notes

1. We focus on mass–elite discrepancy at the country level. Yet, by contributing to the destabilization of party-voter ties, the European issue may also affect individual parties and national party systems.

2. As already pointed out, the topic is still under debate (Hooghe and Marks 2018; Hutter and Kriesi 2019; Whitefield and Rohrschneider 2019).

3. A recent "qualitative turn" has unveiled indifference and ambivalence by relying on focus groups and semistructured interviews (e.g., Gaxie, Hubé, and Rowell 2011). Mainstream approaches to EU public opinion have begun to integrate such insight (Stoeckel 2013; De Vries 2018).

4. However, see Goldberg, Van Elsas, and De Vreese (2020) for a recent exception linked to politicization of EU matters. Inspecting prospective polarization engendered by the latter among parties and citizens of four EU member states, the authors took into account domain-specific scales alongside general European integration.

5. Even congenial wording does not prevent "differential item functioning," that is, respondents expressing the same underlying attitudes through different positions and vice versa (Golder and Stramski 2010). In particular, "differences in the actual political debate on integration may generate differences between countries in what attitudes are indicated by which responses" (Van der Eijk and Franklin 1991, 110).

6. While factor analysis would arguably produce a more stringent test, simple correlation coefficients adequately prove our point.

7. For a complementary study, focusing on the subdimensions rather than dwelling on the individual countries, see Pareschi, Baldini, and Giglioli (2023).

8. Out of necessity, we split into equal halves the proportion of respondents choosing the middle position "5" (Irwin and Thomassen 1975). At the same time, we recall that the midpoint presumably conflates genuinely equidistant citizens with undecided or indifferent ones.

9. Our analyses include "robustness" checks varying the mass-level population (voters only), the measure of central tendency (interpolated medians), and the set of weights (on the importance of such checks, see Shim and Gherghina 2020; Pareschi, Baldini, and Giglioli 2023). Substantive findings are unaffected, except in a very few cases where the figure for a certain country is particularly close to the threshold (5.00 or 50%).

10. Not all these differences are statistically significant; however, the overall patterns are extremely clear.

11. By such a statement, we do not want to suggest that mass attitudes are the dominant factor in an interplay where elites play a subsidiary role. On the contrary, recent work suggests that the foray of European integration into electoral politics should not cause elite agency to be discounted (Hobolt and De Vries 2016; Bartels 2023). As implied by the body of research on *EU mass–elite linkages*, mass–elite dynamics are so complex that any attempt to fully disentangle causes from consequences within this chapter would be untenable. This caveat equally applies to the relationship between the appearance of Eurosceptic actors and the emergence of mass–elite gaps.

12. It is worth emphasizing that these patterns of opinion refer to 2016, well before the Russian invasion of Ukraine which broke out in February 2022.

References

Arnold, Christine, Eliyahu V. Sapir, and Catherine de Vries. 2012. "Parties' Positions on European Integration: Issue Congruence, Ideology or Context?" *West European Politics* 35 (6): 1341–62.

Bakker, Ryan, Seth Jolly, and Jonathan Polk. 2012. "Complexity in the European Party Space: Exploring Dimensionality with Experts." *European Union Politics* 13 (2): 219–45.

Bartels, Larry M. 2023. *Democracy Erodes from the Top: Leaders, Citizens, and the Challenge of Populism in Europe*. Princeton: Princeton University Press.

Best, Heinrich. 2012. "Elite Foundations of European Integration: A Causal Analysis." In *The Europe of Elites*, edited by Heinrich Best, György Lengyel, and Luca Verzichelli, 208–33. Oxford: Oxford University Press.

Best, Heinrich, György Lengyel, and Luca Verzichelli. 2012. "Introduction: European Integration as an Elite Project." In *The Europe of Elites*, edited by Heinrich Best, György Lengyel, and Luca Verzichelli, 1–13. Oxford: Oxford University Press.

Best, Heinrich, and Lars Vogel. 2018. "Representative Elites." In *The Palgrave Handbook of Political Elites*, edited by Maurizio Cotta and John Higley, 339–62. Basingstoke: Palgrave Macmillan.

Boomgaarden, Haio G., Andreas R. T. Schuck, Matthijs Elenbaas, and Claes H. de Vreese. 2011. "Mapping EU Attitudes: Conceptual and Empirical Dimensions of Euroscepticism and EU Support." *European Union Politics* 12 (2): 241–66.

Börzel, Tanja A., and Thomas Risse. 2018. "From the Euro to the Schengen Crises: European Integration Theories, Politicization, and Identity Politics." *Journal of European Public Policy* 25 (1): 83–108.

Bulmer, Simon, and William E. Paterson. 2018. *Germany and the European Union: Europe's Reluctant Hegemon?* London: Red Globe Press.

Carrubba, Clifford J. 2001. "The Electorate Connection in European Union Politics." *Journal of Politics* 63 (1): 141–58.

Costello, Rory, Jacques Thomassen, and Martin Rosema. 2012. "European Parliament Elections and Political Representation: Policy Congruence between Voters and Parties." *West European Politics* 35 (6): 1226–48.

Cotta, Maurizio, and Federico Russo. 2012. "Europe à la Carte? European Citizenship and Its Dimensions from the Perspective of National Elites." In *The Europe of Elites*, edited by Heinrich Best, György Lengyel, and Luca Verzichelli, 14–42. Oxford: Oxford University Press.

Daddow, Oliver. 2018. "Brexit and Britain's Role in the World." In *The Routledge Handbook of the Politics of Brexit*, edited by Patrick Diamond, Peter Nedergaard, and Ben Rosamond, 208–22. London: Routledge.

Devine, Daniel, and Raimondas Ibenskas. 2021. "From Convergence to Congruence: European Integration and Citizen–Elite Congruence." *European Union Politics* 22 (4): 676–99.

De Vries, Catherine E. 2018. *Euroscepticism and the Future of European Integration.* Oxford: Oxford University Press.

De Vries, Catherine E., and Sara B. Hobolt. 2020. *Political Entrepreneurs: The Rise of Challenger Parties in Europe.* Princeton: Princeton University Press.

De Wilde, Pieter, and Michael Zürn. 2012. "Can the Politicization of European Integration Be Reversed?" *Journal of Common Market Studies* 50 (1): 137–53.

Díez Medrano, Juan. 2003. *Framing Europe: Attitudes to European Integration in Germany, Spain, and the United Kingdom.* Princeton: Princeton University Press.

Dolný, Branislav, and Pavol Baboš. 2015. "Voter–Representative Congruence in Europe: A Loss of Institutional Influence?" *West European Politics* 38 (6): 1274–1304.

Down, Ian, and Carole J. Wilson. 2008. "From 'Permissive Consensus' to 'Constraining Dissensus': A Polarizing Union?" *Acta Politica* 43 (1): 26–49.

Eichenberg, Richard C., and Russell J. Dalton. 2007. "Post-Maastricht Blues: The Transformation of Citizen Support for European Integration, 1973–2004." *Acta Politica* 42 (2–3): 128–52.

Engelstad, Fredrik, Trygve Gulbrandsen, Marte Mangset, and Mari Teigen. 2019. Introduction to *Elites and People: Challenges to Democracy*, edited by Fredrik Engelstad, Trygve Gulbrandsen, Marte Mangset, and Mari Teigen, 1–13. Bingley, UK: Emerald Publishing.

EUEngage. 2017a. "Technical Report—Wave 1." Version 4, February.

EUEngage. 2017b. "Interim Report on Elite Survey—Wave 1." February.

Freire, André, Eftichia Teperoglou, and Catherine Moury. 2014. "Awakening the Sleeping Giant in Greece and Portugal? Elites' and Voters' Attitudes towards EU Integration in Difficult Economic Times." *South European Society and Politics* 19 (4): 477–99.

Gaxie, Daniel, Nicolas Hubé, and Jay Rowell, eds. 2011. *Perceptions of Europe: A Comparative Sociology of European Attitudes.* Colchester, UK: ECPR Press.

Goldberg, Andreas C., Erika J. van Elsas, and Claes H. de Vreese. 2020. "Mismatch? Comparing Elite and Citizen Polarisation on EU Issues across Four Countries." *Journal of European Public Policy* 27 (2): 310–28.

Golder, Matt, and Jacek Stramski. 2010. "Ideological Congruence and Electoral Institutions." *American Journal of Political Science* 54 (1): 90–106.

Haas, Ernst B. 1958. *The Uniting of Europe.* Stanford: Stanford University Press.

Hellström, Johan. 2008. "Who Leads, Who Follows? Re-examining the Party–Electorate Linkages on European Integration." *Journal of European Public Policy* 15 (8): 1127–44.

Hobolt, Sara B., and Catherine E. de Vries. 2016. "Public Support for European Integration." *Annual Review of Political Science* 19: 413–32.

Hoeglinger, Dominic. 2016. "The Politicisation of European Integration in Domestic Election Campaigns." *West European Politics* 39 (1): 44–63.

Hoffmann-Lange, Ursula. 2018. "Methods of Elite Identification." In *The Palgrave Handbook of Political Elites*, edited by Maurizio Cotta and John Higley, 79–92. Basingstoke: Palgrave Macmillan.

Hooghe, Liesbet. 2003. "Europe Divided? Elites vs. Public Opinion on European Integration." *European Union Politics* 4 (3): 281–304.

Hooghe, Liesbet, and Gary Marks. 2006. "Europe's Blues: Theoretical Soul-Searching after the Rejection of the European Constitution." *PS: Political Science and Politics* 39 (2): 247–50.

Hooghe, Liesbet, and Gary Marks. 2009. "A Postfunctionalist Theory of European Integration: From Permissive Consensus to Constraining Dissensus." *British Journal of Political Science* 39 (1): 1–23.

Hooghe, Liesbet, and Gary Marks. 2018. "Cleavage Theory Meets Europe's Crises: Lipset, Rokkan and the Transnational Cleavage." *Journal of European Public Policy* 25 (1): 109–35.

Hutter, Swen, and Hanspeter Kriesi. 2019. "Politicizing Europe in Times of Crisis." *Journal of European Public Policy* 26 (7): 996–1017.

Irwin, Galen A., and Jacques Thomassen. 1975. "Issue-Consensus in a Multi-Party System: Voters and Leaders in the Netherlands." *Acta Politica* 10 (4): 389–420.

Krouwel, André, and Koen Abts. 2007. "Varieties of Euroscepticism and Populist Mobilization: Transforming Attitudes from Mild Euroscepticism to Harsh Eurocynicism." *Acta Politica* 42 (2): 252–70.

Marsh, Michael, and Bernhard Wessels. 1997. "Territorial Representation." *European Journal of Political Research* 32 (2): 227–41.

Mattila, Mikko, and Tapio Raunio. 2006. "Cautious Voters–Supportive Parties: Opinion Congruence between Voters and Parties on the EU Dimension." *European Union Politics* 7 (4): 427–49.

Mudde, Cas. 2011. *Sussex v. North Carolina: The Comparative Study of Party-Based Euroscepticism*. EPERN Working Paper no. 23, Sussex.

Müller, Wolfgang C., Marcelo Jenny, and Alejandro Ecker. 2012. "The Elite-Masses Gap in European Integration." In *The Europe of Elites*, edited by Heinrich Best, György Lengyel, and Luca Verzichelli, 167–91. Oxford: Oxford University Press.

Oppermann, Kai. 2018. "Derailing European Integration? Euroscepticism and the Politics of EU Referendums." In *The Routledge Handbook of Euroscepticism*, edited by Benjamin Leruth, Nicholas Startin, and Simon Usherwood, 243–55. Abingdon, UK: Routledge.

Pareschi, Andrea. 2023. "On Framing the EU: A Plea for the Relaunch of Frame Analysis in the Study of Elite and Mass Attitudes on European Integration." *Journal of Contemporary European Research* 19 (1): 62–80.

Pareschi, Andrea, Gianfranco Baldini, and M. F. N. Giglioli. 2023. "Caught between Sovereignty and Solidarity? A Multidimensional Revisitation of EU Mass-Elite Congruence." *Italian Political Science Review/Rivista Italiana di Scienza Politica* 53 (1): 3–23.

Ray, Leonard. 2003. "When Parties Matter: The Conditional Influence of Party Positions on Voter Opinion about European Integration." *Journal of Politics* 65 (4): 978–94.

Real-Dato, José. 2017. "Party-Voters Congruence concerning the European Union: An Analysis of Its Evolution during the Eurozone Crisis Using Elite and Mass Surveys." *Corvinus Journal of Sociology and Social Policy* 8 (3): 85–112.

Riddervold, Marianne, Jarle Trondal, and Akasemi Newsome, eds. 2021. *The Palgrave Handbook of EU Crises*. Basingstoke: Palgrave Macmillan.

Rodríguez-Teruel, Juan, and Jean-Pascal Daloz. 2018. "Surveying and Observing Political Elites." In *The Palgrave Handbook of Political Elites*, edited by Maurizio Cotta and John Higley, 93–113. Basingstoke: Palgrave Macmillan.

Rovny, Jan. 2012. "Who Emphasizes and Who Blurs? Party Strategies in Multidimensional Competition." *European Union Politics* 13 (2): 269–92.

Sanders, David, and Gabor Toka. 2013. "Is Anyone Listening? Mass and Elite Opinion Cueing in the EU." *Electoral Studies* 32 (1): 13–25.

Schmitt, Hermann. 2010. "Better Than It Used to Be? New Evidence on the Congruence of Voters and Their National MPs Regarding the Issue of European Integration." Paper prepared for the Annual Meeting of the American Political Science Association.

Schmitt, Hermann, and Jacques Thomassen. 2000. "Dynamic Representation: The Case of European Integration." *European Union Politics* 1 (3): 318–39.

Semenova, Elena. 2018. "Research Methods for Studying Elites." In *The Palgrave Handbook of Political Elites*, edited by Maurizio Cotta and John Higley, 71–77. Basingstoke: Palgrave Macmillan.

Shim, Jaemin, and Sergiu Gherghina. 2020. "Measuring the Mass-Elite Preference Congruence: Findings from a Meta-Analysis and Introduction to the Symposium." *European Political Science* 19 (4): 509–27.

Skinner, Marianne Sundlisæter. 2013. "Different Varieties of Euroscepticism? Conceptualizing and Explaining Euroscepticism in Western European Non-Member States." *Journal of Common Market Studies* 51 (1): 122–39.

Steenbergen, Marco R., Erica E. Edwards, and Catherine E. de Vries. 2007. "Who's Cueing Whom? Mass-Elite Linkages and the Future of European Integration." *European Union Politics* 8 (1): 13–35.

Stoeckel, Florian. 2013. "Ambivalent or Indifferent? Reconsidering the Structure of EU Public Opinion." *European Union Politics* 14 (1): 23–45.

Szczerbiak, Aleks. 2016. "How Will the EU's 'Rule of Law' Investigation Affect Polish Politics?" *LSE EUROPP* blog, June 2. https://blogs.lse.ac.uk/europpblog/2016/02/06/how-will-the-eus-rule-of-law-investigation-affect-polish-politics

Taggart, Paul. 2006. "Keynote Article: Questions of Europe—the Domestic Politics of the 2005 French and Dutch Referendums and Their Challenge for the Study of European Integration." *Journal of Common Market Studies* 44 (1): 7–25.

Thomassen, Jacques, and Hermann Schmitt. 1997. "Policy Representation." *European Journal of Political Research* 32 (2): 165–84.

Thomassen, Jacques, and Hermann Schmitt. 1999. "Issue Congruence." In *Political Representation and Legitimacy in the European Union*, edited by Hermann Schmitt and Jacques Thomassen, 186–208. Oxford: Oxford University Press.

Usherwood, Simon, and Nick Startin. 2013. "Euroscepticism as a Persistent Phenomenon." *Journal of Common Market Studies* 51 (1): 1–16.

Van der Brug, Wouter, and Joost van Spanje. 2009. "Immigration, Europe and the 'New' Cultural Dimension." *European Journal of Political Research* 48 (3): 309–34.

Van der Eijk, Cees, and Mark N. Franklin. 1991. "European Community Politics and Electoral Representation: Evidence from the 1989 European Elections Study." *European Journal of Political Research* 19 (1): 105–27.

Van der Eijk, Cees, and Mark N. Franklin. 2004. "Potential for Contestation on European Matters at National Elections in Europe?" In *European Integration and Political Conflict*, edited by Gary Marks and Marco R. Steenbergen, 120–40. Cambridge: Cambridge University Press.

Vasilopoulou, Sofia. 2013. "Continuity and Change in the Study of Euroscepticism: Plus ça change?" *Journal of Common Market Studies* 51 (1): 153–68.

Vasilopoulou, Sofia. 2023. "Parties and European Integration." In *The Routledge Handbook of Political Parties*, edited by Neil Carter, Daniel Keith, Gyda M. Sindre, and Sofia Vasilopoulou, 301–11. Abingdon, UK: Routledge.

Whitefield, Stephen, and Robert Rohrschneider. 2019. "Embedding Integration: How European Integration Splits Mainstream Parties." *Party Politics* 25 (1): 25–35.

PART II

Theorizing Causes behind Mass–Elite Discrepancy in Old and New Democracies

CHAPTER 4

Shadow of a Critical Juncture

Asymmetric Politicization and Elite Agency

Jaemin Shim

How can we explain the multiple forms of salient mass–elite discrepancies appearing at certain times? This is the key question this chapter sets out to answer. So far, the previous chapters have conceptually enriched our understanding of mass–elite discrepancies around the globe. Chapter 2 has expanded our conceptual understanding horizontally by demonstrating that specific policy areas and issues where mass–elite discrepancies are observed vary across the globe and take different structures and appear at different time periods. Complementing chapter 2, chapter 3 has expanded the concept of mass–elite discrepancy vertically by showing that the EU integration dimension has multiple subdimensions, each of which is largely autonomous from the general issue of EU integration and has varying mass–elite discrepancy levels.

Directly building on the groundwork laid out in the previous chapters, this chapter aims to generate a theoretical framework from which we can better grasp the varieties of mass–elite discrepancies around the globe. As will be made clear, I draw key insights from historical institutionalism and the specification of the theoretical framework is mainly guided by empirical examples included in this volume.

Based on a meta-analysis, I will share a list of causes behind mass–elite discrepancies that existing scholarship has noted as consequential. After pointing out that the historical approach has largely been neglected, the chapter will then build directly on historical institutionalism in general and the freezing cleavage hypothesis in particular. The main theoretical framework of this volume will be specified with reference to key historical institutionalism concepts such as the "critical juncture" and "path dependency." Finally, I will demonstrate how the proposed theoretical framework can be applied to explain observed mass–elite discrepancies in both old and new democracies.

4.1. Key Causes behind the Mass–Elite Discrepancy

Empirical works on mass–elite discrepancy frequently go beyond descriptive comparison of the masses and elites along a particular political dimension. From 111 studies included in the meta-analysis (see chapter 2 for details), 70 (63 percent) explicitly include explanatory factors and attempt to account for the mass–elite representation gap variation observed in their empirical analysis. Here, "an attempt" is defined as operationalizing potential causes as variables and testing them in the hypothesis form—not simply noting them in passing. The trend over time, based on the three distinct periods noted in chapter 2, demonstrates that explanatory research including a set of causes has increasingly become common in the MED scholarship. Prior to 1990, 41 percent of research examined the observed mass–elite gap with causes, but this rose to 60 percent between 2000 and 2009, and then to 72 percent afterwards. The present chapter includes causes confirmed to be statistically significant (below p-value 0.1) in light of the employed method, for example, survey experiment, multivariate regressions, or simple t-test.

Depending on the level, I categorized each confirmed cause noted in the existing scholarship into country, party/government, individual, issue, and measurement. The unit of calculation was per study, and for those with confirmed causes across different levels, each level was counted separately.[1] The results in figure 4.1 indicate that party/government and country levels harbor most frequently confirmed causes behind mass–elite discrepancies. This was followed by individual and issue-related causes. Very few studies linked a specific measurement employed in the research to the observed mass–elite discrepancy.

Table 4.1 lists most of the confirmed causes and the numbers next to each cause indicate the identification number for a specific study included in the meta-analysis (see appendix in chapter 2 for the full list ranging from 1 to 111).[2] The clustering reflects revealed correlations between the causes or surface-level similarities. The same cause often turned out to be statistically significant, but in different directions in different studies. For these cases, the competing explanations are included in the description—for example, "Cause A leads to higher/lower MED."

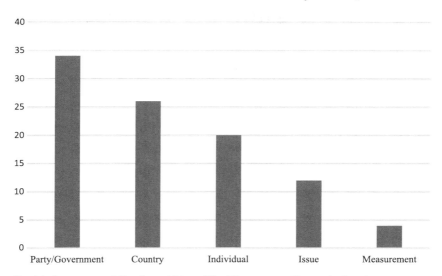

Fig. 4.1. Frequency of Confirmed Mass–Elite Discrepancy Causes by Level

Starting from the country-level causes, these are macro-level causes that can be characterized as economic or political conditions affecting the country of interest as a whole. For this level, four clusters of causes can be identified. First is the age of the democracy. Often conducted in the form of a comparison between Eastern and Western European countries, the existing research points to a larger gap existing in new democracies. Relatedly, the extant scholarship demonstrates that shorter histories of party competition and being a new EU member state result in a larger mass–elite gap. Second, the level of a country's socioeconomic development—often measured using the human development index or the Gross Domestic Product per capita— tends to be negatively associated with the size of the representation gap. The third cluster concerns electoral rules, such as whether a country adopts a majoritarian or proportional electoral rule or, more explicitly, the degree of seat-vote disproportionality. This has been one of the most scrutinized causes in the MED literature. Despite the context sensitivity of electoral rule effect noted in the scholarship (Powell 2013), the evidence drawing from the meta-analysis clearly indicates that majoritarian electoral rules, for example, the first-past-the-post rule, go hand-in-hand with a larger discrepancy. The fourth cause cluster is a time-bound one noting that the mass–elite discrepancy widens when a country experiences an economic crisis.

Party-level causes are meso-level since they largely refer to the way that policy, ideological, and organizational variation between parties is linked to

Table 4.1. List of Confirmed Causes behind Mass–Elite Discrepancies in the Scholarship

Level	Causes
Country	• New democracies/shorter history of party competition have higher MED (5, 43, 104, 109, 50) • Central/Eastern European countries have higher MED than Western European countries (26, 57) • Lower human development index leads to higher MED (43) • Lower socioeconomic development leads to higher MED (50) • Majoritarian electoral rules have higher MED than proportional electoral rules (27, 49, 55, 68, 104, 108) • Large seat-vote disproportionality leads to higher MED (43, 74) • Period of economic crisis leads to higher MED (25)
Party/ government	• Smaller parties have higher (75)/lower MED (8, 14) • Niche parties have higher (75, 84, 28)/lower MED (59, 75) • Government parties have higher (8, 30, 75, 79) /lower (25, 64) MED • Parties with mass organization have lower MED (26, 43, 57) • Centralized parties have lower MED (49) • Institutionalized parties have lower MED (50) • Ideological polarization of party system leads to higher (5, 45)/lower MED (104) • Ideologically extreme parties have lower MED (8, 14, 56, 56, 108) • Higher "effective number of parties" leads to lower MED (28, 43) • Policy-seeking parties have higher MED than vote-seeking parties (25, 33)
Individual	• Middle-class voters have lower MED than working-class voters (56, 57) • High-income voters have lower MED than low-income voters (71, 74) • Educated voters have lower MED (56, 74, 104) • Politically interested voters have lower MED (74, 96, 104, 106) • Politically informed voters have lower MED (56, 71, 86, 96, 110) • Party members have lower MED than party supporters (42) • Partisan voters have lower MED than independent voters (26, 31, 110) • Voting electorates have lower MED than nonvoting electorates (71, 74) • Successful candidates have lower MED than nonsuccessful ones (9, 111) • Politicians with more incumbency/political experience have lower MED (22, 41)
Issue	• Salient issues have lower MED than nonsalient ones (30, 60, 102, 72, 84) • Policy issues lead to higher MED than left–right ideology (81) • Socioeconomic issues have lower MED than sociocultural one (57)
Measurement	• Perception/judgment-based measurement has lower MED than objective measurement (37, 63) • Saliency measurement has lower MED than position measurement (58)

Note: Some caveats to consider. The list should be taken cautiously since it does not contain the full contextual information on measurement choices. Among others, the following three merit particular attention. _First_ is whether the comparison is "partisan voters–parties they support" or "voters–legislators." Depending on which comparison a study looks at, the same cause can turn out to either widen or narrow the mass–elite gap. _Second_, specific causes are oftentimes confirmed only vis-à-vis particular issue areas. For instance, studies confirming that the mass–elite gap grows during a country's economic crisis only examine the socioeconomic issue area. _Third_, although treated as discrete causes in different studies, many causes appear to be highly correlated and could have turned out to be redundant had they been tested in one study.

mass–elite discrepancies. This level consists of the following five clusters and, unlike other levels, exhibits some clearly contradictory findings. First, the foremost regularly observed cause is the linkage between niche (e.g., green, ethno-territorial, pirate parties) or small parties and the level of discrepancy. With highly mixed findings thus far, the jury is still out on whether these parties reduce the mass–elite gap. The second cluster is pertinent to a party's government or opposition status, and upon examining the evidence so far, there is no clear consensus on whether governing—either singly or in coalition form—leads to less or more of a mass–elite gap; some works point to more while others point to less. In contrast, the remaining clusters unequivocally demonstrate that the noted cause led to a reduction in the gap. That is, the third cluster concerns whether the observed gap decreases if parties have mass organization, are centralized, or are institutionalized; in all three regards, the answer points to yes. The fourth cause cluster is germane to parties' polarization and fragmentation and the results evince that fractionalized/polarized party systems yield a closer fit between voters and elites. This is in line with the "responsible party model" (American Political Science Association 1950), which argues that parties ought to provide voters with clear policy alternatives. Relatedly, ideologically extreme parties (e.g., far-right nationalist or far-left anti-austerity parties) tend to have a better representation performance than moderate parties. The last cluster of factors approaches mass–elite discrepancy from the policy, vote, office framework (Strøm and Müller 1999) and confirms the expectation that more vote/office-seeking or catch-all parties result in a smaller representation gap than policy-seeking parties.

Individual-level causes correspond to micro-level factors related to characteristics of masses or elites. At the mass level, two clusters can be identified. First, numerous studies demonstrate that the preferences of low-income, working-class, and lower-educated people tend to be less aligned with their representatives in the legislature. Second, voters who are highly interested in politics or equipped with more political information have higher odds of decreasing the representation gap with elites. Relatedly, existing evidence suggests that there is a clear hierarchy of mass–elite preference matches according to different degrees of political commitment. The preference synchronization is highest for party members followed by partisan voters, then swing voters, and lowest for nonvoters. In the case of elites, first, results demonstrate that electorally unsuccessful candidates tend to be less aligned with voter preferences than successful ones. Second, findings point to the importance of legislators' seniority and incumbency. Legislators with more political experience in general or who are incumbents tend to have less incongruent preferences with the masses.

Issue-level causes link characteristics of specific issues to the mass–elite gap and the following two clusters can be identified. The first cluster relates to the salience of issues. Existing studies clearly show that issues highly salient for voters or parties lead to lower mass–elite discrepancies. In a similar vein, research shows that issues to which voters pay more attention are positively correlated with a lower discrepancy level. Second, among various issue areas, findings demonstrate that socioeconomic issues or a left–right ideology (which closely relates to socioeconomic issues in the Western European setting) lend themselves to a smaller representation gap than other issues.

Measurement-level causes are unique in the sense that, unlike other levels, they view the observed mass–elite gap as a by-product of the way in which research measures the discrepancy. The following two confirmed causes merit our attention. The first is that mass–elite comparisons based on one side's perception/judgment of the other side results in a smaller representation gap vis-à-vis mass–elite comparisons based on self-reports. A good example is research measuring parties' ideological or policy positions based on voters' perceptions. Second, compared to works investigating mass–elite differences in saliency (which is mostly measured by asking which policy areas one prioritizes), those looking at differences in position manifest a wider mass–elite gap.

4.2. The Historical Turn of MED: The Critical Juncture Approach and Conceptual Groundwork

4.2.1. Historical Institutionalism

The previous section identified a large number of explanatory factors that the existing MED literature has demonstrated as significant in explaining mass–elite discrepancy variation. Predominantly, the existing literature has tried to account for the variation in the "size" of a gap. Considering the continuous nature of gap size, it is not surprising that numerous causes across multiple levels were found to contribute to the variation. However, to get a fuller grasp of MED, in addition to the size of a gap, we also need to explain why there is variation in gap content, structure, and timing. For this goal, this volume argues that carefully tracing the historical origin of an observed gap should be the starting point. However, with very few exceptions, for example, Bornschier (2016), the existing scholarship has paid scant attention to the historical origins of incongruence. We try to fill this lacuna by investigating the historical origin of an observed gap with global examples. For this goal, the volume draws on historical institutionalism as a guide to derive a theoretical framework.

Simply put, historical institutionalism raises the importance of contexts within historical situations. Historical institutionalists often define institutions as "formal or informal procedures, routines, norms and conventions embedded in the organizational structure of the polity or political economy" (Hall and Taylor 1996). Insofar as party politics is concerned, electoral rules, party systems, or key enduring political divisions fall under the definition. For analytical purposes, what is particularly useful is that historical institutionalism has multiple concepts that systematically explain how legacies of earlier institutional choices explain the current outcome of interests. As shall be specified later, examples include concepts such as timing and sequence, critical juncture and path dependence, and nonsimultaneity of institutional origin and change (Pierson 2011; Thelen 1999; Orren and Skowronek 1996).

Lack of attention to historical institutionalism is surprising since it has long been noted that the political dimensions on which representation take place vary depending on the specific legacies and trajectories of each country (Kitschelt et al. 1999). Moreover, as pointed out in chapter 2, a large majority of studies explicitly examines the mass–elite gap in key political dimensions where a lasting political divide is observed in the analyzed countries. In view of the fact that lasting political divides are historical in nature, the volume wishes to draw insights from the political cleavage literature. Specifically, it aims to take the temporal dimension of the representation gap seriously by recognizing the unique political circumstances behind the crystallization of key political dynamics at the critical juncture period and their downward consequences.

From the political cleavage literature, the most relevant thesis informing this volume is the "freezing cleavage hypothesis" formulated by Lipset and Rokkan (1967). In their seminal work analyzing political cleavages and party politics in old democracies, the authors demonstrate that the labor-capital cleavage (an important basis of the state vs. market conflict) became the primary diverging point between left- and right-wing parties during the democratic transition in the early twentieth century; this remained consistent for several decades despite major interrupting events such as the Great Depression and two world wars. They argued that the party system is locked-in to the labor vs. capital cleavage because key parties entered national-level politics by addressing then-salient socioeconomic issues and then, having surmounted large start-up costs and created expectations of what mainstream politics is about, dominated the political marketplace.

The freezing cleavage hypothesis clearly combines two key concepts pertinent to historical institutionalism. On the one hand, it reflects the core idea behind "critical juncture" because the thesis explains the equilibrium of class-based political cleavage over a long stretch of time through the timing of the electorate's full mobilization and consolidation of mass democracy's institutional structure (Sartori 1969). On the other hand, it is also a fitting example of the "path dependency" argument—once a certain path is taken, the costs of reversal become increasingly high—which works through a powerful cycle of a self-reinforcing process of "positive feedback" featuring four characteristics: large set-up costs, learning effects, coordination effects, and adaptive expectations (for details, see Arthur 1994). With respect to the freezing cleavage hypothesis, there are two differing viewpoints. On the one hand, the hypothesis is regarded as no more than an "empirical observation" about the history of European party politics (Mair 2001). On the other hand, the hypothesis can go beyond European experiences if we abstract the key idea that the particular political dimension salient during critical junctures becomes crystallized and can have a lasting stamp on subsequent political development (Bornschier 2009). The contributors of this volume side with the latter viewpoint.

It has often been noted that the nature of their formative environment leaves a long-lasting "genetic imprint" on parties (Slater and Wong 2013; Randall, Svåsand, and Khembo 2007; Panebianco 1988; Riedl 2016). In this regard, the students of party politics already have hinted at the possibility of applying the core logic of Lipset and Rokkan's freezing cleavage hypothesis to wider contexts beyond Western Europe. For instance, it has been noted that the key political dynamics created during the democratic transition tend to persist, despite authoritarian interludes, in new democracies in South America, Asia, and Africa (Randall 2001). Similarly, chaotic and messy as they may be, early rounds of electoral competition in new democracies have been approached as critical founding moments when political elites forge long-term political identities and define the nature of subsequent party competition (Zielinski 2002). Echoing these insights, the structure of party competitions in Uruguay, Colombia, and Chile have not changed much since the first two decades of the twentieth century (Bornschier 2009). Likewise, the root of ongoing political division reflects the initial postwar political dimension in Mali, Ghana, and the Philippines (Vengroff 1993; Manacsa and Tan 2005) and the democratic transition period in the 1990s in Taiwan (Cheng and Hsu 2014).

4.2.2. Conceptual Groundwork: Adjusting the Critical Juncture to a Wider Context

In relation to global level mass–elite discrepancies, the two key concepts of the freezing cleavage hypothesis—the critical juncture and path dependency—can reflect broader geographic contexts and be utilized as central pillars of the theoretical framework in this volume. However, in order to reflect the political reality of both old and new democracies, some conceptual groundwork is needed. Specifically, with regard to the "critical juncture," we need to remove our preconceptions and expand our understanding of (1) which periods constitute the critical juncture, (2) what types of political dimensions become crystallized, and (3) how a specific political dimension comes into being.

First, in light of the conventional definition, only few points in time were considered as critical junctures in Lipset and Rokkan's (1967) classic work, namely religious reformation, nationalization, industrial revolution, communist revolution, and mass enfranchisement. Among these, the ones most pertinent to the crystallization of long-lasting political dimension within old European democracies in the twentieth century were the influence of the communist revolution and mass enfranchisement. However, critical junctures during which the primary political dimension is formed do not have to be confined to these specific events, which largely reflect the political trajectory of Western European countries. To be clear, the definition of "critical junctures" can be stated as follows:

> Critical junctures are cast as moments in which uncertainty as to the future of an institutional arrangement allows for political agency and choice to play a decisive causal role in setting an institution on a certain path of development, a path that then persists over a long period of time. (Capoccia 2016, 148)

Consequently, what qualifies as a critical juncture can be inductively defined as long as the period's potentially "decisive causal role" can be linked to the outcome of interest.[3] Therefore, critical junctures can include experiences more frequently observed in non-Western contexts, for example, civil wars, decolonization, reunification, division/succession, foreign occupation/ intervention, and authoritarianization/democratization. Furthermore, critical junctures can be defined in relation to a specific political dimension. Institutions are often composed of heterogenous elements adopted nonsimultaneously, reflecting different needs and constraints at different points in time (Orren and Skowronek 1996). Applying this idea to the multidimensional political space, as specified in chapter 2, each political dimension can have a distinct origin and reflects unique historical contexts at the time of creation. With respect to the change, historical institutionalists note that not all institutional elements necessarily undergo transition at the same time and variation exists in changing speeds (Thelen 2003). From this viewpoint, a critical juncture does not have to be a period during which all key political dimensions are affected.

Second, as mentioned earlier in the freezing cleavage hypothesis, the key political dimension that crystallized in Western Europe concerned socioeconomic issues pertaining to the state vs. market dimension. However, it should be noted that key political dimensions can be shaped in various areas beyond socioeconomic issues. As detailed in chapter 2, in many new democracies, the context during the mass enfranchisement period did not crystallize socioeconomic issues into two opposing sides; instead, the key political dimension has been shaped by other issues ranging from international security to democratic values to religion.

Third, the role of elites should be given more weight in understanding the origin of a particular political dimension during the critical juncture period. As was made clear with the Western European examples in chapter 2, the political cleavage approach largely concluded that the formation of the key political dimension is a bottom-up process reflecting societal structure and voters' attributes (Lipset and Rokkan 1967). However, recent works demonstrate that key political divides are not simple reflections of structural divisions formed in a bottom-up manner. For instance, elites can define political divisions by creating identities, forming communities, and reinforcing the structural and cultural distinctiveness of professional groups and classes (Enyedi 2005; Sartori 1969; Zuckerman 1975; Bartolini 2000; Kriesi 1998). As shall be expounded in greater detail in chapter 5, elite agency is particularly likely to be high in democracies outside Western Europe, owing to common conditions such as weak bottom-up mobilization or lack of continued opportunities to reproduce a political cleavage. Moreover, due to their colonial and Cold War legacies, new democracies' domestic political competition is often more susceptible to the influence of foreign governments (Shim 2021; Shim and Farag 2023).

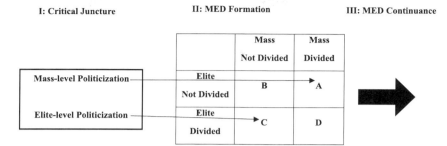

Fig. 4.2. Framework for Explaining Mass–Elite Discrepancy

4.3. Theoretical Framework

4.3.1. Mass–Elite Discrepancy, Critical Juncture, and Elite Agency

Having completed the necessary conceptual groundwork to link the critical juncture concept to the political dimensions on the global level, this section will specify the theoretical framework of the volume. The basic theoretical framework is sketched in figure 4.2 and the discussion here elaborates the two key causal connections indicated by I (critical juncture) and II (MED formation). The next section will elaborate on the third causal connection about why discrepancy persists, which is indicated by III (MED continuance).

Examples drawn from the global MED cases included in this volume (and prominent examples from the meta-analysis) demonstrate that the observed preference gap between masses and elites can be directly linked to the period of asymmetric politicization between elites and masses. Drawing from E. E. Schattschneider's view that politicization implies visible conflicts (1975), "politicization" here is defined as the increasing saliency and polarization[4] of key issues related to the political dimension of interest. To exemplify this with the cases covered in the empirical chapters of this volume, the substantial gap on the religious-secular dimension in Tunisia and Indonesia exists because a segment of the public shifted their position to the religious side and, at the same time, assigned higher weight to this issue. In the case of Bulgaria and Japan, the representation gap became nonnegligible when some elites put efforts to increase the saliency of the issues in question. Besides increasing saliency, in Bulgaria, a significant portion of elites shifted their position to the anti-EU side. In the three cases included in the empirical chapters, the change of position by at least one segment of masses/elites led to polarization within masses/elites

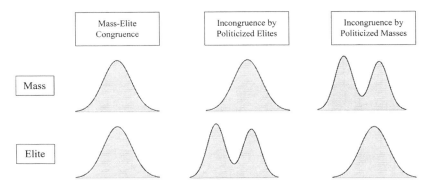

Fig. 4.3. Mass–Elite Incongruence Forms

and resulted in a diverging average position from elites/masses. Figure 4.3 illustrates how polarization on one side leads to position deviation on the other side.

This specified process of salient mass–elite discrepancy formation is historical because the particular timing of mass–elite mismatch can be traced to critical junctures pertinent to the political dimension of interest. What can be treated as a critical juncture requires context-specific understanding since it varies between countries. Empirical chapters included in this volume show that the timing of the critical juncture has varied between covered countries in the past two decades. The mid-2010s was a critical juncture for the EU integration political dimension in Bulgaria given the migrant and Ukraine crisis, which led some elites to rethink Bulgaria's Euro-Atlantic orientation. However, the critical juncture for the normal nation vs. peace state dimension in Japan can be traced to the early 1990s given the changing geopolitical factors in East Asia and the bursting of the economic bubble in Japan. In the case of Indonesia, the redemocratization period between 1998 and 2004 served as a critical juncture for the religious-secular dimension against the backdrop of the increasing global tensions Islam had to face. On the contrary, in Tunisia, it took more than a decade after the turn of the millennium for the same political dimension to see a critical juncture—the Tunisian revolution and the subsequent democratic transition in early 2010. In addition to the diversity in timing, these examples demonstrate that critical junctures are often political-dimension specific. The redemocratization period in Indonesia only rekindled the religious-secular dimension, leaving aside another key political dimension that was evident prior to its authoritarian turn—issues of conflicts between labor and capital. Similarly, the politicization of the EU integration dimension by Bulgarian elites in the mid-2010s did not bring back the pro- vs. anticommunist political dimension that the country was once known for (Spirova 2007; Kanev and Hristova-Valtcheva 2016).

Circumstances surrounding critical juncture periods disrupt the status quo but do not determine which exact path will be taken. In other words, the MEDs observed in the aforementioned examples were not bound to occur. As noted in the definition of the critical juncture, political agency plays a decisive causal role during critical junctures, and in this volume, we argue that elites' deliberate action/inaction to politicize/depoliticize issues related to a political dimension is directly accountable for an observed MED in a particular country at a specific time. In other words, even though it was the masses who politicized issues related to the political dimension of interest, the responsibility for the observed representation gap falls on the shoulder of the elites. This is because, in representative democracies, elected elites are supposed to represent the masses (not the other way around). However, as the examples in the subsequent chapters will demonstrate, political elites also pursue their own political goals, and oftentimes these goals are not aligned with the public.

Given the high level of uncertainty, multiple and contradictory political pressures of varying strengths exist during critical junctures (Capoccia 2015). By identifying the main decision-makers and examining the dynamics of their interactions and subsequent choices, empirical examples in this volume demonstrate what other paths could possibly have been taken instead of the one we observe. Specifically, the volume employs counterfactual reasoning to demonstrate the presence of elite agency. For instance, in the case of Tunisia, the reconstruction of a counterfactual situation draws from Egypt, which was in a similar situation in the early 2010s yet took a path in which elites politicized religion. As for Indonesia, in addition to using neighboring Malaysia as a counterfactual, another period—Indonesia's initial democratization in the 1950s—is chosen to serve as a potential diverging path during which elites politicized religion instead of muting mass-level demand. Going further, South American examples demonstrate elite agency more explicitly by conducting a paired comparison of the most similar cases—Colombia and Uruguay, and Argentina and Peru—with contrasting representation performance.

4.3.2. The Persistence of MED beyond Critical Junctures: Forces behind Path Dependency

So far, I have explained that the origin of MED in specific political dimensions can be traced to critical junctures when elites' deliberate actions or inactions result in deviation from the mass preference. Here, we can pause and ask why the gap did not close afterwards. Put differently, why do elites not reverse their decisions so that they can be more in sync with the masses? Guided by empirical examples in this volume and related literatures, this section will elucidate three key mechanisms through which the created gap persists.

The first mechanism is the marginalization of potentially threatening political opponents. Namely, elites who have politicized or muted a specific political dimension during a critical juncture can afford to establish themselves as mainstream despite their deviation from the masses. In other words, even if other new political forces who mirror masses' preferences emerge after the critical juncture, they are likely to be marginalized from the main political scene. This mechanism is particularly likely to be effective if the discrepancy-bearing critical juncture overlaps with democratization or redemocratization during which the first mover's advantage is present. One of the most noted aspects of path dependency in politics is the utilization of political authority and resources to further power asymmetry (Pierson 2011; Mahoney 2000). That is, winners at the early stage can change the formal institutions and public policies to enhance their powers even more (Hacker and Pierson 2014). As a result, they can alter the resource flows in their favor and decide which issues to focus on and which to leave out (Pierson 2011). Moreover, winners can also dictate how parties should be created, organized, and run by enshrining relevant details in constitutions, party laws, or party finance laws (Pierson 2011). Not surprisingly, research points out that more restrictive regulations, for example, registration requirements, deter the electoral success of new parties (Tavits 2006; Van Biezen and Rashkova 2014).

From this volume, the Japanese case demonstrates how the center-right Liberal Democratic Party depoliticized the normal nation–peace state dimension during the 1960s—the first critical juncture—and instead politicized the rural–urban dimension for its electoral advantage. One of the key reasons this could persist for multiple decades has to do with the marginalization of the party's opponent. For instance, between 1960 and 1990, Japan's center-right Liberal Democratic Party government changed campaign regulations approximately 50 times, most of which were aimed at enhancing the incumbency advantage their members received (McElwain 2008). In a similar vein, based on the Indonesian example, Andreas Ufen details how major parties in a grand coalition successfully block the civil society impact on party politics and raise the bar for new party entry through personalization of politics (chapter 7). Likewise, the Tunisian and South American examples in this volume show how established elites exclude candidates and parties with certain ideological or religious leanings from politics (chapters 5 and 6).

The first mechanism makes it clear that the mass–elite discrepancy created during the critical juncture persists due to the marginalization of other political forces that can potentially reflect the preference of the masses. Added to this, the second and third mechanisms explain why established elites are not likely to change their stance and move in line with the masses. That is, due to deliberate self-selection and socialization, elites are likely to stay homogeneous and sustain inertia. Deliberate self-selection refers to the intention of party leadership to recruit candidates whose policy preferences align with theirs. Evidence drawn from both Western and non-Western contexts points to the prevalence of this pattern (Mauzy and Milne 2002; Ji and Jiang 2020; Lesschaeve et al. 2018). In this volume, the Japanese case shows that left- and right-leaning parties began to have a clear positional divide along the normal nation–peace state dimension from its first postwar critical juncture. How they sustained this divide for nearly seven decades is not surprising because, as noted by McElwain (chapter 8), parties are ideologically invested in the divide and have increasingly become historically embedded. Due to the high saliency of association between certain core issues with particular parties, there will also be a self-selection of aspiring candidates who feel strongly about the core issues, and they will endeavor to stay within the recruitment radar of party leadership. Self-selection mechanisms are not confined to policy-difference-related divides. As will be made clear from the Indonesian case, after the moderation of the religious–secular dimension during its second democratic transition in the early 2000s, success in politics hinged on money. Characterized by Ufen as the politics of personalism and commercialization, Indonesian politics has increasingly favored those with deep pockets at the expense of other qualities (chapter 7). In other words, the critical juncture started a self-reinforcing vicious cycle of plutocracy.

Even if a candidate is elected to office without having congruent preferences on the party's core issues, socialization will serve as another force steering homogenization. For those elected politicians who were ill-informed about the party's core issues and positions, exposure to the party as an incumbent politician will naturally allow them to be better informed. For instance, there will be no shortage of opportunities from which a sitting legislator can learn about the party's policies and positions, for example, from election campaigns and party manifestos, legislative speeches, questions, proposal submissions, voting on specific bills, and party-level social and educational programs designed to socialize their followers to adopt specific sets of values (Atabaki and Zurcher 2004; Claassen 2011). In this regard, the Tunisian case demonstrates how the party members of Ennahda continuously socialized among themselves and with secular politicians to moderate their religious views and made a number of concessions via cooperation with secular forces.

The self-selection and socialization processes are more likely to be facilitated if there is a high level of socioeconomic background homogeneity among political elites. In describing elite circulation, elite theorists have noted whether the scope of elite change is shallow or deep (Higley and Lengyel 2000). Shallow circulation refers to drawing elites from the existing political and social hierarchy, while deep circulation comes down the hierarchical ladder or even includes outsiders such as diasporas and underground movements. Insofar as politics is concerned, shallow elite circulation tends to be the dominant mode. Often noted as an undemocratic feature of representative democracy (Manin 1997), it has long been known that political elites come from more privileged backgrounds in terms of education, class, and previous career (e.g., upper-middle-class, elite-university graduates having a legal background) and possess mainstream ascriptive traits within the society from the perspective of gender, race, and ethnicity (e.g., white male Anglo-Saxons in the US context). For these reasons, elections are known to produce aristocratic effects since public offices are reserved for eminent individuals who are deemed superior to others (Alonso et al. 2011). Existing research notes that these biographical factors affect politicians' worldviews and underpin many of their policy priorities and preferences (Krcmaric et al. 2020). On this, several country examples included in this volume hint at favorable conditions for the continuation of elite-level homogeneity. For instance, Japan is well known for drawing its political elites from a small circle of exclusive universities while having a large portion of hereditary politicians (Smith 2018). In Tunisia, research shows the continuing influence of old regime holdovers in politics after the revolution due to their access to money, networks, and media (Stenslie and Selvik 2019).

Three key mechanisms—opponent marginalization, self-selection, and socialization—attribute the state of mass–elite discrepancy to the path dependency of elites. In other words, the three mechanisms assume that the main parliamentary elites prefer not to change their existing policy positions and explain how that state can continue despite the salient MED. However, elites are by no means always indifferent to their preference incongruence with the public. This is particularly so when their preference divergence from the masses prevents them from reaching a policy outcome they desire. A case in point is Japan, where the ruling elites have been persuading the masses in order to pass the referendum hurdle required for revising the constitution. However, with respect to the ruling elites' discrepancy-closing attempt, Kenneth McElwain (in chapter 8) demonstrates that elites failed due to their message inconsistency and their lack of credibility. From this example, we can draw the lesson that a representation gap can persist in spite of elites' conscious efforts to close it.

4.4. Global Mass–Elite Discrepancies: Summary from New Democracies and Application to Old Democracies

Drawing key insights from historical institutionalism, this chapter has generated a theoretical framework that can explain the varieties of mass–elite-discrepancies observed in salient political dimensions. By doing so, it goes beyond the existing scholarship, which primarily focuses on explaining the gap's size (not varieties) based on explanatory factors insensitive to historical contexts.

To recapitulate the gist of the argument, the key reason behind asymmetric mass–elite discrepancy structure has to do with only one group (mass or elite) politicizing key issues, i.e., asymmetric politicization, concerning a specific political dimension of interest. Specifically, at least one segment of the masses or elites increases the political saliency of issues related to a political dimension and, at the same time, moves its position away from the previous status quo. During this process, the average positional difference between masses and elites becomes prominent. This mass–elite gap emerging process is not ahistorical because the timing of asymmetric politicization overlaps with a critical juncture during which the window of opportunity for change opens for political elites. The volume argues that the asymmetric politicization process during the critical juncture is a result of deliberate action or inaction by elites. Put differently, elites intentionally politicize specific issues without much general public demand, or depoliticize issues with high public demand. The representation gap is an elite-level choice because elites have the agency to take other paths and can prevent the representation gap from emerging or continuing. Finally, with respect to the persistence of the mass–elite gap beyond the critical juncture, global examples from this volume demonstrate three key path dependency reinforcing mechanisms: (1) established elites marginalizing opponents who can mirror mass preferences, (2) established elites self-selecting those who already share similar views regarding politicization/depoliticization of a specific political dimension, and (3) elite-level socializing through which elites with different views can converge and become more homogeneous.

Global examples make it clear that the logic of the critical juncture and elite agency applies to various policy areas in multiple world regions and numerous time points spanning multiple decades. Nevertheless, it should be noted that the proposed theoretical framework draws from experiences of democracies beyond Western Europe. So, one would wonder to what extent the logic described here helps in understanding the prominent mass–elite gap in Western European countries, which is the focus of most of the extant scholarship. After all, Western European democracies have a longer history of party competition and have been through different political trajectories compared to new democracies. Despite numerous differences, I believe the core theoretical ideas grounded in critical juncture and elite agency can help us to understand the state of mass–elite discrepancies in Western Europe too.

As for the old democracies in the West, meta-analysis results and the findings in chapter 3 clearly demonstrate that the mass–elite gap is most prominent in the pro- vs. anti-European integration political dimension (foreign relations issues) and in the authoritarian vs. libertarian political dimension (sociocultural issues), while the structure of the gap for both dimensions largely approximates "divided masses–nondivided elites." In light of the key thesis of this volume, this gap can be attributed to the mainstream parties' strong attachment to the key political dimension that they have politicized during an earlier critical juncture period—the big vs. small government political dimension (socioeconomic issues) in the early twentieth century—and have maintained as the primary axis of conflict. However, this preoccupation came at a cost, since mainstream parties in effect neglected other subsequently emerging political dimensions that increasingly became divisive at the mass level. This resonates well with the observation that elite-level politics today retains much of its old patterns despite mass-level evidence pointing to de-alignment and realignment (Stoll 2010).

There are multiple pieces of relevant supporting evidence. First is the unequal distribution of political space between parties, which does not mirror that of the masses. It has been noted that parties with left-wing positions on economic issues and, at the same time, right-wing positions on sociocultural issues have been historically lacking in Western Europe (Hillen and Steiner 2020). The second piece of evidence concerns the division of issue representation competency between parties. Research shows that mainstream parties are better on socioeconomic issues while niche parties have their edge on sociocultural issues (Van Ditmars and De Lange 2019). The third piece of evidence relates to political elites' sticky policy preferences. As made clear in chapter 3, the origin of the European Union can be traced to a postwar elite-led project. However, along with the euro crisis and the immigration crisis, it has increasingly become an independent political dimension pertinent to foreign relations, often labeled as a new "transnational cleavage" (Hooghe and Marks 2018). Notwithstanding divided masses, vote hemorrhage, and the rise of populist parties, expert survey evidence shows that mainstream European parties have barely changed their positions on EU integration—being pro-EU integration—over time (Hooghe and Marks, 2018). When noticeable changes occurred related to EU issues, it was largely through masses turning to new parties, either through general elections or referendum votes. In this sense, it can be said that populist parties have filled a representation void left by mainstream parties (Mudde 2007).

Western European experiences show that mainstream parties cannot always afford to be nonchalant toward public needs, and that path dependency is not unbreakable. Counterevidence has already accumulated to dismiss any deterministic path-dependency-driven argument. On the one hand, mainstream parties have often accommodated policies advocated by rising leftist or rightist parties whose core issues concern postmaterial or EU integration dimensions (van Spanje 2010; Abou-Chadi and Krause 2020). Moreover, evidence demonstrates that a government's responsiveness particularly goes up when faced with electoral uncertainties due to increased political competition (Hobolt and Klemmensen 2008). On the other hand, research shows that mainstream parties' complacency and neglect of new public demands are often followed by losses of a substantial portion of votes or even office (Bornschier 2010; De Vries and Hobolt 2012). Yet three mainstream party families—the Christian democrats/conservatives, the social democrats/socialists, and the liberals—have proven to be highly resilient in Western European party politics, taking up roughly 70 percent of all votes between 2010 and 2019 (De Vries and Hobolt 2020, 24). The century-long dominance is quite remarkable if we consider how often top private companies have changed during the equivalent period (for instance, changes in Fortune 500 companies in the past decades). In the private sector, top players cannot afford to remain in the market for long if they deviate from the mainstream preferences of the masses. In contrast, the supply-side factor plays a much larger role in defining key players in politics and, as a result, is more likely to avoid the force of, in the language of Schumpeter (2016), "creative destruction." On this, Pierson (2011) rightly points out that path dependency is more likely to be prevalent in politics than in business. Relatedly, the theoretical framework I put forward in this chapter details how, despite political elites' preference divergence from the masses, their replacement may happen in a limited scope and at a slow pace. I hope the present chapter has contributed to our understanding of the origin and continuation of diverse mass–elite discrepancies by expounding on the ways in which elite choices during critical junctures play out in politics.

Notes

1. Even though a study had two different kinds of confirmed causes in one level, it is counted as one. In a similar vein, the same cause getting confirmed, for instance, in multiple regression models in one study is only counted as one.

2. For a more in-depth understanding of the logic and operationalization behind the included causes, the study ID number indicated in the parentheses can be used to trace the corresponding study included in the meta-analysis.

3. Due to the inductive nature of the identification process, firsthand knowledge of the cases is often deemed essential (Capoccia 2015).

4. Polarization here refers to the state of division with two sharply contrasting groups, sets of opinions, or beliefs.

References

Abou-Chadi, T., and W. Krause. 2020. "The Causal Effect of Radical Right Success on Mainstream Parties' Policy Positions: A Regression Discontinuity Approach." *British Journal of Political Science* 50 (3): 829–47.

Alonso, S., J. Keane, and W. Merkel, eds. 2011. *The Future of Representative Democracy*. Cambridge: Cambridge University Press.

American Political Science Association. 1950. "Committee on Political Parties: Towards a More Responsible Two Party System." *American Political Science Review* 44 (supplement).

Arthur, W. B. 1994. "Positive Feedbacks in the Economy." *McKinsey Quarterly* 1: 81–96.

Atabaki, T., and E. J. Zurcher. 2004. *Men of Order: Authoritarian Modernisation in Turkey and Iran, 1918–1942*. London: I.B. Tauris.

Bartolini S. 2000. *The Political Mobilization of the European Left, 1860–1980: The Class Cleavage*. Cambridge: Cambridge University Press.

Binzer Hobolt, S., and R. Klemmensen. 2008. "Government Responsiveness and Political Competition in Comparative Perspective." *Comparative Political Studies* 41 (3): 309–37.

Bornschier, S. 2009. "Cleavage Politics in Old and New Democracies." *Living Reviews in Democracy* (October). Available at https://ethz.ch/content/dam/ethz/special-interest/gess/cis/cis-dam/CIS_DAM_2015/WorkingPapers/Living_Reviews_Democracy/Bornschier.pdf

Bornschier, S. 2010. *Cleavage Politics and the Populist Right. The New Cultural Conflict in Western Europe*. Philadelphia: Temple University Press.

Bornschier, S. 2016. "Historical Polarization and Representation in South American Party Systems, 1900–1990." *British Journal of Political Science* 49 (1): 1–27.

Capoccia, G. 2015. "Critical Junctures and Institutional Change." In *Advances in Comparative-Historical Analysis*, edited by J. Mahoney and K. Thelen. Cambridge: Cambridge University Press.

Capoccia, G. 2016. "Critical Junctures." In *The Oxford Handbook of Historical Institutionalism*, edited by Orfeo Fioretos, Tulia G. Falleti, and Adam Sheingate, 89–106. Oxford: Oxford University Press.

Cheng, T. J., and Y. M. Hsu. 2014. "Long in the Making: Taiwan's Institutionalized Party System." In *Party System Institutionalization in Asia: Democracies, Autocracies, and the Shadows of the Past*, edited by Allen Hicken and Erik Martinez Kuhonta, 108–35. Cambridge: Cambridge University Press.

Claassen, R. L. 2011. "Political Awareness and Electoral Campaigns: Maximum Effects for Minimum Citizens?" *Political Behavior* 33 (2): 203–23.

De Vries, C. E., and S. B. Hobolt. 2012. "When Dimensions Collide: The Electoral Success of Issue Entrepreneurs." *European Union Politics* 13 (2): 246–68.

De Vries, C. E., and S. B. Hobolt. 2020. *The Rise of Challenger Parties in Europe*. Princeton: Princeton University Press.

Deegan-Krause, K., and Z. Enyedi. 2010. "Agency and the Structure of Party Competition: Alignment, Stability and the Role of Political Elites." *West European Politics* 33 (3): 686–710.

Egan, P. J. 2013. *Partisan Priorities: How Issue Ownership Drives and Distorts American Politics*. Cambridge: Cambridge University Press.

Enyedi, Z. 2005. "The Role of Agency in Cleavage Formation." *European Journal of Political Research* 44 (5): 697–720.

Escobar-Lemmon, M. C., and M. M. Taylor-Robinson. 2016. *Women in Presidential Cabinets: Power Players or Abundant Tokens?* Oxford: Oxford University Press.

Greene, Z. D., and M. Haber. 2015. "The Consequences of Appearing Divided: An Analysis of Party Evaluations and Vote Choice. *Electoral Studies* 37: 15–27.

Hacker, J. S., and P. Pierson. 2014. "After the 'Master Theory': Downs, Schattschneider, and the Rebirth of Policy-Focused Analysis. *Perspectives on Politics* 12 (3): 643–62.

Hall, P. A., and R. C. R. Taylor. 1996. "Political Science and the Three Institutionalisms." *Political Studies* 44: 936–57.

Higley, J., and G. Lengyel. 2000. *Elite Configurations after State Socialism: Elites after State Socialism*. Lanham, MD: Rowman and Littlefield.

Hillen, S., and N. D. Steiner. 2020. "The Consequences of Supply Gaps in Two-Dimensional Policy Spaces for Voter Turnout and Political Support: The Case of Economically Left-Wing and Culturally Right-Wing Citizens in Western Europe." *European Journal of Political Research* 59 (2): 331–53.

Hobolt, S., and R. Klemmensen. 2008. "Government Responsiveness and Political Competition in Comparative Perspective." *Comparative Political Studies* 41 (3): 309–37.

Hooghe, L., and G. Marks. 2018. "Cleavage Theory Meets Europe's Crises: Lipset,

Rokkan, and the Transnational Cleavage." *Journal of European Public Policy* 25 (1): 109–35.

Ji, C., and J. Jiang. 2020. "Enlightened One-Party Rule? Ideological Differences between Chinese Communist Party Members and the Mass Public." *Political Research Quarterly* 73 (3): 651–66.

Kahn, K. F. 1992 "Does Being Male Help? An Investigation of the Effects of Candidate Gender and Campaign Coverage on Evaluations of U.S. Senate Candidates." *Journal of Politics* 54: 497–517.

Kanev, Dobrin, and Katia Hristova-Valtcheva. 2016. "Bulgaria." In *Routledge Handbook of European Elections*, edited by Donatella M. Viola, 633–52. New York: Routledge.

Kitschelt, H., Z. Mansfeldova, R. Markowski, and G. Toka. 1999. *Post-Communist Party Systems: Competition, Representation, and Inter-Party Cooperation.* Cambridge: Cambridge University Press.

Krcmaric, D., S. C. Nelson, and A. Roberts. 2020. "Studying Leaders and Elites: The Personal Biography Approach." *Annual Review of Political Science* 23: 133–51.

Kriesi, H. 1998. "The Transformation of Cleavage Politics: The 1997 Stein Rokkan Lecture." *European Journal of Political Research* 33 (2): 165–85.

Lesschaeve, C., P. F. van Erkel, and C. Meulewaeter. 2018. "Thinking Alike: Two Pathways to Leadership-Candidate Opinion Congruence." *Journal of Elections, Public Opinion and Parties* 28 (4): 488–515.

Lipset, S. M., and S. Rokkan, eds. 1967. *Party Systems and Voter Alignments: Cross-National Perspectives.* New York: Free Press.

Mahoney, J. 2000. "Path Dependence in Historical Sociology." *Theory and Society* 29 (4): 507–48.

Mainwaring, S. 1999. *Rethinking Party Systems in the Third Wave of Democratization: The Case of Brazil.* Stanford: Stanford University Press.

Mair, P. 2001. "The Freezing Hypothesis." In *Party Systems and Voter Alignments Revisited*, edited by Lauri Karvonen and Stein Kuhnle, 26–44. London: Routledge.

Manacsa, R. C., and A. C. Tan. 2005. "Manufacturing Parties: Re-examining the Transient Nature of Philippine Political Parties." *Party Politics* 11 (6): 748–65.

Manin, B. 1997. *The Principles of Representative Government.* Cambridge: Cambridge University Press.

Mauzy, D. K., and R. S. Milne. 2002. *Singapore Politics under the People's Action Party.* London: Routledge.

McElwain, K. M. 2008. "Manipulating Electoral Rules to Manufacture Single-Party Dominance." *American Journal of Political Science* 52 (1): 32–47.

Meyer, T. M., and W. C. Müller. 2013. "The Issue Agenda, Party Competence and Popularity: An Empirical Analysis of Austria 1989–2004." *Journal of Elections, Public Opinion & Parties* 23 (4): 484–500.

Mudde, C. 2007. *Populist Radical Right Parties in Europe.* Cambridge: Cambridge University Press.

Norris, P., J. Curtice, D. Sanders, M. Scammell, and H. A. Semetko. 1999. *On Message: Communicating the Campaign.* London: Sage.

Olson, M. 1989. "Collective Action." In *The Invisible Hand*, edited by John Eatwell, Murray Milgate, and Peter Newman, 61–69. London: Palgrave Macmillan.

Orren, K., and S. Skowronek. 1996. "Institutions and Intercurrence: Theory Building in the Fullness of Time." In *Political Order*, edited by Ian Shapiro and Russell Hardin, 111–46. New York: New York University Press.

Panebianco, A. 1988. *Political Parties: Organization and Power*. Cambridge: Cambridge University Press.

Petrocik, J. R. 1996. "Issue Ownership in Presidential Elections, with a 1980 Case Study." *American Journal of Political Science* 40 (3): 825–50.

Pierson, P. 2011. *Politics in Time: History, Institutions, and Social Analysis*. Princeton: Princeton University Press.

Powell, G. B., Jr. 2013. "Representation in Context: Election Laws and Ideological Congruence between Citizens and Governments." *Perspectives on Politics* 11 (1): 9–21.

Rakner, L., Svåsand, L., and N. S. Khembo. 2007. "Fissions and Fusions, Foes and Friends: Party System Restructuring in Malawi in the 2004 General Elections." *Comparative Political Studies* 40 (9): 1112–37.

Randall, V. 2001. "Party Systems and Voter Alignments in the New Democracies of the Third World." In *Party Systems and Voter Alignments Revisited*, edited by Lauri Karvonen and Stein Kuhnle, 258–79. London: Routledge.

Riedl, R. 2016. "Political Parties, Regimes, and Social Cleavages." In *The Oxford Handbook of Historical Institutionalism*, edited by Orfeo Fioretos, Tulia G. Falleti, and Adam Sheingate, 223–38. Oxford: Oxford University Press.

Rovny J. 2012. "Who Emphasizes and Who Blurs? Party Strategies in Multidimensional Competition." *European Union Politics* 13: 269–92.

Sartori, G. 1969. "From the Sociology of Politics to Political Sociology." *Government and Opposition* 4 (2): 195–214.

Schattschneider, E. E. 1975. *The Semisovereign People: A Realist's View of Democracy in America*. Boston: Wadsworth.

Schumpeter, J. A. 2016. *Capitalism, Socialism and Democracy*. New York: Columbia University Press.

Shim, J. 2021. "Mass-Elite Representation Gap in Old and New Democracies: Two Caveats for a Global Level Comparison." *East Asia Today*. Heidelberg University Transcultural Studies Working Paper Series.

Shim, J., and M. Farag. 2022. "Blind Spots in the Study of Political Representation: Actors and Political Dimensions." Paper presented at the 2022 Annual Meeting of the Swiss Political Science Association.

Shim, J., and M. Farag. 2023. "Beyond Clientelism and Personalism: Political Divisions beyond Western Democracies." Paper presented at the 2023 Annual Meeting of the Swiss Political Science Association.

Slater, D., and J. Wong. 2013. "The Strength to Concede: Ruling Parties and Democratization in Developmental Asia." *Perspectives on Politics* 11 (3): 717–33.

Smith, D. M. 2018. *Dynasties and Democracy: The Inherited Incumbency Advantage in Japan*. Stanford: Stanford University Press.

Spirova, Maria. 2007. *Political Parties in Post-Communist Societies: Formation, Persistence, and Change*. New York: Palgrave Macmillan.

Stenslie, S., and K. Selvik. 2019. "Elite Survival and the Arab Spring: The Cases of Tunisia and Egypt." In *Elites and People: Challenges to Democracy*, edited by Fredrik

Engelstad, Trygve Gulbrandsen, Marte Mangset, and Mari Teigen. Leeds, UK: Emerald Publishing.

Stoll, H. 2010. "Elite-Level Conflict Salience and Dimensionality in Western Europe: Concepts and Empirical Findings." *West European Politics* 33 (3): 445–73.

Strøm, Kaare, and Wolfgang C. Müller. 1999. "Political Parties and Hard Choices." In *Policy, Office, or Votes: How Political Parties in Western Europe Make Hard Decisions*, edited by Kaare Strøm and Wolfgang C. Müller, 1–35. Cambridge: Cambridge University Press.

Tavits, M. 2006. "Party System Change: Testing a Model of New Party Entry." *Party Politics* 12 (1): 99–119.

Thelen, K. 1999. "Historical Institutionalism in Comparative Politics." *Annual Review of Political Science* 2: 369–404.

Thelen, K. 2003. "How Institutions Evolve: Insights from Comparative Historical Research." In *Comparative Historical Analysis in the Social Sciences*, edited by J. Mahoney and D. Rueschemeyer, 208–40. New York: Cambridge University Press.

Van Biezen, I., and E. R. Rashkova. 2014. "Deterring New Party Entry? The Impact of State Regulation on the Permeability of Party Systems." *Party Politics* 20 (6): 890–903.

Van Ditmars, M. M., and S. L. De Lange. 2019. "Differential representation? The Gaps between Mainstream and Niche Party Representatives and Their Voters in the Netherlands." *Acta Politica* 54:295–314.

Van Spanje, J. 2010. "Contagious Parties: Anti-Immigration Parties and Their Impact on Other Parties' Immigration Stances in Contemporary Western Europe." *Party Politics* 16 (5): 563–86.

Vengroff, R. 1993. "Governance and the Transition to Democracy: Political Parties and the Party System in Mali." *Journal of Modern African Studies* 31 (4): 541–62.

Zielinski, J. 2002. "Translating Social Cleavages into Party Systems: The Significance of New Democracies." *World Politics* 54 (2): 184–211.

Zuckerman, A. 1975. "Political Cleavage: A Conceptual and Theoretical Analysis." *British Journal of Political Science* 5 (2): 231–48.

CHAPTER 5

Polarization, Political Cleavages, and Elites in Old and New Democracies

Simon Bornschier

The appeal of the cleavage concept lies in its capacity to link individual political behavior to large-scale divisions in society by conceiving of individuals as members of various social groups. In their seminal work, Lipset and Rokkan (1967; Rokkan 1970, 1999) explained how party systems in Western Europe formed and came to represent the programmatic preferences of voters, thereby achieving a high degree of mass–elite correspondence (Dalton 1985). Because it was developed to explain the configuration of party systems in Western Europe, Lipset and Rokkan's model cannot be directly applied to other contexts (but see Geddes 2003). While the point of departure in the original model was the critical junctures defined by the twin processes of the national and industrial revolutions, subsequent theorizing on Western Europe identified the educational revolution beginning in the 1960s (Allardt 1968; Kriesi 1999; Bornschier 2010; Stubager 2009, 2010), the multifaceted process of globalization (Kriesi et al. 2008, 2012; de Wilde et al. 2019), and the transnationalization of governance (Hooghe and Marks 2018) as further critical junctures that shaped party systems. Contrary to accounts that emphasize a generalized process of dealignment, or the prevalence of antiestablishment dynamics and issue competition,[1] scholars working within the cleavage account generally assess the capacity of party systems to represent voters' substantive policy preferences more positively.

If we detach this perspective from the critical junctures that were relevant in Western Europe, the cleavage approach can fruitfully be applied to other regions, and to newer democracies in particular. To make the cleavage approach travel to other contexts, which forms the prime focus of this volume, it needs to be adapted in two ways. For one thing, the approach needs to be contextualized to account for critical junctures that are often different from the national and industrial revolutions (Randall 2001; van Eerd 2017; this volume, chap. 4). More fundamentally, this requires a shift from macrohistorical sociology and a concern with similarities and differences between societies and their party systems to a more actor-centered perspective that acknowledges that critical junctures may afford elites considerable leeway to shape political cleavages (Chhibber and Torcal 1997; Torcal and Mainwaring 2003; Enyedi 2005; Deegan-Krause 2006; Bornschier 2009; Deegan-Krause and Enyedi 2010; Bargsted and Somma 2016). The agency-oriented approach is also in line with definitions of critical junctures prevalent in recent theorizing (Collier and Collier [1991] 2002; Capoccia and Kelemen 2007; Mahoney 2000; Roberts 2017). As noted in the previous chapter, mass–elite discrepancy largely depends upon elite leeway during the critical juncture, which takes the form of intentionally muting mass-level social divides or politicizing divides without much mass-level demand. This chapter focuses on the former.

The first part of this chapter seeks to contribute to theorizing on elite agency in the politicization of social divides and their translation into party systems. Specifically, it lays out key conditions under which elite agency increases. It takes as a point of departure the undisputed importance of elite strategy in situations when cleavages are cross-cutting, a common scenario in developing and advanced democracies alike. It then moves on to discussing how new and old democracies differ by addressing the interplay between mobilization from below and elite strategic action. In most new democracies, large-scale processes of social change and suffrage expansion were less intimately related than was the case in the old democracies. Second, elites are also afforded more leeway in new democracies due to the frequent restrictions on political pluralism and party competition. It is here that a different strategic configuration of elite actors impinges directly on the quality of substantive representation. Finally, I address the process in which cleavages are reproduced over generations, and how prior democratic experiences shape the degree to which redemocratization constitutes a critical juncture in its own right, or merely reproduces earlier mass–elite configurations.

The empirical part of the chapter substantiates some of these theoretical claims by analyzing the mobilization of the economic cleavage in South America in the first decades of the twentieth century. Often noted as a region whose party development sequence most closely resembles that of Western Europe (Randall 2001), South America can be distinguished from other non-Western regions by its early decolonization experience in the early nineteenth century, the emergence of working-class organization in the early twentieth century, and prominent socioeconomic divides at the mass level. The empirical analysis consists of paired comparisons of South American countries and is intended to illustrate the range of possible outcomes in mass–elite congruence or divergence when parties have substantial autonomy from society in defining their policy positions. The results demonstrate that elite choices are central in determining whether mass pressure from below results in mobilization of competitive divides at the elite level, or whether it results in congruence between parties and voters, in the terms set out in figure 4.2 in chapter 4. Specifically, parties played the predominant role in mobilizing left-leaning voters in Uruguay and Colombia, pulling them into a coalition with the middle class. The Colorados in Uruguay maintained their course and were able to retain this constituency, while the Liberals in Colombia colluded with their former archenemies after a civil war, leaving left-wing voters without representation. Similarly, the comparison between the Argentine Peronists and Peru's American Popular Revolutionary Alliance (APRA) again underlines the leeway for elite agency: party leaders unconstrained by party organizations with strong mechanisms of internal accountability may in some cases remain congruent with their constituents, and in others abandon them. Finally, both the Venezuelan and the Colombian cases demonstrate that elite pacts intended to restore democracy after interruptions of democratic rule can put the party system on the track of growing mass–elite divergence, because these pacts often restrict open contestation and competition. In Venezuela, this eventually paved the way for the emergence of Chavismo.

5.1. Elite Agency in Old and New Democracies

Mobilization from below and from above interact both in the initial formation of cleavages, as well as in their subsequent perpetuation or their fading, as we will see. Politics is always a struggle about meaning and about which of the manifold dividing lines in society are politicized, as Schattschneider ([1960] 1975) recognized long ago. Agency is thus crucial in old and new democracies alike. At the most elementary level, individuals need interpretative frames in order to engage in collective political action. These frames allow them to interpret grievances and to form political preferences to alleviate those grievances. This involves the formation of collective identities that help to define the boundaries of the group in question (see also Tarrow 1992). Leadership by elites is crucial in this process, as many cleavage theorists highlight (e.g., Chhibber and Torcal 1997; Torcal and Mainwaring 2003; Enyedi 2005; Deegan-Krause 2006; Zuckerman 1975). Beyond the collective action problem, elite agency is also crucial because every individual belongs to multiple groups that are potentially relevant politically. Following Stryker (1980, 2000), we can think of identities such as those linked to class, religion, or ethnicity as arranged in a hierarchy of salience. Elites matter both in the initial mobilization of cleavages, when they provide interpretative frames to make some group identities salient at the expense of others (Deegan-Krause and Enyedi 2010, 697; Bornschier et al. 2024). Here, the space for agency is limited by the legacies of the mobilization of prior cleavages, as is evident in the well-known notion of cross-cutting cleavages. On the other hand, the continued salience of a division depends on the degree to which political conflict stabilizes the salience hierarchy of identities at the individual level (Bornschier 2010; see also Coser 1956; Sartori 1968; Bartolini 2005). Indeed, the extensive literature that has documented how the strength of class voting in the old democracies depends on the degree of continued elite political conflict speaks in favor of this hypothesis (e.g., van der Brug 2010; Evans and Tilley 2011; Adams, De Vries, and Leiter 2011; Evans and de Graaf 2013).

In this section, I start out by expanding on the first notion, namely that new divisions interact with existing cleavages, whereby the latter determine the mobilization space for the former. This mechanism is common to old and new democracies. I then go on to discuss some of the reasons why political elites have more room for agency in new democracies.

5.1.1. Cross-Cutting Cleavages

Political agency occupies a central role in the initial mobilization of cleavages, and especially where social divisions are strongly cross-cutting. While we find state-market and religious cleavages almost everywhere in Europe, the degree to which cleavages cross-cut or reinforce each other depends crucially on elite strategies (see, e.g., Lipset and Rokkan 1967; Rokkan 1999; Casal Bértoa 2014; Manow 2015). Outside Europe, an analogous (if rare) case of a very gradual process of suffrage extension and the sequential mobilization of a religious and an economic cleavage is Chile (Scully 1992). More broadly, a large number of divisions are potentially relevant in political terms in any society, and party systems are always more responsive to some conflicts than to others (Schattschneider ([1960] 1975). This also has implications for the representation of voters' substantive interests. To the degree that competitive divides are cross-cutting, voters face trade-offs in terms of choosing a party that best represents their interests: depending on parties' political offer, they may be able to maximize proximity to a party along the dimension that matters most to them only at the expense of reducing proximity along another dimension that is of secondary importance to them. We must therefore be careful to identify the relevant divides for voters, because we might otherwise misinterpret the lack of saliency enjoyed by a divide with a lack of responsiveness on the part of parties.

All of this makes the measurement of how well party systems represent voter preferences a very complicated task in old and new democracies alike. The presence of several competing dimensions with varying levels of salience, as well as the dynamic and evolving nature of party system divides, makes the identification of what Jaemin Shim (chapter 2, this vol.) calls *mass–elite policy discrepancies on key political dimensions* far from trivial. This might be illustrated with reference to the populist right in Western Europe: for those supporting the radical populist right in Western Europe, the economic dimension is indeed secondary to the cultural one. While their anti-universalistic preferences are represented well by right-wing populist parties, this is not necessarily the case with regard to the economic dimension (Ivarsflaten 2005; Bornschier 2010; but see Enggist and Pinggera 2021).[2] Overall, radical right parties have moved to the left on the economic dimension, but depending on the country, this may alienate some of their supporters, and these parties may therefore be reluctant to move too far to the left in the economic domain. A similar situation was well known in postwar Western Europe when religion was still a salient cleavage—indeed, more salient than the economic divide in many countries.[3] Consequently, religious voters often faced a dilemma in terms of representation due to the cross-cutting nature of economic and religious cleavages. While the identification and measurement of competitive divides in new democracies is more demanding than in established democracies (Bornschier 2020), examples of cross-cutting cleavage abound. For instance, as noted in the previous chapters, numerous cleavages concerning foreign relations and defense cross-cut socioeconomic divides. By displaying more variance in terms of their strength, political cleavages in new democracies shed light on the nontrivial role of elite agency in cleavage formation.

5.1.2. Weak Bottom-up Mobilization

Critical junctures constitute moments in which the interaction between demands from below and elite agency crystallizes. They are moments in which elites acquire more room for agency (Collier and Collier [1991] 2002; Mahoney 2000; Capoccia and Kelemen 2007; Deegan-Krause and Enyedi 2010; Roberts 2017; this volume, chap. 4). If the social groups in question already enjoy the right to vote, critical junctures usually occur over several "critical elections," as realignment theory postulates (Key 1959; Martin 2000; Mayhew 2000). Even in the classical cleavage model, which most of the time adopts a social group perspective, political actors play a key role in politicizing social divisions, in particular by forging coalitions of more specific electoral segments into cleavage groups (Lipset and Rokkan 1967; Rokkan 1999; Enyedi 2005, 700–701). Many new democracies differ from this historical model, first, in that mobilization from below involved more than just one group or class. Second, weaker institutionalization meant that mobilization was more likely to occur in sudden outbursts, increasing the risk of an authoritarian reaction (Weyland 2012, 2014). The following paragraphs discuss how these two factors play out.

The leeway for political agency at critical junctures depends on the one hand on the nature of bottom-up social mobilization. Mobilization from below can either involve previously excluded groups that are clearly defined in terms of their group boundaries and political demands, or broader segments of the population. Although there is some variance across countries, the historical mobilization of the European working class is closer to the first scenario (Bartolini 2000a). The broader the groups demanding inclusion, the more important agency becomes in crafting coalitions and in developing a discourse that gives coherence to their demands. The difference between the class cleavage and the older cleavages in Western Europe illustrates this nicely. The cleavages triggered by the national revolution and the sectoral cleavage between agriculture and industry resulted in high levels of diversity between party systems—it is here that Lipset and Rokkan (1967; Rokkan 1999) discuss elite alliance options and choices extensively. Although the vigor of the subsequent class cleavage depended heavily on the strength and configuration of these older cleavages, the authors hardly discuss elite agency with respect to the class cleavage. It is almost as if they took its manifestation, which coincided with the forceful mobilization of the labor movement, for granted.[4] The more that critical junctures coincide with large-scale processes of social change and the formation of new social groups, the more restricted the leeway for political agency seems to be. This will become even clearer when we compare the European process of cleavage formation with that elsewhere and with respect to South America in the empirical part of this chapter. Although the formation of social groups along the class cleavage was aided by the consciousness-raising struggle for suffrage extension in Europe (Rueschemeyer, Huber Stephens, and Stephens 1992; Collier 1999), the critical junctures were large-scale processes of *socioeconomic*, rather than more strictly political, change.

In more recent instances of democratization, the extension of suffrage resulted from more genuine conflicts over political inclusion, although these were often coupled with socioeconomic demands. In sub-Saharan Africa, the struggle for independence against colonial powers constitutes a critical juncture or "genetic moment" that set in motion a path-dependent reproduction of these initial divisions (van Eerd 2017). Similarly, elite-driven political conflicts in the early rounds of electoral competition turned path-dependent in numerous East Asian and Eastern European countries (Slater and Wong 2013; Randall 2001; Zielinski 2002). In South America, where independence was achieved in the early nineteenth century, this process occurred decades before steps toward a broader suffrage were attained.[5] Levels of industrialization were low relative to Europe at the time when pressures for democratization and redistribution mounted in the first decades of the twentieth century (Collier and Collier 2002; Rueschemeyer, Huber Stephens, and Stephens 1992). Suffrage expansion is then more heavily shaped by the strategic choices of elites that seek to bolster their support relative to others (Dix 1989; Collier 1999), rather than by a massive growth of the working class. The resulting cross-class nature of demands for political inclusion affords elites an important role in forging coalitions between different classes, some of which may be less organized than others. Likewise, in Africa, leaders combined Marxist ideology, however distant from social reality due to the fragility of the industrial working class, with nationalism in the struggle against colonialism and the definition of the postcolonial order (van Eerd 2017, 66–72). Asian countries highly resemble this in the sense that communism often deviated from the original doctrine (Belogurova 2014; Scalapino 1965) and became connected to nationalism during the anticolonial struggle. The class character of mobilization from below was far less clear-cut in new democracies; rather, demands for inclusion as well as for specific policies involved diverse social groups. This is all the more true when democratization occurs in the process of decolonization, where it often involves a direct transition to a regime with universal suffrage, sidestepping the establishment of a competitive oligarchic regime (Geddes 2011, 606; see also Randall 2001). In new democracies, elites are thus afforded a more important role as they forge broad social coalitions around substantive political demands.

The socially heterogeneous basis of pressures from below, and the resulting difficulty in specifying policy-oriented demands beyond political reform, means that critical junctures are strongly defined by the struggle between elite actors. Political reform can result from the efforts of established elites to broaden their support, in a pattern Collier (1999) refers to as "electoral support mobilization." But political newcomers will also find it easier to appeal to the masses than when social groups have preexisting linkages to parties deriving from older cleavages. In particular, populist actors are much more likely to rally broad coalitions in new, as opposed to older, democracies (Bornschier 2018). Populist parties generally offer leaders more room for maneuver, since parties of this type have a weaker formal organization to hold leaders to account than mass-organic parties (Levitsky and Roberts 2011). Although populist movements differ in the degree to which they establish strong partisan organizations, Roberts (2006, 137) suggests that "given the weight of personalistic authority, partisan vehicles formed by populist movements are inevitably instruments that serve their leaders' interests." Hence, they offer their leaders—and usually one leader—more decision-making autonomy than classical left-wing mass parties. Charismatic leadership allows voters to project their desires and demands onto the leader (Madsen and Snow 1991; Kitschelt 2000), a psychological mechanism (Conover and Feldman 1982) that results in a greater potential for mass–elite discrepancy along competitive dimensions.

5.1.3. Elite-Led Transitions and Curtailed Political Competition

The more central role occupied by elite agency is coupled with a greater repressive capacity. In part, this is due to weaker mobilization from below, but also to the strength and greater independence of nonparliamentary elites such as the military (Rueschemeyer, Huber Stephens, and Stephens 1992; Geddes 1999; Geddes, Wright, and Frantz 2018). In part, this reflects the experience of numerous new democracies with top-down democratic transitions led by the military or a revolutionary/nationalist party. This difference renders the elite strategic game more complex in many new democracies; but, overall, it further reinforces the ability of elites to channel mass mobilization from below. What is more, in revolutionary moments in which the masses mobilize, the stakes for elites are often high because mobilization is weakly channeled by political organizations (Weyland 2012), impinging on the way they assess the balance between the costs of toleration and the cost of repression of opposition (cf. Dahl 1971).

Pacted transitions to democracy constitute key instances where elites decisively shape the contours of future party competition (Rustow 1970; O'Donnell and Schmitter 1986; Bejarano 2011; Bornschier 2019). To the extent that it results in the exclusion or marginalization of key actors, this mode of transition from authoritarian rule or civil war is damaging for representation. Not only are certain interests excluded from parliamentary representation, the more far-reaching consequence is that a lack of real contestation strongly weakens the incentives of established parties to respond to voter preferences. Cases in point are the exclusion of communist or other radical left parties in many countries in twentieth-century South America, which will be analyzed in detail in the empirical part of this chapter. By contrast, in Spain's democratic transition, the socialist and communist parties—"to the outrage of the Franquist hardliners" (O'Donnell 1992, 27)—were able to push for their legalization in the negotiations.

The contingent logic of pacted democratization does not apply only to representation along economic divides. As a case in point, the difficult translation of religious divides into politics in the MENA region has important implications for representation along the highly salient religious-secular divide in these countries (see Farag, this volume; Wegner and Cavatorta 2019). Regardless of the policy dimension involved, curtailing competition narrows the political spectrum by excluding certain political demands. More damaging still is the impact on the strategic incentives of the established parties: with their more radical competitors outlawed, the costs for colluding ideologically with their competitors are almost absent in the short run, because those voters lacking representation have nowhere else to go (Bornschier 2019). Curtailing competition therefore risks the gradual dealignment of party systems, and it also destroys parties' incentives to adapt to new social demands.[6] As a consequence, restricted competition in the medium or long run leads to representation deficits. These culminated in the breakdown of the party system and the election of Hugo Chávez as a political outsider in Venezuela (Morgan 2011; Bornschier 2018, 2019), and in a progressive deinstitutionalization of the party system in Colombia (Bejarano and Pizarro 2005; Pizarro Leongómez 2006), as we will see later.

An alternative to outright bans on certain parties is for established elites to insulate their voters from programmatic appeals by their competitors by investing in nonprogrammatic linkages (Shefter 1977; Kitschelt 2000). Often, this strategy is sufficient to restrict programmatic pluralism. Again, the examples of Venezuela and Colombia will show that this strategy can extend incumbent advantage even as formal restrictions on competition are lifted. Another case in point is Brazil, where rampant clientelism was able to retard the emergence of a party mobilized from below during the entire post-1945 semidemocratic regime and well into the 1980s (Chalmers 1972; Schmitter 1971; Weyland 1996; Hagopian 1996). This pattern can also be observed in the East and Southeast Asian regions. As will be made clear by Kenneth McElwain (chapter 8), Japan's LDP furthered its electoral advantage through pork barrel projects and patronage, thereby muting ideological issues. Similarly, Andreas Ufen's analysis of the Indonesia case (chapter 7) shows how key party elites dampened the mass-level religious cleavage, while maintaining their dominant position over time through clientelistic, oligarchic, and personalistic forms of politics.

5.1.4. Democratic Breakdown and Discontinuity in Political Cleavage Reproduction

Ongoing party differentiation and interparty conflict—which I will call "polarization" here—is crucial to keep programmatic alignments between parties and voters alive, as I have emphasized above. In a process that operates similarly in old and new democracies, polarization nourishes the ideological schemas that guide voters and help them to navigate the political space (Bornschier 2010, 2019). Strong programmatic linkages also put pressure on parties to adapt to voters' evolving preferences and new demands, because mass–elite discrepancy leads to voters shifting to other parties. Because of frequent authoritarian backlashes and the fragility of programmatic linkages, however, the reproduction of cleavages according to this mechanism is much more difficult in new democracies.

One reason, which follows from the preceding discussion on the openness of competition, is that each transition back to democracy after an authoritarian interlude offers the possibility for elites to exclude actors from future competitive elections. Whether this is the case or not depends also on the international system. Some historical periods are more propitious to democracy, and in particular to differing degrees of open or restricted competition. The Cold War era was particularly inimical to democracy and open contestation (Levitsky and Way 2010; Boix 2011; Mainwaring and Pérez-Liñán 2013; Weyland 2019), in that strong pressures existed in the Western

Hemisphere to exclude communist parties from competition. This affected redemocratization processes in South America and put other countries that experienced uninterrupted democratic rule at an advantage, since it proved much more difficult to outlaw radical competitors in these contexts. In addition, due to the overriding focus on winning the regime competition, Western democracies turned a blind eye to many authoritarian governments in their hemisphere. As a result, military coups d'état overturning civilian regimes, for example in South Korea and Indonesia, did not face resistance from the West.

More generally, authoritarian backlashes and interruptions in the electoral calendar mitigate the reproductive mechanism that underlies cleavages. Based on data from Argentina, Lupu and Stokes (2010) show that every interruption in the electoral calendar weakened the formation of programmatic partisan identities. The same argument is made by van Eerd (2017) with respect to the countries he studies in Africa. Likewise, Ufen (chapter 7) demonstrates how the institutionalization of economic and religious cleavages in Indonesia was halted by the authoritarian turn in the 1950s.

In the next section, I flesh out how three specificities of the South American context account for a more important role for elite strategic action than in the old democracies. Because the region first democratized in the early twentieth century, the relevant period to focus on is the initial period of party system formation in the advent of mass politics, rather than the period of redemocratization in the 1980s.

5.2. Empirical Analysis: Elite Agency and Substantive Policy Representation in South America

Although there are exceptions, the working class played an important role in the final step to manhood suffrage in Western Europe (Rueschemeyer, Huber Stephens, and Stephens 1992; Collier 1999), making mobilization from below and the crystallization of the class cleavage coincide. In this context, the fact that elites are held accountable by powerful social movements from below restricts their room for maneuver. Because large scale-processes of social change and suffrage expansion coincided less in South America, mobilization from below was generally weaker and had a more strongly multiclass character. In the empirical section of this chapter, I present evidence for three structuralist configurations in early twentieth-century South America—the critical juncture of democratization—that make elite agency more important than in the Lipset-Rokkan universe.

First, democratization pushed by established parties—a pattern labeled "electoral support mobilization" by Collier (1999)—is more prevalent in South America than in the old democracies. As a consequence, the quality of substantive policy representation after the extension of the franchise depends heavily on elite choices. Second, pacted transitions to democracy impinge heavily on the openness of competition, since the political survival of the parties entering the pact often depends on their ability to exclude competitors. As explained, this results in a loss of programmatic responsiveness and dealigns the party system in the long run. Third, when suffrage expansion occurs in leaps—because it is not triggered by the sequential mobilization of social groups for inclusion, but rather by more strictly political dynamics and populist mass mobilization—electoral coalitions tend to be more heterogeneous. Mass-organic parties of the left then face strong competition by populist left parties, which affords considerable discretion to charismatic leaders. In the next section, based on a number of paired comparisons, I demonstrate that these contexts make mass–elite congruence heavily dependent on elites' strategic decisions. The comparison is focused on the economic state–market cleavage due to the fact that conflicts surrounding the religious cleavage had largely been pacified in South America, with a few exceptions (cf. Middlebrook 2000).

5.2.1. Electoral Support Mobilization and Elite Agency

The one case in South America that experienced a gradual expansion of suffrage similar to most European countries and the subsequent emergence of strong religious and economic cleavages is Chile (Scully 1992). Elsewhere, suffrage expansion coincided less with the critical junctures of state formation and industrialization, giving elites considerably more leeway in terms of agency. Even in the earliest cases of democratization outside Europe and North America, leaders had more foresight when the working class started to organize. Seeking to take advantage of the growth of this potential new political constituency, elites adopted platforms to incorporate the working class into broad multiclass alliances. I demonstrate this pattern by drawing on the cases of Uruguay and Colombia, which present interesting similarities and contrasts that underline both the importance of elite strategic action in general and the role of open contestation in shaping elite choices.

In the context of party systems that mirrored the nineteenth-century conflict between Liberals and Conservatives, the Liberals in Colombia and their equivalent in Uruguay, the Colorados, took steps to appeal to the nascent working class and other progressive social groups (Collier and Collier 2002). Their shift to the left precluded the growth of a strong left and, in terms of their configuration, party systems in both countries remained "elitist" (Roberts 2014, chap. 4). In Uruguay, José Battle y Ordóñez moved the Colorado Party decisively to the left and initiated a far-reaching project of social reform in the first years of the twentieth century, with the intent of preempting mass unrest by reducing inequality (Collier and Collier 2002, 271–314). This immediately triggered resistance from the Blancos, the other traditional party, which displayed more of a center-right profile. The result was a polarization of the party system along the economic state–market dimension that was sustained for roughly half a century (Bornschier 2019). When the Colorados moved to the center in the 1960s, they rapidly lost their dominant position in the left-wing spectrum to a competitor, the Frente Amplio (Luna 2007; Lanzaro and Piñeiro 2017). This process of realignment testifies to the programmatic nature of party competition: as soon as the Colorados increased the distance from their traditional electorate, open competition resulted in the growth of a new left-wing pole in the party system (Bornschier n.d., chap. 5).

While Uruguay was a forerunner in terms of development and the emergence of an urban working class, Colombia lagged behind in this respect. The fact that the Liberals in Colombia only moved to the left in the 1930s is thus rooted in the timing and extent of industrialization. Regardless of these differences, however, what Colombia and Uruguay have in common is that the opening toward the working class occurred when the labor movement was still weak (Collier and Collier 2002, 93–99). Colombia only experienced partial democratization, yet it conforms to the same pattern in which a middle-class party hopes to win electorally from rallying emerging social groups. In Colombia, safeguards for union organization and the right to strike were cornerstones of the polarization that occurred between the two traditional parties (Collier and Collier 2002, 289–95, 299–303). Individual agency was crucial: in the 1946 presidential elections, the Liberals were split between their moderate wing and the populist figure of Jorge Eliécer Gaitán (Hartlyn 1988, 36). Gaitán had initially formed a party of his own, the Revolutionary Leftist National Union, but now led the Liberals' progressive wing, which pursued a successful strategy of populist mass mobilization (Betz 2018). But, contrary to Uruguay, the party system did not sustain the resulting polarization. Gaitán's assassination in 1948, after winning the 1947 parliamentary elections, triggered the twenty-year civil war known as

"La Violencia." The civil war ended the country's experiment of offering representation along the entire political spectrum.

By absorbing the progressive momentum brought about by the initial growth of the working class and other progressive sectors, the traditional parties succeeded in dominating politics for decades in both countries. However, the crucial difference is that this occurred in the context of open contestation and the presence of competing left-wing parties in Uruguay, while the traditional parties restricted competition in Colombia when they engineered the country's return to democracy. In the pacted transition of 1958, the Liberals and the Conservatives outlawed and repressed the left (e.g., Hartlyn 1988, 54–65; Bejarano 2011, 90–129). According to Bejarano (2011), the communists themselves were too weak to forcefully demand their inclusion, while the Cold War political climate produced powerful pressures from within and without the country to outlaw them. In Uruguay, on the other hand, the two established parties never outlawed the communists, forcing the Colorados to remain responsive to left-wing voters if they were not to lose them to left-wing competitors (Collier and Collier 2002, 453–56; Bornschier n.d., chap. 5).

As a consequence, politics in Colombia began to center more and more on clientelist exchanges, and programmatic responsiveness was lost (Wilde 1978; Martz 1997; Morgan 2011, 216–25; Collier and Collier 2002, 671–73). Empirical assessments of the responsiveness of parties to voter preferences after the redemocratization wave in the 1980s reveal a striking contrast between Uruguay and Colombia in terms of party system responsiveness, with Uruguay consistently scoring at the top, while the performance of Colombia is dismal (Bornschier 2013; Bornschier 2019, 170; Kitschelt et al. 2010; Luna and Zechmeister 2010). The comparison between the two cases shows that where democratization occurs at lower levels of industrialization and working-class mobilization, elite choices are crucial even in the "older" democracies outside Western Europe.[7] In both cases, elite actors managed to rally the nascent working class behind middle-class parties. While the Uruguayan party system withstood the resulting polarization, establishing power-sharing after the civil war in Colombia required safeguards for the established parties and resulted in the exclusion of the communist left (Hartlyn 1988). The degree of mass–elite congruence thus depended crucially on whether the competitive situation provides incentives for parties to remain responsive to their voters, or whether restrictions in contestation allow them to abandon their voters with no immediate electoral cost.

5.2.2. Elite Pacts and Restrictions on Competition

Colombia is not the only case of return to democracy that involves an elite pact between parties with roots in a prior (semi-)democratic regime. Venezuela witnessed a similar pact when it returned to democracy in 1958 after a 10-year dictatorship that followed its short-lived democratic experiment between 1945 and 1948 known as the "Trienio," which was characterized by a very high degree of polarization (Coppedge 1994). As in Colombia, the pact agreed upon by the signatory parties in Venezuela narrowed the political spectrum by excluding the communist parties, although it was less rigid than that in Colombia in not outlawing all opposition parties (Bejarano 2011; Karl 1986). Nonetheless, the outcome was similar in two respects: programmatic distinctiveness was lost and politics centered almost exclusively on the distribution of clientelistic benefits (Coppedge 1994, chap. 6; Roberts 2003; Lyne 2008, chap. 3; Morgan 2011, chap. 4; Ellner 2008, chap. 3). Indeed, the three signatory parties of the pact not only agreed on a number of policy principles but also to the sharing of both power and patronage resources, including "access to state jobs and contracts, a partitioning of ministries, and a complicated spoils system which would ensure the political survival of all signatories" (Karl 1986, 213). During most of the decade that followed redemocratization in 1958, Venezuela was governed by coalition cabinets including Acción Democrática (AD, which was strongly left-wing back in the 1940s, but centrist after 1958), the Christian Democratic Comité de Organización Política Electoral Independiente (COPEI, born out of opposition against AD in the 1940s and taking more conservative positions both in the economic and the religious domain, but converging ideologically with AD from 1958 onward), and at times the smaller Unión Republicana Democrática (Lyne 2008, 112).

Open contestation was reestablished in Venezuela in 1968, and parts of the communist left merged into the Movement for Socialism. However, at that point, the inherited loyalties from the phase of polarization, along with AD's and COPEI's capacity to deliver particularistic benefits to their voters, allowed them to govern the country for another three decades until the devastating blow delivered to them by Hugo Chávez in the 1998 elections, from which they did not recover. For Mona Lyne, the prevalence of clientelism explains why "two decades of economic decline [in the 1980s and 1990s] fail to generate parties challenging the status quo" (2008, 67). The inability of parties to represent voters' substantive policy preferences thus only became fully apparent when alternative linkage strategies failed as well

(Morgan 2011). Indeed, an empirical analysis of party placements in a mass-level survey shows that as early as the 1983 elections, Acción Democrática, the former left-wing pole in the party system, was perceived as rather right-wing by voters (Bornschier n.d.).

In summary, to the extent that elite pacts impose restrictions on competition, they harm substantive policy representation. By weakening parties' incentives to retain their original spatial positions, the parties involved in these pacts can abandon their voters without immediate cost, as we have seen in the Colombian case. Quantitative analyses of the quality of representation in the 1990s (the first point in time for which cross-national data is available) show that the performance of party systems in this respect was dismal in Venezuela and Colombia (Luna and Zechmeister 2005; Kitschelt et al. 2010; Bornschier 2013). The two cases also underline the point made earlier regarding the importance of historical timing: democratization was much less likely to involve full contestation and electoral competition after the advent of the Cold War. In particular, after the Cuban Revolution, the fear of communism fostered elite suspicion toward radical actors that might succumb to revolutionary action (cf. Weyland 2019).

5.2.3. Populist Leadership and Divergent Choices

The importance of elite agency is also put in evidence by a third configuration, where labor demands are articulated by competing parties on the left. As we have already seen in Uruguay and Colombia, working-class organization emerged in the first two decades of the twentieth century throughout South America, at a point when industrial occupation was still extremely limited. In certain countries, this was due to the spatial concentration of the working class in mining enclaves (Rueschemeyer, Huber Stephens, and Stephens 1992, chap. 5), but early organization was also aided by the example of similar organizations and ideologies from abroad, as well as the presence of migrants from Europe. Consequently, communist parties linked to unions existed in most countries (Collier and Collier 2002). Given the more heterogeneous nature of social groups potentially available for progressive social and political projects, however, these parties found themselves in strong competition with populist left-wing actors with weaker formal party organizations. Indeed, the struggle for political and economic inclusion in the early twentieth century had an anti-oligarchic character as it rallied broad swaths of the population against elite parties representing only a small strata of society (Roberts 2002, 2014). It is here that we witness the first historical instances of populist mobilization (Jansen 2017). Populist appeals were often more successful than communist or socialist mass parties in attracting a broad coalition pushing for social and political change, such as lower-class urban constituencies outside manufacturing, as well as middle-class sectors favoring social protection and anti-oligarchical political reform. Weaker party organizations, in turn, afforded charismatic leaders more leeway for agency than was the case for organized working-class parties. While I would argue that left-wing populist parties at least in theory are able to offer similar levels of substantive policy representation as mass-organic parties, whether they do so depends more heavily on discretionary elite choices.

In this section, I focus on two emblematic examples of left-wing populist mobilization, the APRA in Peru and Peronism in Argentina. APRA established a dominant position in the Peruvian labor movement in the 1930s and was initially a staunchly left-wing party. The Peronists (or, by their official names, the Partido Justicialista or Partido Peronista) in Argentina were founded by Juan Domingo Perón, who originally came to power as the labor minister of a non-elected military government in 1943. Although the status of the Peronists as a left-wing party is sometimes disputed (e.g., Ostiguy 2009), Perón's policies clearly favored the industrial working class and protectionist sectors more generally, and the Peronists became the dominant force in the Argentine labor movement (Gibson 1996; O'Donnell 1999). The two cases demonstrate the ability of charismatic leaders to sidestep organized working-class organizations and appeal to a broad coalition that might be considered the natural constituency of mass parties of the left (see also Roberts 2006). After substantiating this claim, I show how the contrasting trajectories of the Argentine and Peruvian party systems are due to the strategic choices of charismatic leaders that can determine whether populist movements remain responsive to their voters in the longer term.

Although Argentina was much more developed in the early twentieth century, Argentina and Peru are similar in that Peru exhibited an atypically high level of labor movement development relative to its level of industrialization in the 1930s, which was due to the country's status as mineral export economy (Rueschemeyer, Huber Stephens, and Stephens 1992). Left-wing parties representing the interests of the middle and working classes had formed in the 1920s in Peru, the most important being the Socialist Party. Allied with the General Confederation of Peruvian Workers, it became the Communist Party of Peru in 1930. Like the Peronists later on, APRA, formed in 1924 by Haya de la Torre, succeeded in establishing a predominant position in the labor movement by the 1930s (Collier and Collier 2002, 325–27).

The 1931 presidential elections are considered a watershed in Peruvian politics. The established elite had been wiped out by two successive dictatorships between 1919 to 1931 that were shaped by the rivalry between two authoritarian rulers. With the embryonic precoup party system destroyed and the communists barred from participating in the election by the military junta, the political field was wide open (Jansen 2017, chap. 3). The result was that two candidates without links to established parties—Haya de la Torre and former military dictator Sánchez Cerro—ran against each other, pushing each other to pursue innovative mobilization strategies involving mass rallies across much of the country (Jansen 2017, 48–55, chaps. 4–5). Jansen identifies this election as the first instance of populist mobilization in South America and possibly beyond, in the contemporary use of the term. In this and later elections, APRA was thus able to forge an anti-oligarchic and anti-imperialist alliance including the middle and the working classes (Rueschemeyer, Huber Stephens, and Stephens 1992, 184, 186, 191, 193–94). Because its organizational basis was so clearly middle class, Di Tella (2004, 188–99) considers APRA the archetypical case of a radical middle-class party. When the 1931 election was over, Haya de la Torre did not accept its result, claiming that he had won the contest. He organized a military insurrection, launching a tradition of violence that persisted alongside efforts to moderate and gain acceptance from the political establishment (Collier and Collier 2002, 151; Coppedge 1998, 195).

Organization in Argentina's labor movement had surged since 1930, when the Confederación General del Trabajo (General Labor Confederation), the country's first national labor confederation, was formed. In part due to the influence of anarcho-syndicalism, however, the labor movement had remained largely outside party politics. Juan Domingo Perón took advantage of this fact by rallying the labor movement after a brief antilabor phase of the military government he was part of. Later on, the General Labor Confederation later became closely linked to Peronism (McGuire 1995, 208; Collier and Collier 2002, 331–35), yet due to the weak organizational structure of the party itself, Perón maintained extensive control over the party's course. Similarly to Haya de la Torre in Peru, Perón's charisma enabled him to unite a new social coalition and to establish what Madsen and Snow (1991) call the "charismatic bond." A spontaneous mass rally on October 17, 1945, after Perón had been deposed by his rivals within the military, marks the "mythical founding event of Peronism," according to Ostiguy (2009, 21). Perón gave a famous speech after his liberation the same day. "Within a few days [after the demonstration on October 17], several union leaders announced the formation of a Labor Party, which almost immediately nominated Perón as its presidential candidate" (Madsen and Snow 1991, 50). The speech showed his unique capacity to appeal to the lower classes by utilizing colloquial style, while employing highly elaborate rhetorics and symbols (Ostiguy 2009, 20–21). The lower classes in Argentine society were given expression in politics for the first time. But in their elaborate analysis of the "charismatic bond" between a leader and his followers, Madsen and Snow (1991) underline that the link between Perón and his voters was not maintained on the basis of illusion, but rather by the policies enacted by the Peronist government to improve the situation of the lower classes.

Both the Peronists and APRA were thus multiclass parties: while APRA united the working and the middle classes in an anti-oligarchical coalition, the Peronists formed a sectoral coalition between the working class and protectionist groups in the countryside. Mass support suggests that both APRA's and the Partido Justicialista's programmatic profile resonated with voters. Although we have no measure of congruence, there is little to suggest that, during their initial mobilization, these movements represented left-wing voters to a lesser extent than the communist or socialist parties they displaced. But without a party apparatus of the kind characteristic of mass-organic parties to hold leaders to account, the choices made by the two movements' founding fathers played a pivotal role in maintaining or diluting substantive policy representation.

The crucial difference between the two cases in terms of the long-term representation of left-wing interests was that APRA moved to the center in a delusionary quest to gain acceptance by the military establishment, while the Argentine Peronists stubbornly pushed polarization, despite similar military involvement in politics. Even faced with the threat that democracy could be overturned, the Peronist party never moderated its programmatic position after its rise in the 1940s, and only on one occasion did the Peronists form a short-lived alliance with political opponents. Contrary to most other cases in which labor parties were faced with a strong conservative reaction following the incorporation of the labor movement into politics, according to Collier and Collier (2002, 494), Perón did not exclude the left from his movement. This constitutes another factor that mitigated moderation. In terms of this pluralism inside the Peronist party, Argentina resembles Uruguay, where we have seen that competition with the communists prevented the Colorados from abandoning their left-wing stance on economic policy. In Peru, on the other hand, the only way for APRA to have a chance of governing once repression softened was to moderate its profile, and it is this route that Haya de la Torre chose (Collier and Collier 2002,

327–28, 474–83, 694–709). When the APRA-supported government came to adopt austerity politics after the 1956 elections, APRA even helped to restrain opposition from the labor movement. Collier and Collier (2002, 477) compare this agreement with the right to the pacts between AD and COPEI in Venezuela, and between Liberals and Conservatives in Colombia, although the agreement in Peru remained informal and APRA denied that a pact had been agreed upon.

Overall, then, the openness of political competition was crucial in setting party systems in South America on a path toward strong or weak programmatic representation. Elite political actors and their repressive capacities were not the only things to impinge on the direction that countries took at this forking path; the strategic behavior of left-wing parties was relevant as well. The discretionary power that leaders of populist parties enjoy is of course an advantage when it comes to forging large social coalitions. But it also makes representation outcomes more contingent on these leaders' choices, leading to higher odds for representation failure.

5.3. Conclusion

While it is hardly disputed today that mobilization from below and from above invariably interact in cleavage formation, we know less about the factors shaping the relative weight of bottom-up and top-down processes. By enlarging the universe of cases, studying cleavage formation in new democracies beyond the "usual suspects" helps to shed light on various ways in which the role of elite political agency remains hidden if we consider only the advanced democracies. The aim of this chapter was to advance this discussion and to theorize why elites may have greater leeway in shaping the representation of salient social divides in new democracies and how this impinges on the substantive representation of citizen preferences.

There are at least three ways in which the experience of new democracies differs from those considered in Lipset and Rokkan's (1967) treatment of the European cases. First, the social groups the franchise was extended to often did not correspond to specific social classes or sectoral interests. As a consequence, the social basis of cleavages is more heterogeneous, and elites acquire a more important role in forging these diverse coalitions and in holding them together. The diversity of these groups also gives an advantage to populist movements with charismatic figureheads. While they may be effective in representing hitherto neglected preferences, the leaders of populist movements face weaker accountability mechanisms internal to the party than those of classical mass parties that would commit them to a specific policy stance. While this does not rule out that such leaders will remain responsive to their constituents, it does mean that they have the opportunity to strategically abandon their constituents if need be, for example when democracy is in danger. This first difference between old and the new democracies is thus directly linked to a second difference: a greater repressive capacity on the part of the established elites in new democracies. Established elites have more opportunities to manipulate the extent to which elections are open and truly competitive, again with important consequences for the representation of citizen preferences. Third, frequent reversals of democratization mitigate the reproduction of cleavages expressed in party systems and consequently offer more room for political maneuvering on the elite side.

This brief comparative analysis of South American case studies in the early twentieth century offered in this chapter illustrates that differences in the way elites mobilize mass-level political cleavages in the region have been important, and that these contrasts were consequential for representation. The following four full-fledged empirical chapters based on new democracies in four world regions will further demonstrate the influence of elites on muting mass-level political divisions or, sometimes, even creating their own elite-level political divisions.

Notes

1. The literature on these topics is too extensive to quote in full. For a recent overview, see Ford and Jennings (2020), and Bornschier et al. (2024).

2. Enggist and Pinggera (2021) show a higher degree of alignment of voters and radical right parties with respect to welfare state preferences than is usually assumed.

3. France and Switzerland are cases in point; see Bartolini (2000a, 494); Knutsen (2004, 228); Lijphart (1979).

4. Elite agency and coalition formation certainly matter for party systems, but more in terms of the makeup of the left than in shaping whether the class cleavage manifests itself at all and how salient it becomes with respect to the older cleavages (see Bartolini 2000a).

5. Conflicts over state structure after independence can be considered critical antecedents in that they shaped the antagonism between liberals and conservatives, but this conflict in general did not survive mass politics and impinged on later critical junctures only indirectly (Bornschier 2019; on "critical antecedents," see Slater and Simmons 2010).

6. Bartolini (1999; 2000b) refers to this mechanism by means of the concept of "vulnerability" as a precondition for competition.

7. The same is true in the cases of particularly early democratization in Western democracies. In Switzerland and the United States, for example, established parties

initially appealed to and mobilized the working class, delaying or partially preempting the formation of left-wing parties relative to the timing of industrialization (see Rueschemeyer, Huber Stephens, and Stephens 1992, chap. 4; see also Collier 1999).

References

Adams, James, Catherine E. De Vries, and Debra Leiter. 2011. "Subconstituency Reactions to Elite Depolarization in the Netherlands: An Analysis of the Dutch Public's Policy Beliefs and Partisan Loyalties, 1986–98." *British Journal of Political Science* 42 (1): 81–105. https://doi.org/10.1017/S0007123411000214

Allardt, Erik. 1968. "Past and Emerging Political Cleavages." In *Party Systems, Party Organizations, and the Politics of New Masses, Beiträge Zur 3. Internationalen Konferenz Über Vergleichende Politische Soziologie, Berlin, 15–20. Januar 1968*, edited by Otto Stammer, 66–76. Berlin: Institut für politische Wissenschaft, Freien Universität Berlin.

Bargsted, Matías A., and Nicolás M. Somma. 2016. "Social Cleavages and Political Dealignment in Contemporary Chile, 1995–2009." *Party Politics* 22 (1): 105–24. https://doi.org/10.1177/1354068813514865

Bartolini, Stefano. 1999. "Collusion, Competition, and Democracy, Part I." *Journal of Theoretical Politics* 11 (4): 435–70. https://doi.org/10.1177/0951692899011004001

Bartolini, Stefano. 2000a. *The Political Mobilization of the European Left, 1860–1980: The Class Cleavage*. Cambridge: Cambridge University Press.

Bartolini, Stefano. 2000b. "Collusion, Competition, and Democracy, Part II." *Journal of Theoretical Politics* 12 (1): 33–65. https://doi.org/10.1177/0951692800012001002

Bartolini, Stefano. 2005. "La formation des clivages." *Revue Internationale de Politique Comparée* 12 (1): 9–34. https://doi.org/10.3917/ripc.121.0009

Bejarano, Ana María. 2011. *Precarious Democracies: Understanding Regime Stability and Change in Colombia and Venezuela*. Notre Dame: University of Notre Dame Press.

Bejarano, Ana María, and Eduardo Pizarro. 2005. "From 'Restricted' to 'Besieged': The Changing Nature of the Limits to Democracy in Colombia." In *The Third Wave of Democratization in Latin America: Advances and Setbacks*, edited by Frances Hagopian and Scott Mainwaring, 235–60. Cambridge: Cambridge University Press.

Belogurova, Anna. 2014. "Communism in South East Asia." In *The Oxford Handbook of the History of Communism*, edited by Stephen Anthony Smith, 437–50. Oxford: Oxford University Press.

Betz, Hans-Georg. 2018. "Populist Mobilization across Time and Space." In *The Ideational Approach to Populism: Concept, Theory, and Analysis*, edited by Kirk A. Hawkins, Ryan E. Carlin, Levente Littvay, and Cristóbal Rovira Kaltwasser. Abingdon, UK: Routledge.

Boix, Carles. 2011. "Democracy, Development, and the International System." *American Political Science Review* 105 (4): 809–28. https://doi.org/10.1017/S0003055411000402

Bornschier, Simon. 2009. "Cleavage Politics in Old and New Democracies." *Living Reviews in Democracy* 1 (1). https://doi.org/10.5167/uzh-26412

Bornschier, Simon. 2010. *Cleavage Politics and the Populist Right: The New Cultural Conflict in Western Europe.* Philadelphia: Temple University Press.

Bornschier, Simon. 2013. "Trayectorias históricas y responsiveness del sistema de partidos en siete países de América Latina." *América Latina Hoy* 65 (December): 45–77. https://doi.org/10.14201/alh2013654577

Bornschier, Simon. 2018. "Populist Success in Latin America and Western Europe: Ideational and Party-System-Centered Explanations." In *The Ideational Approach to Populism: Concept, Theory, and Analysis*, edited by Kirk A. Hawkins, Ryan E. Carlin, Levente Littvay, and Cristóbal Rovira Kaltwasser, 202–37. Abingdon, UK: Routledge.

Bornschier, Simon. 2019. "Historical Polarization and Representation in South American Party Systems, 1900–1990." *British Journal of Political Science* 49 (1): 153–79. https://doi.org/10.1017/S0007123416000387

Bornschier, Simon. 2020. "Combining Deductive and Inductive Elements to Measure Party System Responsiveness in Challenging Contexts: An Approach with Evidence from Latin America." *European Political Science* 19 (4): 540–49. https://doi.org/10.1057/s41304-020-00272-z

Bornschier, Simon. N.d. "From Historical Polarization to the Left Turn: Explaining Party System Responsiveness in Latin America." Book manuscript. University of Zurich.

Bornschier, Simon, Lukas Haffert, Silja Häusermann, Marco Steenbergen, and Delia Zollinger. 2024. *Cleavage Formation in the 21st Century—How Social Identities Shape Voting Behavior in Contexts of Electoral Realignment.* Cambridge: Cambridge University Press.

Capoccia, Giovanni, and R. Daniel Kelemen. 2007. "The Study of Critical Junctures: Theory, Narrative, and Counterfactuals in Historical Institutionalism." *World Politics* 59 (3): 341–69. https://doi.org/10.1017/S0043887100020852

Casal Bértoa, Fernando. 2014. "Party Systems and Cleavage Structures Revisited: A Sociological Explanation of Party System Institutionalization in East Central Europe." *Party Politics* 20 (1): 16–36. https://doi.org/10.1177/1354068811436042

Chalmers, Douglas A. 1972. "Parties and Society in Latin America." *Studies in Comparative International Development* 7 (2): 102–28. https://doi.org/10.1007/BF02800529

Chhibber, Pradeep, and Mariano Torcal. 1997. "Elite Strategy, Social Cleavages, and Party Systems in a New Democracy: Spain." *Comparative Political Studies* 30 (1): 27–54. https://doi.org/10.1177/0010414097030001002

Collier, Ruth Berins. 1999. *Paths toward Democracy: The Working Class and Elites in Western Europe and South America.* Cambridge: Cambridge University Press.

Collier, Ruth Berins, and David Collier. 2002. *Shaping the Political Arena. Critical Junctures, the Labor Movement, and Regime Dynamics in Latin America.* 2nd ed. Notre Dame: University of Notre Dame Press.

Conover, Pamela Johnston, and Stanley Feldman. 1982. "Projection and the Perception of Candidates' Issue Positions." *Western Political Quarterly* 35 (2): 228–44. https://doi.org/10.1177/106591298203500209

Coppedge, Michael. 1994. *Strong Parties and Lame Ducks: Presidential Partyarchy and Factionalism in Venezuela*. Stanford: Stanford University Press.

Coppedge, Michael. 1998. "The Evolution of Latin American Party Systems." In *Politics, Society, and Democracy: Latin America*, edited by Scott Mainwaring and Arturo Valenzuela, 171–206. Boulder: Westview Press.

Coser, Lewis A. 1956. *The Functions of Social Conflict: An Examination of the Concept of Social Conflict and Its Use in Empirical Sociological Research*. New York: Free Press.

Dahl, Robert A. 1971. *Polyarchy: Participation and Opposition*. New Haven: Yale University Press.

Dalton, Russell J. 1985. "Political Parties and Political Representation: Party Supporters and Party Elites in Nine Nations." *Comparative Political Studies* 18 (3): 267–99. https://doi.org/10.1177/0010414085018003001

Deegan-Krause, Kevin. 2006. *Elected Affinities: Democracy and Party Competition in Slovakia and the Czech Republic*. Stanford: Stanford University Press.

Deegan-Krause, Kevin, and Zsolt Enyedi. 2010. "Agency and Structure of Party Competition: Alignment, Stability and the Role of Political Elites." *West European Politics* 33 (3): 686–710. https://doi.org/10.1080/01402381003654742

de Wilde, Pieter, Ruud Koopmans, Wolfgang Merkel, Oliver Strijbis, and Michael Zürn. 2019. *The Struggle over Borders: Cosmopolitanism and Communitarianism*. Cambridge: Cambridge University Press.

Di Tella, Torcuato S. 2004. *History of Political Parties in Twentieth-Century Latin America*. New Brunswick, NJ: Transaction.

Dix, Robert H. 1989. "Cleavage Structures and Party Systems in Latin America." *Comparative Politics* 22 (1): 23–37. https://doi.org/10.2307/422320

Ellner, Steve. 2008. *Rethinking Venezuelan Politics: Class, Conflict, and the Chávez Phenomenon*. Boulder, CO: Lynne Rienner.

Enggist, Matthias, and Michael Pinggera. 2021. "Radical Right Parties and Their Welfare State Stances—Not So Blurry after All?" *West European Politics* 45 (1): 102–28. https://doi.org/10.1080/01402382.2021.1902115

Enyedi, Zsolt. 2005. "The Role of Agency in Cleavage Formation." *European Journal of Political Research* 44 (5): 697–720. https://doi.org/10.1111/j.1475-6765.2005.00244.x

Evans, Geoffrey, and Nan Dirk de Graaf, eds. 2013. *Political Choice Matters: Explaining the Strength of Class and Religious Cleavages in Cross-National Perspective*. Oxford: Oxford University Press.

Evans, Geoffrey, and James Tilley. 2011. "How Parties Shape Class Politics: Explaining the Decline of the Class Basis of Party Support." *British Journal of Political Science* 42: 137–61. https://doi.org/10.1017/S0007123411000202

Ford, Robert, and Will Jennings. 2020. "The Changing Cleavage Politics of Western Europe." *Annual Review of Political Science* 23. https://doi.org/10.1146/annurev-polisci-052217-104957

Fust, Sebastian. 2021. "Searching for Stability and Predictability in Latin American Party Systems: Introducing a Linkage-Based Comparative Approach." PhD diss., University of Zurich. https://doi.org/10.5167/uzh-209707

Geddes, Barbara. 1999. "What Do We Know about Democratization after Twenty Years?" *Annual Review of Political Science* 2: 115–44. https://doi.org/10.1146/annurev.polisci.2.1.115

Geddes, Barbara. 2003. *Paradigms and Sand Castles: Theory Building and Research Design in Comparative Politics*. Ann Arbor: University of Michigan Press.

Geddes, Barbara. 2011. "What Causes Democratization." In *The Oxford Handbook of Political Science*, edited by Robert E. Goodin, 593–615. Oxford: Oxford University Press. https://doi.org/10.1093/oxfordhb/9780199604456.013.0029

Geddes, Barbara, Joseph Wright, and Erica Frantz. 2018. *How Dictatorships Work: Power, Personalization and Collapse*. Cambridge: Cambridge University Press.

Gibson, Edward L. 1996. *Class and Conservative Parties: Argentina in Comparative Perspective*. Baltimore: Johns Hopkins University Press.

Hagopian, Frances. 1996. *Traditional Politics and Regime Change in Brazil*. Cambridge: Cambridge University Press.

Hartlyn, Jonathan. 1988. *The Politics of Coalition Rule in Colombia*. Cambridge: Cambridge University Press.

Hooghe, Liesbet, and Gary Marks. 2018. "Cleavage Theory Meets Europe's Crises: Lipset, Rokkan, and the Transnational Cleavage." *Journal of European Public Policy* 25 (1): 109–35. https://doi.org/10.1080/13501763.2017.1310279

Ivarsflaten, Elisabeth. 2005. "The Vulnerable Populist Right Parties: No Economic Realignment Fuelling Their Success." *European Journal of Political Research* 44 (3): 465–92. https://doi.org/10.1111/j.1475-6765.2005.00235.x

Jansen, Robert S. 2017. *Revolutionizing Repertoires: The Rise of Populist Mobilization in Peru*. Chicago: University of Chicago Press.

Karl, Terry Lynn. 1986. "Petroleum and Political Pacts: The Transition to Democracy in Venezuela." In *Transitions from Authoritarian Rule: Latin America*, edited by Guillermo O'Donnell, Philippe C. Schmitter, and Laurence Whitehead, 196–219. Baltimore: Johns Hopkins University Press.

Key, V. O. 1959. "Secular Realignment and the Party System." *Journal of Politics* 21 (2): 198–210. https://doi.org/10.2307/2127162

Kitschelt, Herbert. 2000. "Linkages between Citizens and Politicians in Democratic Polities." *Comparative Political Studies* 33 (6–7): 845–79. https://doi.org/10.1177/001041400003300607

Kitschelt, Herbert, Kirk A. Hawkins, Juan Pablo Luna, Guillermo Rosas, and Elizabeth J. Zechmeister. 2010. *Latin American Party Systems*. Cambridge: Cambridge University Press.

Knutsen, Oddbjørn. 2004. *Social Structure and Party Choice in Western Europe: A Comparative Longitudinal Study*. Basingstoke: Palgrave Macmillan.

Kriesi, Hanspeter. 1999. "Movements of the Left, Movements of the Right: Putting the Mobilization of Two New Types of Social Movement into Political Context." In *Continuity and Change in Contemporary Capitalism*, edited by Herbert Kitschelt, Peter Lange, Gary Marks, and John D. Stephens, 398–423. Cambridge: Cambridge University Press.

Kriesi, Hanspeter, Edgar Grande, Martin Dolezal, Marc Helbling, Dominic Höglinger, Swen Hutter, and Bruno Wüest. 2012. *Political Conflict in Western Europe*. Cambridge: Cambridge University Press.

Kriesi, Hanspeter, Edgar Grande, Romain Lachat, Martin Dolezal, Simon Bornschier, and Timotheos Frey. 2008. *Western European Politics in the Age of Globalization*. Cambridge: Cambridge University Press.

Lanzaro, Jorge, and Rafael Piñeiro. 2017. "Uruguay: A Counterexample of Malaise in Representation: A Propitious Transformation of the Old Party Democracy." In *Malaise in Representation in Latin American Countries*, edited by Alfredo Joignant, Mauricio Morales, and Claudio Fuentes, 211–31. New York: Palgrave Macmillan.

Levitsky, Steven, and Kenneth M. Roberts. 2011. "Latin America's 'Left Turn': A Framework for Analysis." In *The Resurgence of the Latin American Left*, edited by Steven Levitsky and Kenneth M. Roberts, 1–28. Baltimore: Johns Hopkins University Press.

Levitsky, Steven, and Lucan A. Way. 2010. *Competitive Authoritarianism: Hybrid Regimes after the Cold War*. Cambridge: Cambridge University Press.

Lijphart, Arend. 1979. "Religious vs. Linguistic vs. Class Voting: The 'Crucial Experiment' of Comparing Belgium, Canada, South Africa, and Switzerland." *American Political Science Review* 73 (2): 442–58. https://doi.org/10.2307/1954890

Lipset, Seymour Martin, and Stein Rokkan. 1967. "Cleavage Structures, Party Systems, and Voter Alignments: An Introduction." In *Party Systems and Voter Alignments*, edited by Seymour Martin Lipset and Stein Rokkan, 1–64. New York: Free Press.

Luna, Juan P., and Elizabeth J. Zechmeister. 2005. "Political Representation in Latin America: A Study of Elite-Mass Congruence in Nine Countries." *Comparative Political Studies* 38 (4): 388–416. https://doi.org/10.1177/0010414004273205

Luna, Juan Pablo. 2007. "Frente Amplio and the Crafting of a Social Democratic Alternative in Uruguay." *Latin American Politics and Society* 49 (4): 1–30. https://doi.org/10.1111/j.1548-2456.2007.tb00390.x

Luna, Juan P., and Elizabeth J. Zechmeister. 2010. "Political Representation in Latin America." In *Latin American Party Systems*, edited by Herbert Kitschelt, Kirk A. Hawkins, Juan Pablo Luna, Guillermo Rosas, and Elizabeth J. Zechmeister, 119–44. Cambridge: Cambridge University Press.

Lupu, Noam, and Susan C. Stokes. 2010. "Democracy, Interrupted: Regime Change and Partisanship in Twentieth-Century Argentina." *Electoral Studies* 29: 91–104. https://doi.org/10.1016/j.electstud.2009.07.005

Lyne, Mona M. 2008. *The Voter's Dilemma and Democratic Accountability: Latin America and Beyond*. University Park: Pennsylvania State University Press.

Madsen, Douglas, and Peter G. Snow. 1991. *The Charismatic Bond: Political Behaviour in Time of Crisis*. Cambridge: Harvard University Press.

Mahoney, James. 2000. "Path Dependence in Historical Sociology." *Theory and Society* 29 (4): 507–48. https://www.jstor.org/stable/3108585

Mainwaring, Scott, and Aníbal Pérez-Liñán. 2013. *Democracies and Dictatorships in Latin America: Emergence, Survival, and Fall*. New York: Cambridge University Press.

Manow, Philip. 2015. "Workers, Farmers and Catholicism: A History of Political Class Coalitions and the South-European Welfare State Regime." *Journal of European Social Policy* 25 (1): 32–49. https://doi.org/10.1177/0958928714556969

Martin, Pierre. 2000. *Comprendre les évolutions électorales: La théorie des réalignements revisitée*. Paris: Presses de Sciences Po.

Martz, John D. 1997. *The Politics of Clientelism: Democracy and State in Colombia*. New Brunswick, NJ: Transaction.

Mayhew, David. 2000. "Electoral Realignments." *Annual Review of Political Science* 3: 449–74. https://doi.org/10.1146/annurev.polisci.3.1.449

McAllister, Ian. 2007. "Social Structure and Party Support in the East Asian Democracies." *Journal of East Asian Studies* 7 (2): 225–49. https://doi.org/10.1017/S1598 240800008729

McGuire, James. 1995. "Political Parties and Democracy in Argentina." In *Building Democratic Institutions: Party Systems in Latin America*, edited by Scott Mainwaring and Timothy R. Scully, 200–246. Stanford: Stanford University Press.

Middlebrook, Kevin J. 2000. "Conservative Parties, Elite Representation, and Democracy in Latin America." In *Conservative Parties, the Right, and Democracy in Latin America*, edited by Kevin J. Middlebrook, 1–50. Baltimore: Johns Hopkins University Press.

Morgan, Jana. 2011. *Bankrupt Representation and Party System Collapse*. University Park: Pennsylvania State University Press.

O'Donnell, Guillermo. 1992. "Transitions, Continuities, and Paradoxes." In *Issues in Democratic Consolidation: The New South American Democracies in Comparative Perspective*, edited by Scott Mainwaring, Guillermo O'Donnell, and J. Samuel Valenzuela, 17–56. Notre Dame: University of Notre Dame Press.

O'Donnell, Guillermo. 1999. "State and Alliances in Argentina, 1956–1976." In *Counterpoints: Selected Essays on Authoritarianism and Democratization*, edited by Guillermo O'Donnell, 3–33. Notre Dame: University of Notre Dame Press.

O'Donnell, Guillermo, and Philippe C. Schmitter. 1986. *Transitions from Authoritarian Rule: Tentative Conclusions about Uncertain Democracies*. Baltimore: Johns Hopkins University Press.

Ostiguy, Pierre. 2009. "Argentina's Double Ideological Spectrum: Party System, Political Identities, and Strategies, 1944–2007." Kellogg Institute for International Studies, Working Paper #361. https://www.academia.edu/29136348/The_High -Low_Political_Divide_Rethinking_Populism_and_Anti-Populism

Pizarro Leongómez, Eduardo. 2006. "Giants with Feet of Clay: Political Parties in Colombia." In *The Crisis of Democratic Representation in the Andes*, edited by Scott Mainwaring, Ana María Bejarano, and Eduardo Pizarro Leongómez, 78–99. Stanford: Stanford University Press.

Randall, Vicky. 2001. "Party Systems and Voter Alignments in the New Democracies of the Third World." In *Party Systems and Voter Alignments Revisited*, edited by Lauri Karvonen and Stein Kuhnle, 238–60. London: Routledge.

Roberts, Kenneth M. 2002. "Social Inequalities without Class Cleavages in Latin America's Neoliberal Era." *Studies in Comparative International Development* 36 (4): 3–33. https://doi.org/10.1007/BF02686331

Roberts, Kenneth M. 2003. "Social Correlates of Party System Demise and Populist Resurgence in Venezuela." *Latin American Politics and Society* 45 (3): 35–57. https://doi.org/10.1111/j.1548-2456.2003.tb00249.x

Roberts, Kenneth M. 2006. "Populism, Political Conflict, and Grass-Roots Organization in Latin America." *Comparative Politics* 38 (2): 127–48. https://doi.org/10.23 07/20433986

Roberts, Kenneth M. 2014. *Changing Course in Latin America: Party Systems in the Neoliberal Era*. New York: Cambridge University Press.

Roberts, Kenneth M. 2017. "Pitfalls and Opportunities: Lessons from the Study of Critical Junctures in Latin America." *Qualitative and Multi-Method Research* 15 (1): 12–15. https://escholarship.org/uc/item/3qk7w7j0

Rokkan, Stein. 1970. *Citizens, Elections, Parties: Approaches to the Comparative Study of the Processes of Development.* Oslo: Universitetsforlaget.

Rokkan, Stein. 1999. *State Formation, Nation-Building, and Mass Politics in Europe: The Theory of Stein Rokkan, Based on His Collected Works.* Edited by Peter Flora with Stein Kuhnle and Derek Urwin. Oxford: Oxford University Press.

Rueschemeyer, Dietrich, Evelyne Huber Stephens, and John D. Stephens. 1992. *Capitalist Development and Democracy.* Cambridge: Polity Press.

Rustow, Dankwart A. 1970. "Transitions to Democracy: Toward a Dynamic Model." *Comparative Politics* 2 (3): 337–63.

Sartori, Giovanni. 1968. "The Sociology of Parties: A Critical Review." In *Party Systems, Party Organizations, and the Politics of New Masses, Beiträge Zur 3. Internationalen Konferenz Über Vergleichende Politische Soziologie, Berlin, 15–20. Januar 1968,* edited by Otto Stammer, 1–25. Berlin: Institut für politische Wissenschaft, Freien Universität Berlin.

Scalapino, Robert A. 1965. *Communism in Asia: Toward a Comparative Analysis.* Berkeley: University of California Press.

Schattschneider, E. E. 1975. *The Semisovereign People: A Realist's View of Democracy in America.* London: Wadsworth.

Schmitter, Philippe C. 1971. *Interest Conflict and Political Change in Brazil.* Stanford: Stanford University Press.

Scully, Timothy R. 1992. *Rethinking the Center: Party Politics in Nineteenth- and Twentieth-Century Chile.* Stanford: Stanford University Press.

Shefter, Martin. 1977. "Party and Patronage: Germany, England, and Italy." *Politics & Society* 7 (4): 403–51. https://doi.org/10.1177/003232927700700402

Slater, Dan, and Erica Simmons. 2010. "Informative Regress: Critical Antecedents in Comparative Politics." *Comparative Political Studies* 43 (7): 886–917. https://doi.org/10.1177/0010414010361343

Slater, Dan, and Joseph Wong. 2013. "The Strength to Concede: Ruling Parties and Democratization in Developmental Asia." *Perspectives on Politics* 11 (3): 717–33.

Stryker, Sheldon. 1980. *Symbolic Interactionalism: A Social Structural Version.* Menlo Park, CA: Benjamin/Cummings Publishing.

Stryker, Sheldon. 2000. "Identity Competition: Key to Differential Social Movement Participation?" In *Self, Identity, and Social Movements,* edited by Sheldon Stryker, Timothy J. Owens, and Robert W. White, 21–39. Minneapolis: University of Minnesota Press.

Stubager, Rune. 2009. "Education-Based Group Identity and Consciousness in the Authoritarian-Libertarian Value Conflict." *European Journal of Political Research* 48 (2): 204–33. https://doi.org/10.1111/j.1475-6765.2008.00834.x

Stubager, Rune. 2010. "The Development of the Education Cleavage: Denmark as a Critical Case." *West European Politics* 33 (3): 505–33. https://doi.org/10.1080/01402381003654544

Tarrow, Sidney. 1992. "Mentalities, Political Cultures, and Collective Action Frames: Constructing Meanings through Action." In *Frontiers in Social Movement Theory,* edited by Aldon D. Morris and Carol McClurg Mueller, 174–202. New Haven: Yale University Press.

Torcal, Mariano, and Scott Mainwaring. 2003. "The Political Recrafting of Social Bases of Party Competition: Chile, 1973–95." *British Journal of Political Science* 33 (1): 55–84. https://doi.org/10.1017/S0007123403000036

van der Brug, Wouter. 2010. "Structural and Ideological Voting in Age Cohorts." *West European Politics* 33 (3): 586–607. https://doi.org/10.1080/01402381003654593

van Eerd, Jonathan. 2017. *The Quality of Democracy in Africa: Opposition Competitiveness Rooted in Legacies of Cleavages.* Basingstoke: Palgrave Macmillan.

Walle, Nicolas van de. 2007. "Meet the New Boss, Same as the Old Boss? The Evolution of Political Clientelism in Africa." In *Patrons, Clients, and Policies: Patterns of Democratic Accountability and Political Competition*, edited by Herbert Kitschelt and Steven I. Wilkinson, 50–67. Cambridge: Cambridge University Press.

Wegner, Eva, and Francesco Cavatorta. 2019. "Revisiting the Islamist–Secular Divide: Parties and Voters in the Arab World." *International Political Science Review* 40 (4): 558–75. https://doi.org/10.1177/0192512118784225

Weyland, Kurt. 1996. *Democracy without Equity: Failures of Reform in Brazil.* Pittsburgh: University of Pittsburgh Press.

Weyland, Kurt. 2012. "The Arab Spring: Why the Surprising Similarities with the Revolutionary Wave of 1848?" *Perspectives on Politics* 10 (4): 917–34. https://doi.org/10.1017/S1537592712002873

Weyland, Kurt. 2014. *Making Waves: Democratic Contention in Europe and Latin America since the Revolutions of 1848.* Cambridge: Cambridge University Press.

Weyland, Kurt. 2019. *Revolution and Reaction: The Diffusion of Authoritarianism in Latin America.* Cambridge: Cambridge University Press.

Wilde, Alexander W. 1978. "Conversations among Gentlemen: Oligarchical Democracy in Colombia." In *The Breakdown of Democratic Regimes: Latin America*, edited by Juan J. Linz and Alfred Stepan, 28–81. Baltimore: Johns Hopkins University Press.

Zielinski, Jakub. 2002. "Translating Social Cleavages into Party Systems: The Significance of New Democracies." *World Politics* 54 (2): 184–211. https://doi.org/10.1353/wp.2002.0005

Zuckerman, Alan. 1975. "Political Cleavage: A Conceptual and Theoretical Analysis." *British Journal of Political Science* 5 (2): 231–48. https://doi.org/10.1017/S000712340008140

Critical Junctures and Mass–Elite Discrepancy

Religious and Foreign Policy Issues

CHAPTER 6

Mass–Elite Religious–Secular Discrepancy in Tunisia

The Revolution as a Critical Juncture

Mahmoud Farag

On December 17, 2010, Mohamed Bouazizi, a Tunisian street vendor, set himself on fire, sparking what came to be the Jasmine Revolution that toppled President Zine El Abidine Ben Ali, who had ruled Tunisia since 1987. After Ben Ali's fall, Tunisia embarked on a democratic transition that was completed successfully in late 2011, after electing the National Constituent Assembly (NCA). The revolution, however, brought one of Tunisia's long-standing questions to the public agenda: the relationship between Islam and politics (Allani 2009, 257). Throughout its history, secularization was imposed in an aggressive, top-down manner on Tunisian society following the French model (Ben Yahmed and Yerkes 2018). The rise of Ennahda, Tunisia's oldest and largest Islamist movement, and their victory in the 2011 NCA elections not only surprised Tunisians and the international community, it also galvanized the fears of secularists and former regime members (Cavatorta and Merone 2013, 857). Ennahda, nevertheless, managed to form a governing coalition with secular parties in 2011 and to join, as a junior partner, in a coalition led by Nidaa Tounes, a secular party, after coming second in the 2014 elections. This coalition was surprising given the religious–secular divide that dominated Tunisia both before and after the revolution.

The religious–secular divide is, in fact, the most important and consistent political dimension in the Middle East, including in Tunisia (Wegner and Cavatorta 2019, 1–2). However, the recent transition to democracy in

Tunisia, in which religious and secular forces were celebrated for coming together (Bellin 2013), indicates that the religious–secular divide has been minimized at the elite level. In other words, elite-level compromise and cooperation during Tunisia's democratic transition point to the possibility of mass–elite discrepancy. This calls for empirically examining the religious–secular dimension at both mass and elite levels.

Tunisia is well suited for the study of mass–elite discrepancy in new democracies. Tunisia was the only Arab country that successfully completed its democratic transition after the 2011 Arab Spring (Stepan 2012), before sliding back to autocracy in 2021.[1] Nevertheless, looking at Tunisia's period of democratic reign allows for an exploration of whether there is a discrepancy between masses and elites on the religious–secular dimension and to what extent the revolution, as a critical juncture, contributed to such a discrepancy. Also, studying Tunisia provides important insights into how the religious–secular dimension evolves at both the mass and the elite levels during democratization, which is significant not only for Arab but for all Muslim-majority countries.

The core argument of this chapter is that mass–elite discrepancy on the religious–secular dimension is a direct result of the Tunisian revolution, as a critical juncture. The revolution's political uncertainty opened a window of opportunity for Ennahda to embark on a process of ideological transformation by making concessions as part of their cooperation with secular forces. Elite-led socialization had path-dependent effects on mass–elite discrepancy and led to the continued moderation of secular and Islamist elites. Thus, the chapter uncovers the frequently overlooked role of critical junctures in developing mass–elite discrepancy.

This chapter makes both empirical and theoretical contributions to the literature on party politics and to the burgeoning literature on the Middle East and North Africa (MENA) region. Empirically, it offers one of the few attempts to measure mass–elite discrepancy in Tunisia. In so doing, it contributes to the recent wave of scholarship attempting to use MENA cases to inform the study of comparative politics in general (Bank and Busse 2021) and the analysis of mass–elite congruence in particular (Rasmussen, Reher, and Toshkov 2019). By triangulating the analysis of party manifestos with data on legislative proposals and voting, the chapter reveals a mass–elite discrepancy that could not be captured by only using party manifestos. This triangulation overcomes the weakness sometimes attributed to party manifestos of only capturing issue salience (Laver 2003b, 73), given the wider view in the literature about roll-call data and bill sponsorship as accurate estimates of elite attitudes (Carroll and Poole 2014).

Theoretically, the chapter uncovers the frequently overlooked role of critical junctures in developing mass–elite discrepancy. This finding supports earlier arguments about the need to account for the role of agency in cleavage formation or pacification (Bornschier 2009; Zuckerman 1975; see also chapters 4 and 5 in this volume). In new democracies with less institutionalized secondary organizations, elites have more leeway to identify the main political dimensions of electoral competition (Chhibber and Torcal 1997). Treating a recent event, such as the Tunisian Revolution, as a critical juncture and explaining its effect on mass–elite discrepancy shows how the political dimensions are not shaped primarily by bottom-up structural factors, as classically argued by Lipset and Rokkan. In other words, taking the role of elites during critical junctures seriously avoids the social determinism that has shaped the cleavage literature by bridging both the bottom-up force of structures with the top-down discretion of elite agency (Bornschier 2009, 10). Adopting a critical juncture perspective also implies path dependency (Mahoney 2000; Pierson 2000) because the mass–elite discrepancy is most likely to persist over time. Specifically, as made clear in the theoretical framework of this volume in chapter 4, the representation gap can persist because elites are likely to be locked-in to the political dynamics created during the critical juncture period.

This chapter surveys the literature on the religious–secular divide in the Arab world from the perspective of both masses and elites. It then outlines the mass–elite discrepancy on the religious–secular political dimension in Tunisia. Employing a critical juncture perspective, it traces the origin of the mass–elite discrepancy to the Tunisian revolution, and concludes by discussing the implications of the key findings.

6.1. The Religious–Secular Divide: Mass and Elite Attitudes

This section contextualizes the religious–secular divide by providing an overview of political Islam before outlining the current state of the literature. Tracing the rise of political Islam can clarify the origins of the religious–secular political dimension. The main distinction to be made here should be between Islam as a religion and political Islam as an ideology. Ayubi (1991, 2) argues forcefully that Islam is not and has never been a political religion, and it was Islamists who constructed Islam's political nature as a reaction to the fall of the Ottoman Empire. Political Islam goes beyond theology and focuses on political activism, justified and promoted through selective religious entrepreneurship (Browers 2005, 84). Thus, Islamist actors prioritize the control of state institutions in order to advance their agenda (Bayat 2013b, 592). Bayat (2013a, 4) defines political Islam in terms of its ideological project as "the ideologies and movements that work towards the aim of establishing an Islamic order—a religious state, sharia law and moral codes in Muslim societies and communities." These goals, from an Islamist perspective, can be achieved via social and political actions such as party formation and electoral competition (Albrecht and Wegner 2006, 124). Islamists, thus, are purely political actors who use religion to advance their political agenda (Mecham 2014, 202). Islamists also reinforce their ideological appeal via social services to increase their popularity (Salloukh 1997, 124; Brooke 2019).

Islamist movements that consciously and deliberately use Islamic vocabulary and principles have emerged as the main vehicles of political opposition in the Middle East (Crystal 1994, 285; Abukhalil 1997, 156).[2] According to Albrecht and Schlumberger (2004, 386), non-co-opted Islamist groups are the only social actors who have managed to maintain some financial and organizational independence from Arab authoritarian regimes. Due to their popular support and organizational capacity, it is actually the nonviolent Islamist groups, rather than the violent ones, who have challenged most authoritarian regimes (Albrecht and Wegner 2006, 123).

With very few exceptions, the existing literature on the religious–secular divide in the Arab world studies mass and elite attitudes separately, with the mass–elite discrepancy not being compared simultaneously. On the one hand, early studies on mass attitudes were mostly "based on impressionistic and anecdotal information . . . systematic empirical inquiries into the nature, distribution, and determinants of political attitudes in the Arab world are rare" (Tessler 2002b, 337). The first wave to empirically examine mass divides in the Arab world used the World Values Survey (Tessler 2002a; Jamal 2006) or original survey data to examine how the religious orientations of the masses shape their attitudes toward democracy (Tessler 2002b). The emergence of the Arab Barometer in the mid-2000s represented the first systematic attempt to examine comparative mass attitudes across the Arab world (Jamal and Tessler 2008; Tessler and Jamal 2006).

Many subsequent analyses using survey data from the various Arab Barometer waves have focused on gauging the religious–secular divide at the mass level or in tandem with their effect on attitudes toward democracy (Rahman 2018; Robbins 2017; Solomon and Tausch 2021; Tessler 2010; Ciftci 2013; Ciftci, Wuthrich, and Shamaileh 2018). Other studies have attempted to capture the stability and change of Arab attitudes toward democracy (Benstead 2015; Robbins 2015; Tessler, Jamal, and Robbins

2012). The 2011 Arab Spring also came with opportunities to collect new data on mass attitudes and to test a new set of hypotheses. Using new data from Egypt and Tunisia, Hoffman and Jamal (2014) examine whether religion encourages or discourages protest activity. Masoud (2014) examines why Egyptian voters favored Islamists and not leftists, despite the former's preference for neoliberal economic policies.

On the other hand, the scholarship on elite attitudes in the Arab world has focused primarily on two themes: first, whether the political inclusion of Islamists leads to their behavioral and ideological moderation (al-Anani 2019; Pahwa 2017; Schwedler 2006, 2011; Tepe 2019; Tezcür 2010), and second, the dynamics of cross-ideological cooperation between secularists and Islamists (Abdelrahman 2009; Kraetzschmar 2014; Lust 2011b; Buehler 2018; Clark 2010; Durac 2019). The majority of those studies are primarily based on ethnographic research and analysis of party documents including manifestos (Tadros 2012).

Charles Kurzman and colleagues have made the only systematic effort to compile, code, and analyze the manifestos of Islamist parties across the Islamic world (Kurzman and Naqvi 2010; Kurzman and Türkoğlu 2015). They coded the manifestos on 13 issues, mainly focusing on the Islamist gray zones identified by Brown, Hamzawy, and Ottaway (2006) around the implementation of sharia, attitudes toward democracy, and their stand on women's rights and minority rights, in addition to identifying the top three issues in each manifesto. While Kurzman and Naqvi (2010) observed the liberalization of Islamist parties, their most recent analysis concluded that liberalization had stagnated (Kurzman and Türkoğlu 2015). There have been recent attempts to analyze Islamist party manifestos, with a particular focus on their economic policies (Ben Salem 2020; Daher 2020; Tobin 2020; Cavatorta and Resta 2020).

The scholarship on Tunisia also reflects the wider focus on either mass attitudes or elite attitudes, without combining both strands. Findings so far reveal that mass attitudes in Tunisia are structured along three dimensions: religious–secular, political reform–support for the status quo, and modernity–authenticity (Abduljaber and Arbor 2018, 99). At the same time, elite attitudes, represented by political parties in Tunisia, are structured along two dimensions: cultural modernist vs. conservative, and socioeconomic (van Hamme, Gana, and Ben Rebbah 2014).

Wegner and Cavatorta (2019) offer the single most ambitious attempt to compare mass–elite divides in the Arab world using survey data on seven Arab countries. They conclude that "ideological congruence exists but that it is, by and large, limited to an Islamist–Secular core content, with supporters of Islamist and Secular Left parties having significantly different attitudes towards the role of religion in politics" (Wegner and Cavatorta 2019, 3). They, nevertheless, admit that their "classification of Islamist and Secular Left party platforms is—in the absence of a comprehensive coding effort of such platforms—a simplistic approximation of the values promoted by these parties." This chapter overcomes that limitation by coding party manifestos and triangulating the analysis with data on legislative proposals and voting. The next section moves to analyze the mass–elite discrepancy on the religious–secular political dimension in Tunisia.

6.2. Mass–Elite Religious–Secular Discrepancy in Tunisia

6.2.1. Measuring Mass–Elite Discrepancy: Arab Barometer Surveys and Election Manifestos

The focus of this section is to examine whether there is a discrepancy between elites and masses on the religious–secular dimension. At the mass level, mass issue positions are examined using data from three Arab Barometer survey waves: II, III, and IV.[3] The Arab Barometer surveys the attitudes, values, and judgments of Arab citizens on a wide array of topics. It is divided into several sections including general topics on economic conditions, safety, and trust; the evaluation of political institutions and public attitudes; elections and the House of Representatives; media; democracy; social, cultural, and religious topics; current affairs, the Arab world, and international relations; the Tunisian Revolution; identity; and demographics and personal information of respondents. It includes, on average, over 200 questions covering the nine sections. The Tunisian surveys took place in 2011, 2013, and 2016, with an average sample of 1,200 respondents representing the 24 governorates. The analysis focuses on the religious–secular dimension to the exclusion of other dimensions, given its significance as outlined in the introduction.

The Arab Barometer provides more relevant data than its counterparts, which are the World Values Survey and the Afrobarometer. The World Values Survey includes Tunisia in its sixth wave (2010–14). It asks questions on the importance of religion, acceptance toward people of different religions, the meaning of religion, compatibility between religion and science, and teaching religion in public schools. The Afrobarometer asks similar questions about whether Tunisia would be better off if religious people held public office, on the compatibility between democracy and Islam, and on preferring a system governed by Islamic law. However, the questions in the Arab Barometer on the exact application of personal and penal laws according to Islamic sharia, the preference for religious parties, and allowing banks to charge interest are a better approximation of the religious–secular dimension since Islamic law is one of the main gray zones of Islamist movements (Brown, Hamzawy, and Ottaway 2006). In addition, the availability of Arab Barometer data over three waves (2011, 2013 and 2016) enables the tracing of changing public attitudes toward the religious–secular dimension.

To identify mass attitudes on the religious–secular dimension, this chapter analyzes eight questions pertinent to the role of religion in politics (see appendix 6.1). Table 6.1 presents the position of masses and elites on the religious–secular dimension. The mass-level data is the percentage (mean) of all eight issues that underlie the religious–secular dimension for each survey. The general picture is divisive but, at the same time, the Tunisian mass public has developed more religious positions over time. The number of Tunisians who support the government and parliament enacting Islamic sharia law in general and for personal status matters in particular is nearly double the number of those who are against doing so. Moreover, Tunisians, in general, have a stronger preference for religious, not secular, political parties despite a decrease in 2016. However, Tunisians have been against enacting penal laws according to Islamic sharia and are in favor of allowing banks to charge interest, despite this being regarded as anti-Islamic by some religious scholars.

The divisive mass attitudes captured by the Arab Barometer reflect the many real-life conflicts between Islamists and secularists in Tunisia after 2011. In December 2011, for instance, thousands of secular university students protested in front of Tunisia's Constituent Assembly against Islamist students' calls for female colleagues to wear the Islamic head covering known as the hijab (Ahram Online 2011). In January 2012, thousands of Tunisians organized a secular rally in opposition to the growing influence of Salafis in Tunisia, which led to the trial of a television director for broadcasting the French animated film *Persepolis*, which contained a brief scene depicting God that many here have deemed blasphemous (Shadid 2012). In March 2012, thousands of Salafis and conservative Islamists organized a demonstration calling for the explicit adoption of Islamic sharia law in the then-draft constitution (Hürriyet Daily News 2012).

In 2018, thousands of male and female Islamists protested at the Tunisian parliament against a report by the Commission of Individual Liberties and Equality, which called for legalizing homosexuality and equal inheritance rights for men and women, both of which are seen as going against Islamic principles (France24 2018). These different instances all corroborate

Table 6.1. Mass–Elite Discrepancy on the Religious–Secular Dimension (2011–16)

| | Mass level Survey (percentage) | | Elite level Manifesto (# of statements) | | | |
| | | | Religious | | Secular | |
	Religious	Secular	Ennahda	Nidaa Tounes	Ennahda	Nidaa Tounes
2011	50.41	32.59	—	—	—	—
2012	—	—	—	—	—	—
2013	55.82	34.81	—	—	—	—
2014	—	—	55	14	0	0
2015	—	—	—	—	—	—
2016	56.00	33.14	—	—	—	—

Source: Arab Barometer (survey waves II, III, IV) for mass-level data. Author calculations for elite-level data.
Note: Mass-level data do not add to 100 percent due to the "declined" and "don't know" answers in the survey.

the Arab Barometer surveys that indicate there is a religious–secular divide at the mass level in Tunisia.

Elite attitudes in Tunisia are gauged by examining the policy positions of the two biggest political parties in Tunisia: Ennahda (*Renaissance* in Arabic) and Nidaa Tounes (*Call for Tunisia* in Arabic). The focus on Ennahda and Nidaa Tounes is justified, since these are the two biggest Islamist and secular parties, respectively. Ennahda was founded in 1972 under the name "Islamic Group" and is currently the biggest and oldest Islamist movement turned political party in Tunisia. Nidaa Tounes was formed in 2012 by former Tunisian president Beji Caid Essebsi as the largest secular party to counter the rise of Ennahda. Tunisia held its Constituent Assembly elections in October 2011, which saw the victory of Ennahda with 37.04 percent of the vote (89 seats). The next party, the Congress for the Republic (CPR), received only 8.71 percent of the vote (29 seats). Together with the CPR and another secular party, the Democratic Forum for Labour and Liberties (Ettakatol), Ennahda formed a coalition government. In the 2014 parliamentary elections, Nidaa Tounes and Ennahda combined received 65.35 percent of the vote (37.56% for Nidaa Tounes and 27.79% for Ennahda), which translated to 155 seats or 71.4 percent of the parliament's seats (International Foundation for Electoral Systems 2014). In fact, the party that received the largest share of the votes after Nidaa Tounes and Ennahda was the Free Patriotic Union, which received only 4.13 percent of the vote.

One straightforward way to measure elite attitudes is via analyzing legislator surveys and public speeches (Bankov and Gherghina 2020). Given the lack of such data in Tunisia, this chapter analyzes the policy positions of political parties and triangulates them with legislative proposals and related voting patterns. Party policy positions are one of the many established ways to measure elite attitudes (Laver 2003a). Using the Manifesto Project's coding instructions, this chapter analyzes the manifestos of both Ennahda and Nidaa Tounes, which were released ahead of the 2014 parliamentary elections (Werner, Lacewell, and Volkens 2015).[4] Taking these manifestos as the political parties' primary statements, the analysis quantifies the number of messages and positions (Werner, Lacewell, and Volkens 2015, 2). The coding answers the following questions: "What message is the party/presidential candidate trying to convey to voters? Which are the issues the party/presidential candidate regards as important?" (Werner, Lacewell, and Volkens 2015, 5). The basic unit of analysis is the quasi sentence that delivers a certain, differentiated message and which should not, in any case, exceed a grammatical sentence (Werner, Lacewell, and Volkens 2015, 6). The Manifesto Project coding includes 56 subcategories representing seven major policy domains: (1) external relations, (2) freedom and democracy, (3) political system, (4) economy, (5) welfare and quality of life, (6) fabric of society, and (7) social groups.

To gauge the positions of Ennahda and Nidaa Tounes on the religious–secular dimension, this chapter first uses certain positional subcategories in the 2014 manifestos of both parties. While party manifestos are usually an expression of saliency (Laver 2003b, 73), advocates of saliency theory argue that "emphasis equals direction" and that the position of political actors can be derived from the salience they attach to issues (Budge 2003). Relatedly, several methods have been developed to measure the issue positions of political actors based on their party manifestos (Dinas and Gemenis 2010). The fact that many subcategories in the latest Manifesto Project's coding instructions include positional coding, either positive or negative, justifies using manifesto data as one data point to identify party positions, as illustrated in appendix 6.2.

On the religious–secular dimension, Ennahda scored 55 compared to 14 by Nidaa Tounes on the religious side, while no manifesto statement on the secular side existed for either party. This shows that Ennahda is further to the right, with its manifesto maintaining a more Islamist position than Nidaa Tounes. However, although Nidaa Tounes is the biggest secular party in Tunisia, its position on the religious–secular dimension does not concur with a position based on a nonexistent statement favoring the secularist side. Because of this, contrary to the masses, it is clear that the two parties are not divided on the religious–secular dimension.

6.2.2. Triangulating Elite-Level Findings: Roll-Call Votes and Bill Sponsorship

The results appear to reveal a mass–elite congruence with the overall direction being on the mass side, namely, as pro-religious. However, as noted, the measurement of elites' policy positions with party manifestos is not yet a widely accepted method. For instance, since the origin and purpose of data generation are highly strategic, scholars often question the validity of party manifesto data in capturing parties' issue positions (Laver and Garry 2000; Gabel and Huber 2000). Bearing this in mind, I consulted legislative voting patterns by parties, another method often utilized to capture elite-level positions (e.g., Talbert and Potoski 2002).

First, the chapter uses a newly acquired dataset of the 2014–16 legislative voting of both Ennahda and Nidaa Tounes.[5] Between 2014 and 2016, there has been a total of 134 bills voted on by the Tunisian parliament. Almost two-thirds (62.6%) of the laws passed by the parliament's majority, namely Nidaa Tounes and Ennahda, concern economic loans and agreements. Pure economic policies and laws account for the second-largest group of adopted bills (14.1%). Next comes democratic-freedom-related bills such as the access to information bill, the higher judicial council law, and the revision of other laws to be in line with the constitution (8.2%). In fact, no bills reflect the pro- or anti-Islamist positions of elites. Oftentimes, confining analysis only to legislative voting can conceal positional differences since contentious legislative proposals can be filtered out prior to the voting stage. Bearing this concern in mind, I examined all legislative proposals during the three years of observation; the result shows that not a single pro- or anti-Islamist law proposal was submitted to the parliament. This stands in stark contrast to the constitutional drafting process, finished in 2013, which showed Ennahda initially having stronger positions on Islamist issues such as references to Islamic sharia law, women's rights, and religious blasphemy (Marks 2014). In other words, while the manifestos of both parties appear to reflect the positions of the masses, their legislative voting patterns reveal the silencing of the religious–secular division, which clearly points to the existence of a mass–elite discrepancy.

This analysis raises a number of questions. If there is a mass divide around the religious–secular dimension, why did Nidaa Tounes downplay its secular identity? The same applies to Ennahda. Why did Ennahda not express its Islamist identity even more in the 2014 manifesto, and why did it not try to push for an Islamist agenda in the parliament that was similar to what it tried during the constitutional drafting process? The next section sheds light on how the Tunisian Revolution, as a critical juncture, facilitated the moderation of Ennahda, leading it to attempt to pacify the religious–secular divide at the elite level, which subsequently resulted in a mass–elite religious–secular discrepancy.

6.3. The Tunisian Revolution and the Mass–Elite Religious–Secular Discrepancy: A Critical Juncture Explanation

Building on the theoretical framework of this volume, this section explains the mass–elite discrepancy from a critical juncture perspective. By allowing for the agency and choice of political forces, critical junctures overcome the social determinism that has characterized cleavage research in new democracies (Bornschier 2009, 2). Critical junctures, with their inherent uncertainty, allow for a decisive causal human choice that will leave its path-dependent imprint for decades (Capoccia 2016).[6]

To put the Tunisian revolution in context, this section first presents a brief historical background for Ennahda. Rached Ghannouchi cofounded Ennahda under the name of the Islamic Group in 1972, having been influenced by the Muslim Brotherhood in Egypt. Its predominant focus was initially social and religious, but it started to take political positions, particularly after the repression of a general strike in 1978, and in 1979 it changed its name to the Islamic Tendency Movement (Abdel Ghafar and Hess 2018, 8–9). It went public in 1980, holding a press conference and seeking official registration as a political party, which the government rejected, subsequently detaining most of its leaders; by 1987, the government attempted to execute some of them, including Ghannouchi himself. After Zine El Abidine Ben Ali became Tunisia's president as a result of overthrowing Habib Bourguiba in 1987, relations with the regime deteriorated once more. In 1988, the Islamic Tendency Movement changed its name to the current Ennahda and ran in parliamentary elections, leading to a two-decade cycle of repression with many of its members living in exile, detained, or in hiding.[7] Ennahda has evolved and moderated its ideology over time, from an illiberal, undemocratic movement in the 1970s to accepting democratic procedures and social pluralism in the late 1980s (Cavatorta and Merone 2013, 858). However, in the 1989 elections, Ennahda held extreme views regarding women's rights and the role of religion in public life, which induced public hostility (Allani 2009, 264–65).

6.3.1. Elite-Level Moderation of Religious–Secular Cleavage:
The 2010–2011 Tunisian Revolution and Democratic Transition

The beginning of the critical juncture in Tunisia is the massive popular mobilization between December 18, 2010 and January 14, 2011, and the subsequent fall of Ben Ali's regime. In such a context, the existing political institutions were broken, and human agency played a pivotal role in establishing new institutions (Bellin 2013, 2). This is particularly true for Islamists in the Middle East, including Ennahda, in the aftermath of the Arab uprisings—not only because Islamists got to power through ballots but because of how bargaining with other secular forces, including members of the old regime, would affect their ideology and tactics (al-Anani 2012, 467).

The peak of the critical juncture lies in Ennahda's electoral victory in the 2011 NCA elections and the adoption of pragmatism that favored both the movement's survival and the success of the democratic transition. When the revolution took everyone by surprise in 2011, "Ennahda had to both rebuild itself and develop a clear platform," as noted by a member of the movement's executive bureau (Abdel Ghafar and Hess 2018, 14). The metaphor used after Ennahda came first in the NCA elections was "going from the prison to the palace," according to Lotfi Abedyda, director of Ennahda's headquarters in Sfax (Marks 2014, 12). The 2011 NCA elections were dominated by ideological debates (Murphy 2013). However, to maximize votes, what Ennahda did was a textbook example of positional alignment, "not by changing their opinions on a particular question but by persuading them [voters] that the question is less important than another" (Deegan-Krause and Enyedi 2010, 697). By de-emphasizing the religious–secular divide, Ennahda aimed to keep their core voters and also to reach out to new groups of voters who traditionally would not buy into Ennahda's pure religious rhetoric.

After winning the 2011 elections, Ennahda found out that many political parties were unwilling to cooperate with them and join a coalition government (Abdel Ghafar and Hess 2018, 19). However, together with the CPR and another secular party, Ettakatol, Ennahda formed a coalition government. Upon government formation and during the constitutional drafting process, Ennahda similarly made several religion-related concessions including removing the reference to sharia, revising the article on women's rights to support equality rather than complementarity, and removing the criminalization of blasphemy (Marks 2014).

All these concessions led Hamid (2016) to observe that Ennahda has conceded its Islamism. Of all Ennahda members in the Constituent Assembly, Nejib Mrad, their most conservative member, was the only one who voted against the constitution (Grewal 2020, 526). But it took much effort from the national, moderate leadership to bring their regional cadres on board with these concessions and to convince them that they are not contradicting their Islamic principles (Marks 2014, 1). This deliberate effort also included sidelining Ennahda's conservative voices and not nominating them for the 2014 parliamentary elections (Grewal 2020). Ennahda's moderation continued to be observed. For instance, in the 2014 parliamentary elections, it was issues and programs, not ideology, that guided Ennahda's campaign (Abdel Ghafar and Hess 2018, 16). After Ennahda came in second, it agreed to Nidaa Tounes's offer to enter a coalition government (Ajroudi and Allahoum 2018), which led to stark divisions and defections within the latter party (Marks 2015a).

6.3.2. The Reasons behind Political Moderation: Uncertainty-Induced Compromise to Maintain Power

Why did leading political actors pacify the religious–secular cleavage in Tunisia during the critical juncture? I argue that the key motivation behind political moderation stems from the elites' motivation to reduce political risks in the middle of an uncertain revolutionary landscape. The following examples demonstrate this.

Tunisia witnessed a deep political crisis within the governing coalition led by Ennahda in 2013, which eventually led the secular opposition to boycott the NCA. The crisis was aggravated by the military coup against the Muslim Brotherhood president, Mohamed Morsi, in Egypt and the assassination of two Tunisian leftist leaders, Chokri Belaid and Mohamed Brahmi, in February and July 2013, respectively. When the transition was on the brink of failure, a Tunisian National Dialogue Quartet composed of the Tunisian General Labor Union, the Tunisian Confederation of Industry, Trade and Handicrafts, the Tunisian Human Rights League, and the Tunisian Order of Lawyers mediated between Ennahda and other political forces including Nidaa Tounes (Marks 2015b).

At that point, Ennahda could have chosen to defend its electoral mandate to rule based on its majority in the NCA or it could have played the religion card to mobilize its supporters against the secularist opposition, or both. However, Ennahda agreed to hand over their coalition-led government to a technocratic government that would supervise the parliamentary and presidential elections (Allinson 2015, 303). In doing this, Ennahda had in mind Egypt's coup and feared something similar might happen in Tunisia (Abdel Ghafar and Hess 2018, 31). It was, therefore, the post-2011 uncertainty associated with the political landscape of Tunisia and the regional anti-Islamist sentiment following the fall of the Muslim Brotherhood in Egypt that led Ennahda to concede.

The many concessions by Ennahda during the constitutional drafting can also be attributed to political uncertainty. To successfully navigate the transition to democracy, Ennahda's leadership decided to make concessions to their secular counterparts. Counterfactually, Ennahda could have chosen to enforce its religious views in the constitution. It chose, however, not to because it was uncertain about what the secularists would do.[8] Similarly, after the 2014 election, Ennahda leaders accepted the coalition, fearing that self-exclusion would lead to a renewed phase of repression, similar to what happened before 2011 (McCarthy 2015). At the same time, secularists, at least their moderate factions, chose to include Ennahda because they were uncertain what Ennahda's exclusion would mean to Tunisia. Tunisia's secularists have always feared the replication of the decade-long civil war in neighboring Algeria had they chosen to exclude the Islamists from power (Allani 2009, 258). This seemed particularly imminent given the active operations of Ansar al-Sharia, a militant Islamist group in Tunisia (Cavatorta 2015).

6.3.3. A Lasting Mass–Elite Discrepancy: Elite-Level Socialization

Socialization between Tunisian political elites clearly contributed to the continuing political moderation of the religious–secular divide. Both the gradual moderation of Ennahda and its rejection of harsh repressive tendencies since 1989, and the accompanying cross-ideological cooperation between Ennahda and secular parties, happened long before the Tunisian revolution in 2010. In 2003, representatives of Ennahda, the Congress for the Republic Party, the Democratic Forum for Labor and Liberties (Ettakatol), and the Progressive Democratic Party—the major, non-co-opted Tunisian parties—agreed to form an oppositional alliance and to set aside their differences, which they thought were less important than opposing the incumbent regime (Marks 2014, 11).

In 2005, the same political parties formed a wider cross-ideological alliance, called the October 18 Collectif, which lasted for five years (Haugbølle and Cavatorta 2011, 336). The fact that Ennahda had formed an oppositional coalition with other secular parties, including the CPR and Ettakatol in 2003 and once again in 2005, facilitated the formation of a joint governing coalition after the revolution. Grewal (2020) shows convincingly how such socialization was facilitated with some of the Ennahda, CPR, and Ettakatol members living in exile, which gave them more freedom to meet and interact beyond the control of the Tunisian regime. The socialization between secular parties and Ennahda before the revolution led to the further moderation of Ennahda once the revolution happened.

The fact that socialization between elites began prior to the 2010–11 critical juncture does not deny the primary importance of elite agency. On this point, another neighboring Muslim-majority country, Egypt, can serve as a counterfactual. The experience of Egypt's Muslim Brotherhood offers a good contrast to Tunisia's Ennahda. Before 2011, the Egyptian regime manipulated secularists' attitudes toward the Muslim Brotherhood (Lust 2011a, 177). In the 2000s, and despite historical hostility between secularists and Islamists, cooperation had been on the rise (Browers 2009, 3). This had manifested itself in the creation of opposition movements that brought secularists, particularly socialists, and Islamists together, such as the Egyptian Movement for Change (Kifaya), the United National Front for Change, and the National Association for Change (Albrecht and Wegner 2006). In that regard, Egypt, similar to Tunisia, witnessed cross-ideological cooperation prior to the critical juncture.

Both countries had popular revolutions that led to the fall of their ruling regimes. However, during the critical juncture of the Arab Spring, Egypt did not choose the politics of pragmatism. It polarized the religious–secular divide and subsequently failed to transition into a democracy. The Muslim Brotherhood in Egypt did not compromise. It monopolized the parliament, the constitutional drafting committee, and the presidency to the exclusion of other politically relevant groups, including the Salafis (Brown 2013). The polarization between Islamists and secularists continued, and secularists formed the National Salvation Front in late 2012 (Dunne and Radwan 2013, 98).

On July 3, 2013, the military, backed by secularists and making use of the millions who took to the streets, removed President Morsi. Brown (2013, 53) summarizes this by saying that it was "not so much that Egypt's political actors lacked democratic commitments (though some did), but more that they deeply distrusted their adversaries and regarded real democratic processes as full of potential pitfalls." To summarize, while both Tunisia and Egypt witnessed pre-2011 cross-ideological cooperation, the divergence in outcomes with respect to the focus of this chapter, namely mass–elite discrepancy, became possible when elite cooperation in Tunisia was coupled with elite pragmatism during the critical juncture itself.

The open question, notwithstanding, is to explain why elite-level moderation was not echoed at the mass level. There is a well-established literature on how elite cues shape the political positions of the masses (Tappin 2023). There are two plausible reasons why this was not the case in Tunisia. First, elite moderation took place in a context of political uncertainty after the revolution. The competition for power, therefore, shaped elite preferences toward moderation, something that the masses lacked. Moreover, prerevolution cooperation between elites took place in exile (Grewal 2020), something that most Tunisians living in the country did not experience. Second, the widespread repression of Tunisia's political secular and Islamist opposition groups pre-2011 led to the evolution of shared identities and reduced polarization (Nugent 2020). Since the majority of Tunisia's population was not a victim of such politically motivated repression, no similar identities were formed.

6.4. Conclusion

The chapter has attempted to answer two questions: first, whether there was a mass–elite discrepancy on the religious–secular political dimension in Tunisia between 2010 and 2016; and second, if it existed, to what extent did the Tunisian revolution, as a critical juncture, create such a discrepancy. Using data from the Arab Barometer survey waves of 2011, 2013, and 2016, and from three types of elite-level data (i.e., party manifestos, roll-call votes, and bill sponsorship), the chapter uncovered mass–elite discrepancy on the religious–secular dimension. Employing a critical juncture perspective, the chapter demonstrated that the 2011 revolution impacted Ennahda and led to its ideological moderation. The uncertainty of Tunisia's post-2011 political landscape incentivized political elites to come together to hold power during the democratic transition. This led to the emergence of a mass–elite discrepancy, which persisted through continuing elite-level socialization. The critical juncture, as an analytical concept, refines Lipset and Rokkan's structural determinism by showing that critical junctures open arenas for human agency that can later become path dependent.

In new democracies, Zielinski (2002, 200–201) argues, "the early rounds of electoral competition determine not only who wins or loses a particular election but also, and perhaps more importantly, which social cleavages will be depoliticized and which will be established as a permanent base for political conflict." This chapter used the case of Tunisia to demonstrate how elite choices are likely to be path dependent on the political dynamics created around the critical juncture as a result of elite-level socialization—one of the three key "locking-in" mechanisms specified in chapter 4. It is yet to be seen whether the current mass–elite discrepancy will continue, given the recent democratic backsliding in Tunisia.

Survey evidence has documented Tunisians' disillusionment with democracy and the ruling elites, and their increasing support for military intervention and outsider eclecticism (Albrecht et al. 2021). In fact, the public has voiced its dissatisfaction with the performance of Ennahda and Nidaa Tounes, including their inability to address many social and economic problems, in two ways. First, Tunisians took to the streets in 2018 over price hikes (Burke and Cordall 2018) and in 2021 over police brutality and unemployment (Cordall 2021). Second, and most importantly, Tunisians have started moving away from voting for Ennahda and Nidaa Tounes. In the 2019 parliamentary elections, both Ennahda and Nidaa Tounes lost many votes. While still the largest party represented in the parliament, Ennahda received only 19.63 percent of the votes compared to 27.79 percent in 2014. Nidaa Tounes suffered an even bigger loss as they only received 1.51 percent of the votes compared to 37.56 percent in 2014.

Such losses are largely due to two reasons: the death of Nidaa Tounes's founder and late president Beji Caid Essebsi, who died four months before elections, and the emergence of two new secular political parties, Heart of Tunisia and Tahya Tunis. This has also been coupled with the increasing popularity of older parties such as the Free Destourian Party and the Democratic Current. The 2019 election of the populist president Kais Saied was a clear signal about the struggles facing secular and Islamist political parties (Grubman 2022). Their failure to even form a unified front against the 2021 civilian coup by President Saied can be interpreted as a move away from previous elite moderation and the consolidation of another cleavage along the democratic–authoritarian dimension (Marzouki 2022).

The findings in this chapter not only have implications for Tunisia but also for the Middle East as a whole. Given the pervasive religious–secular divide, at both the mass and elite levels in several Arab countries, the Tunisian case shows that political elites during critical junctures are able to pacify long-standing divisions given the right combination of conditions prior to and during the critical juncture period. With a troubled democratic transition underway in Sudan and protests that have erupted in several other countries such as Algeria, Morocco, Lebanon, and Iraq, secular and Islamist elites have similar opportunities to pacify their divides. However, one lesson we can learn from this chapter is that unless the pacification attempts occur in parallel at the mass level, they are bound to create their own problem—the mass–elite representation gap.

Appendix 6.1. Questions Related to Mass-Level Attitudes

Table A6.1. Eight Questions Related to the Religious–Secular Dimension in Tunisia (2011–16)

1	The government and parliament should enact laws in accordance with Islamic law.
2	The government and parliament should enact penal laws in accordance with Islamic law.
3	The government and parliament should enact personal status laws (marriage, divorce) in accordance with Islamic law.
4	The laws of Tunisia should be based equally on sharia and the will of the people.
5	Preference for a religious political party over a nonreligious party.
6	Banks should be allowed to charge interest to meet the demands of the modern economy.
7	Tunisia is better off if religious people hold public positions in the state.
8	Democracy is a (Western) system that contradicts the teachings of Islam.

Source: Arab Barometer.

For ordinal questions such as those in Q605.2 in table A6.2, I combined respondents who strongly agreed or agreed to enact laws in accordance with Islamic law, anI combined respondents who strongly disagreed or disagreed, while excluding the "don't know" and "declined" answers. For Q605, I combined the respondents who answered that laws should be either entirely or mostly based on sharia, and those who answered that laws should be based entirely or mostly on the will of people, against those who prefer that laws should be based equally on the will of people.

Table A6.2. Sample Questions from the 2011 Arab Barometer Survey

Question code	Question	Type of answer
Q605.2 (2011 and 2013 surveys)	The government and the Shura Council should enact laws in accordance with Islamic law?	Ordinal: Likert scale (strongly agree, agree, disagree, strongly disagree, I don't know, declined to answer)
Q605 (2016 survey)	Which of the following statements is the closest to your point of view?	1. The laws of our country should be based entirely on the sharia. 2. The laws of our country should be based mostly on the sharia. 3. The laws of our country should be based equally on sharia and the will of the people. 4. The laws of our country should be based mostly on the will of the people. 5. The laws of our country should be based entirely on the will of the people. 98. I don't know 99. Declined to answer

Source: Arab Barometer.

Appendix 6.2. Calculating Elite Attitudes on the Religious–Secular Dimension

The religious–secular dimension is measured using the positional subcategories below from the manifestos of both Ennahda and Nidaa Tounes:

[*601 (National way of life: positive) + 603 (Traditional morality: positive)*]

(-)

[*602 (National way of life: negative) + 604 (Traditional morality: negative)*]

Notes

1. On July 25, 2021, amid antigovernment demonstrations, Tunisia witnessed a power grab by President Kais Saied whereby he suspended the parliament, dissolved the government, and later accumulated massive legislative powers (Tamburini 2022). According to V-Dem's Regimes of the World, Tunisia was an electoral *democracy* between 2012 and 2020, but since 2021 has been relegated to an electoral *autocracy* (Lührmann, Tannenberg, and Lindberg 2018).

2. Roy (2012, 6) argues that the Middle East is the only region where the strongest opposition groups are ideologically religious groups. He thinks that Islamists might be compared to the Spanish and Portuguese communist parties of the late 1970s.

3. The Arab Barometer is a nonpartisan research network that has been carrying out face-to-face public opinion surveys in the Arab world since 2006. More information can be found at http://www.arabbarometer.org

4. More information can be found on the Manifesto Project's website, https://manifesto-project.wzb.eu/

5. The full text of law proposals and legislative voting in the Tunisian parliament has been made available by Al-Bawsala (in Arabic and French) at https://majles.marsad.tn/ar/legislation/

6. For an overview of the causal logic of critical junctures and elite-level lock-in, see chapter 4 of this volume.

7. It is worth noting, however, that Tunisia remained an autocracy and never had democratic elections before 2011. It scored on average 0.2 on V-Dem's electoral democracy index during its postindependence history between 1956 until 2011.

8. This was one step in a longer moderation process that led Ennahda to disband its cultural and religious activities and to focus only on politics, and to calling its members "Muslim democrats" (Ghannouchi 2016).

References

Abdel Ghafar, Adel, and Bill Hess. 2018. *Islamist Parties in North Africa: A Comparative Analysis of Morocco, Tunisia, and Egypt*. Analysis paper. Doha: Brookings Doha Center.

Abdelrahman, Maha. 2009. "'With the Islamists?—Sometimes. With the State?—Never!' Cooperation between the Left and Islamists in Egypt." *British Journal of Middle Eastern Studies* 36 (1): 37–54. https://doi.org/10.1080/13530190902749556

Abduljaber, Malek, and Ann Arbor. 2018. "The Determinants of Political Cleavages in Jordan, Tunisia, and Yemen: An Analysis of Political Attitudes Structure in the Arab World." *Domes* 27 (1): 97–120. https://doi.org/10.1111/dome.12132

Abukhalil, As'ad. 1997. "Change and Democratisation in the Arab World: The Role of Political Parties." *Third World Quarterly* 18 (1): 149–64. https://doi.org/10.1080/01436599715109

Ahram Online. 2011. "Thousands in Tunisia Protest against Religious Fundamentalism." *Ahram Online*, 2011. http://english.ahram.org.eg/NewsContent/2/8/28272/World/Region/Thousands-in-Tunisia-protest-against-religious-fun.aspx

Ajroudi, Asma, and Ramy Allahoum. 2018. "Tunisia's Nidaa Tounes in Shambles amid Political Turbulence." 2018. *Al-Jazeera*, December 5. https://www.aljazeera.com/indepth/features/tunisia-nidaa-tounes-shambles-political-turbulence-181202090020299.html

al-Anani, Khalil. 2012. "Islamist Parties Post-Arab Spring." *Mediterranean Politics* 17 (3): 466–72. https://doi.org/10.1080/13629395.2012.725309

al-Anani, Khalil. 2019. "The Inclusion-Moderation Thesis: Muslim Brotherhood in

Egypt." In *Oxford Research Encyclopedia of Politics*. Oxford: Oxford University Press.

Albrecht, Holger, Dina Bishara, Michael Bufano, and Kevin Koehler. 2021. "Popular Support for Military Intervention and Anti-Establishment Alternatives in Tunisia: Appraising Outsider Eclecticism." *Mediterranean Politics* 28 (3): 1–25. https://doi .org/10.1080/13629395.2021.1974691

Albrecht, Holger, and Oliver Schlumberger. 2004. "Waiting for Godot: Regime Change without Democratization in the Middle East." *International Political Science Review* 24 (4): 371–92.

Albrecht, Holger, and Eva Wegner. 2006. "Autocrats and Islamists: Contenders and Containment in Egypt and Morocco." *Journal of North African Studies* 11 (2): 123–41. https://doi.org/10.1080/13629380600704688

Allani, Alaya. 2009. "The Islamists in Tunisia between Confrontation and Participation: 1980–2008." *Journal of North African Studies* 14 (2): 257–72. https://doi.org /10.1080/13629380902727510

Allinson, Jamie. 2015. "Class Forces, Transition and the Arab Uprisings: A Comparison of Tunisia, Egypt and Syria." *Democratization* 22 (2): 294–314. https://doi.org /10.1080/13510347.2015.1010812

Ayubi, Nazih. 1991. *Political Islam: Religion and Politics in the Arab World*. London: Routledge.

Bank, André, and Jan Busse. 2021. "MENA Political Science Research a Decade after the Arab Uprisings: Facing the Facts on Tremulous Grounds." *Mediterranean Politics* 26 (5): 1–24. https://doi.org/10.1080/13629395.2021.1889285

Bankov, Petar, and Sergiu Gherghina. 2020. "Post-Accession Congruence in Bulgaria and Romania: Measuring Mass-Elite Congruence of Opinions on European Integration through Mixed Methods." *European Political Science* 19 (4): 562–72.

Bayat, Asef, ed. 2013a. *Post-Islamism: The Changing Faces of Political Islam*. Oxford: Oxford University Press.

Bayat, Asef. 2013b. "The Arab Spring and Its Surprises." *Development and Change* 44 (3): 587–601. https://doi.org/10.1111/dech.12030

Bellin, Eva. 2013. *Drivers of Democracy: Lessons from Tunisia*. Middle East Brief 75. Waltham, MA: Crown Center for Middle East Studies, Brandeis University.

Ben Salem, Maryam. 2020. "'God Loves the Rich.' The Economic Policy of Ennahda: Liberalism in the Service of Social Solidarity." *Politics and Religion* 13 (4): 695–718. https://doi.org/10.1017/S1755048320000279

Ben Yahmed, Zeineb, and Sarah Yerkes. 2018. "God or Man in Tunisia?" *Diwan: Middle East Insights from Carnegie*. https://carnegie-mec.org/diwan/77113

Benstead, Lindsay J. 2015. "Why Do Some Arab Citizens See Democracy as Unsuitable for Their Country?" *Democratization* 22 (7): 1183–1208. https://doi.org/10 .1080/13510347.2014.940041

Bornschier, Simon. 2009. "Cleavage Politics in Old and New Democracies." *Living Reviews in Democracy* 1. http://www.cis.ethz.ch/content/dam/ethz/special-interest /gess/cis/cis-dam/CIS_DAM_2015/WorkingPapers/Living_Reviews_Democracy /Bornschier.pdf

Brooke, Steven. 2019. *Winning Hearts and Votes: Social Services and the Islamist Political Advantage*. Ithaca: Cornell University Press.

Browers, Michaelle. 2005. "The Secular Bias in Ideology Studies and the Case of Islamism." *Journal of Political Ideologies* 10 (1): 75–93. https://doi.org/10.1080/13 56931052000310254

Browers, Michaelle. 2009. *Political Ideology in the Arab World: Accommodation and Transformation.* Cambridge Middle East Studies 31. Cambridge: Cambridge University Press. https://doi.org/10.1017/CBO9780511626814

Brown, Nathan J. 2013. "Egypt's Failed Transition." *Journal of Democracy* 24 (4): 45–58.

Brown, Nathan J., Amr Hamzawy, and Marina Ottaway. 2006. *Islamist Movements and the Democratic Process in the Arab World: Exploring Gray Zones.* Washington, DC: Carnegie Endowment for International Peace.

Budge, Ian. 2003. "Validating the Manifesto Research Group Approach: Theoretical Assumptions and Empirical Confirmations." In *Estimating the Policy Position of Political Actors,* edited by Michael Laver, 50–65. London: Routledge.

Buehler, Matt. 2018. *Why Alliances Fail: Islamist and Leftist Coalitions in North Africa.* Syracuse, NY: Syracuse University Press.

Burke, Jason, and Simon Speakman Cordall. 2018. "Tunisia Rocked by Protests over Price Rises." *The Guardian,* January 10. https://www.theguardian.com/world/20 18/jan/10/tunisia-rocked-second-night-protests-over-price-rises-austerity-meas ures

Capoccia, Giovanni. 2016. "Critical Junctures." In *The Oxford Handbook of Historical Institutionalism,* edited by Karl-Orfeo Fioretos, Tulia G. Falleti, and Adam D. Sheingate, 89–106. Oxford: Oxford University Press.

Carroll, Royce, and Keith T. Poole. 2014. "Roll-Call Analysis and the Study of Legislatures." In *The Oxford Handbook of Legislative Studies,* edited by Shane Martin, Thomas Saalfeld, and Kaare W. Strøm, 103–25. Oxford: Oxford University Press.

Cavatorta, Francesco. 2015. "Salafism, Liberalism, and Democratic Learning in Tunisia." *Journal of North African Studies* 20 (5): 770–83. https://doi.org/10.1080/13 629387.2015.1081464

Cavatorta, Francesco, and Fabio Merone. 2013. "Moderation through Exclusion? The Journey of the Tunisian Ennahda from Fundamentalist to Conservative Party." *Democratization* 20 (5): 857–75. https://doi.org/10.1080/13510347.2013.80 1255

Cavatorta, Francesco, and Valeria Resta. 2020. "Beyond Quietism: Party Institutionalisation, Salafism, and the Economy." *Politics and Religion* 13 (4): 796–817. https:// doi.org/10.1017/S1755048320000292

Chhibber, Pradeep, and Mariano Torcal. 1997. "Elite Strategy, Social Cleavages, and Party Systems in a New Democracy." *Comparative Political Studies* 30 (1): 27–54. https://doi.org/10.1177/0010414097030001002

Ciftci, Sabri. 2013. "Secular-Islamist Cleavage, Values, and Support for Democracy and Shari'a in the Arab World." *Political Research Quarterly* 66 (4): 781–93. https://doi.org/10.1177/1065912912470759

Ciftci, Sabri, F. Michael Wuthrich, and Ammar Shamaileh. 2018. "Islam, Religious Outlooks, and Support for Democracy." *Political Research Quarterly* 115 (4). https://doi.org/10.1177/1065912918793233

Clark, Janine A. 2010. "Threats, Structures, and Resources: Cross-Ideological Coali-

tion Building in Jordan." *Comparative Politics* 43 (1): 101–20. https://doi.org/10
.5129/001041510X12911363510475

Cordall, Simon Speakman. 2021. "'Things Are Getting Worse': Tunisia Protests Rage
on as Latest Victim Named." *The Guardian*, January 27. https://www.theguardian
.com/global-development/2021/jan/27/things-are-getting-worse-tunisia-protests
-rage-on-as-latest-victim-named

Crystal, Jill. 1994. "Authoritarianism and Its Adversaries in the Arab World." *World
Politics* 46 (2): 262–89. https://doi.org/10.2307/2950675

Daher, Joseph. 2020. "Hezbollah, Neoliberalism and Political Economy." *Politics and
Religion* 13 (4): 719–47. https://doi.org/10.1017/S1755048320000218

Deegan-Krause, Kevin, and Zsolt Enyedi. 2010. "Agency and the Structure of Party
Competition: Alignment, Stability and the Role of Political Elites." *West European
Politics* 33 (3): 686–710. https://doi.org/10.1080/01402381003654742

Dinas, Elias, and Kostas Gemenis. 2010. "Measuring Parties' Ideological Positions
with Manifesto Data." *Party Politics* 16 (4): 427–50. https://doi.org/10.1177/13
54068809343107

Dunne, Michele, and Tarek Radwan. 2013. "Egypt: Why Liberalism Still Matters."
Journal of Democracy 24 (1): 86–100. https://doi.org/10.1353/jod.2013.0017.

Durac, Vincent. 2019. "Opposition Coalitions in the Middle East: Origins, Demise,
and Afterlife?" *Mediterranean Politics* 24 (4): 534–44. https://doi.org/10.1080/13
629395.2019.1639969

France24. 2018. "Thousands Protest Tunisia Gender Equality Proposals." *France24*,
November 8. https://www.france24.com/en/20180811-tunisia-gender-equality-re
form-homosexuality-fundamentalists-protest-demonstration-tunis

Gabel, Matthew J., and John D. Huber. 2000. "Putting Parties in Their Place: Inferring Party Left-Right Ideological Positions from Party Manifestos Data." *American
Journal of Political Science* 44 (1): 94–103. https://doi.org/10.2307/2669295

Ghannouchi, Rached. 2016. "From Political Islam to Muslim Democracy: The
Ennahda Party and the Future of Tunisia." *Foreign Affairs* 95: 58. https://www.for
eignaffairs.com/articles/tunisia/political-islam-muslim-democracy

Grewal, Sharan. 2020. "From Islamists to Muslim Democrats: The Case of Tunisia's
Ennahda." *American Political Science Review* 114 (2): 519–35. https://doi.org/10
.1017/S0003055419000819

Grubman, Nate. 2022. "Transition Arrested." *Journal of Democracy* 33 (1): 12–26.
https://doi.org/10.1353/jod.2022.0001

Hamid, Shadi. 2016. *Islamic Exceptionalism: How the Struggle over Islam Is Reshaping
the World*. New York: St. Martin's Press.

Haugbølle, Rikke Hostrup, and Francesco Cavatorta. 2011. "Will the Real Tunisian
Opposition Please Stand Up? Opposition Coordination Failures under Authoritarian Constraints." *British Journal of Middle Eastern Studies* 38 (3): 323–41. https://
doi.org/10.1080/13530194.2011.621696

Hoffman, Michael, and Amaney A. Jamal. 2014. "Religion in the Arab Spring:
Between Two Competing Narratives." *Journal of Politics* 76 (3): 593–606.

Hürriyet Daily News. 2012. "Thousands Rally for Shariah in Tunisia." *Hürriyet Daily
News*, March 26. https://www.hurriyetdailynews.com/thousands-rally-for-shariah
-in-tunisia-16907

International Foundation for Electoral Systems. 2014. "IFES Election Guide: Election for Tunisian Assembly of People's Representatives 2014." http://www.electiongui de.org/elections/id/2746/

Jamal, Amaney A. 2006. "Reassessing Support for Islam and Democracy in the Arab World? Evidence from Egypt and Jordan." *World Affairs* 169 (2): 51–63.

Jamal, Amaney A., and Mark Tessler. 2008. "The Democracy Barometers (Part II): Attitudes in the Arab World." *Journal of Democracy* 19 (1): 97–110. https://doi .org/10.1353/jod.2008.0004

Kraetzschmar, Hendrik, ed. 2014. *The Dynamics of Opposition Cooperation in the Arab World*. London: Routledge.

Kurzman, Charles, and Ijlal Naqvi. 2010. "Do Muslims Vote Islamic?" *Journal of Democracy* 21 (2): 50–63. https://doi.org/10.1353/jod.0.0163

Kurzman, Charles, and Didem Türkoğlu. 2015. "After the Arab Spring: Do Muslims Vote Islamic Now?" *Journal of Democracy* 26 (4): 100–109.

Laver, Michael, ed. 2003a. *Estimating the Policy Position of Political Actors*. London: Routledge.

Laver, Michael. 2003b. "Position and Salience in the Policies of Political Actors." In *Estimating the Policy Position of Political Actors*, edited by Michael Laver, 66–75. London: Routledge.

Laver, Michael, and John Garry. 2000. "Estimating Policy Positions from Political Texts." *American Journal of Political Science* 44 (3): 619. https://doi.org/10.2307 /2669268

Lührmann, Anna, Marcus Tannenberg, and Staffan I. Lindberg. 2018. "Regimes of the World (RoW): Opening New Avenues for the Comparative Study of Political Regimes." *Politics and Governance* 6 (1): 60–77. https://doi.org/10.17645/pag.v6 i1.1214

Lust, Ellen. 2011a. "Missing the Third Wave: Islam, Institutions, and Democracy in the Middle East." *Studies in Comparative International Development* 46 (2): 163– 90. https://doi.org/10.1007/s12116-011-9086-z

Lust, Ellen. 2011b. "Opposition Cooperation and Uprisings in the Arab World." *British Journal of Middle Eastern Studies* 38 (3): 425–34. https://doi.org/10.1080/135 30194.2011.621704

Mahoney, James. 2000. "Path Dependence in Historical Sociology." *Theory and Society* 29 (4): 507–48. https://doi.org/10.1023/A:1007113830879

Marks, Monica. 2014. *Convince, Coerce, or Compromise? Ennahdha's Approach to Tunisia's Constitution*. Analysis Paper 10. Doha: Brookings Doha Center.

Marks, Monica. 2015a. "Tunisia Opts for an Inclusive New Government." *Washington Post*, February 3. https://www.washingtonpost.com/news/monkey-cage/wp /2015/02/03/tunisia-opts-for-an-inclusive-new-government/?utm_term=.a56c16 c7f5b9

Marks, Monica. 2015b. "What Did Tunisia's Nobel Laureates Actually Achieve?" *Washington Post*, October 27. https://www.washingtonpost.com/news/monkey-ca ge/wp/2015/10/27/what-did-tunisias-nobel-laureates-actually-achieve/?utm_ter m=.4e5774e65cbe

Marzouki, Moncef. 2022. "Is Democracy Lost?" *Journal of Democracy* 33 (1): 5–11. https://doi.org/10.1353/jod.2022.0000

Masoud, Tarek. 2014. *Counting Islam: Religion, Class, and Elections in Egypt*. Problems of International Politics. Cambridge: Cambridge University Press. https://doi.org/10.1017/CBO9780511842610

McCarthy, Rory. 2015. "What Happens When Islamists Lose an Election?" *Washington Post*, June 11. https://www.washingtonpost.com/news/monkey-cage/wp/2015/06/11/what-happens-when-islamists-lose-an-election/?utm_term=.c5b21e c7d945

Mecham, Quinn. 2014. "Islamist Movements." In *The Arab Uprisings Explained: New Contentious Politics in the Middle East*, edited by Marc Lynch, 201–17. Columbia Studies in Middle East Politics. New York: Columbia University Press.

Murphy, Emma C. 2013. "The Tunisian Elections of October 2011: A Democratic Consensus." *Journal of North African Studies* 18 (2): 231–47. https://doi.org/10.1080/13629387.2012.739299

Nugent, Elizabeth R. 2020. *After Repression: How Polarization Derails Democratic Transition*. Princeton: Princeton University Press.

Pahwa, Sumita. 2017. "Pathways of Islamist Adaptation: The Egyptian Muslim Brothers' Lessons for Inclusion Moderation Theory." *Democratization* 24 (6): 1066–84. https://doi.org/10.1080/13510347.2016.1273903

Pierson, Paul. 2000. "Increasing Returns, Path Dependence, and the Study of Politics." *American Political Science Review* 94 (2): 251–67. https://doi.org/10.2307/2586011

Rahman, Natalya. 2018. "Democracy in the Middle East and North Africa: Five Years after the Arab Uprisings." Arab Barometer, October. http://www.arabbarometer.org/wp-content/uploads/Democracy_Public-Opinion_Middle-east_North-Africa_2018.pdf

Rasmussen, Anne, Stefanie Reher, and Dimiter Toshkov. 2019. "The Opinion-Policy Nexus in Europe and the Role of Political Institutions." *European Journal of Political Research* 58 (2): 412–34. https://doi.org/10.1111/1475-6765.12286

Robbins, Michael. 2015. "After the Arab Spring: People Still Want Democracy." *Journal of Democracy* 26 (4): 80–89.

Robbins, Michael. 2017. "Youth, Religion and Democracy after the Arab Uprisings: Evidence from the Arab Barometer." *Muslim World* 107 (1): 100–126. https://doi.org/10.1111/muwo.12180

Roy, Olivier. 2012. "The Transformation of the Arab World." *Journal of Democracy* 23 (3): 5–18. https://doi.org/10.1353/jod.2012.0056

Salloukh, Bassel F. 1997. "Studying Arab Politics: The End of Ideology or the Quest for Alternative Methods?" *Critique: Critical Middle Eastern Studies* 6 (10): 109–25. https://doi.org/10.1080/10669929708720103

Schwedler, Jillian. 2006. *Faith in Moderation: Islamist Parties in Jordan and Yemen*. Cambridge: Cambridge University Press. https://doi.org/10.1017/CBO9780511550829

Schwedler, Jillian. 2011. "Can Islamists Become Moderates? Rethinking the Inclusion-Moderation Hypothesis." *World Politics* 63 (2): 347–76. https://doi.org/10.1017/S0043887111000050

Shadid, Anthony. 2012. "Tunisia Faces a Balancing Act of Democracy and Religion." *New York Times*, January 31. https://www.nytimes.com/2012/01/31/world/africa/tunisia-navigates-a-democratic-path-tinged-with-religion.html

Solomon, Hussein, and Arno Tausch. 2021. "Political Islam in the Arab MENA Countries: The Evidence from the Arab Barometer (5) Data about the 'Unword' of Middle East Research?" In *Arab MENA Countries: Vulnerabilities and Constraints against Democracy on the Eve of the Global COVID-19 Crisis*, edited by Hussein Solomon and Arno Tausch, 182–232. Perspectives on Development in the Middle East and North Africa (MENA) Region. Singapore: Springer.

Stepan, Alfred C. 2012. "Tunisia's Transition and the Twin Tolerations." *Journal of Democracy* 23 (2): 89–103. https://doi.org/10.1353/jod.2012.0034

Tadros, Mariz. 2012. *The Muslim Brotherhood in Contemporary Egypt: Democracy Redefined or Confined?* Durham Modern Middle East and Islamic World Series 25. London: Routledge.

Talbert, Jeffery C., and Matthew Potoski. 2002. "Setting the Legislative Agenda: The Dimensional Structure of Bill Cosponsoring and Floor Voting." *Journal of Politics* 64 (3): 864–91. https://doi.org/10.1111/0022-3816.00150

Tamburini, Francesco. 2022. "'How I Learned to Stop Worrying and Love Autocracy': Kais Saied's 'Constitutional Self-Coup' in Tunisia." *Journal of Asian and African Studies* 58 (6). https://doi.org/10.1177/00219096221079322

Tappin, Ben M. 2023. "Estimating the Between-Issue Variation in Party Elite Cue Effects." *Public Opinion Quarterly* 86 (4): 862–85. https://doi.org/10.1093/poq/nfac052

Tepe, Sultan. 2019. "The Inclusion-Moderation Thesis: An Overview." In *Oxford Research Encyclopedia of Politics*. Oxford: Oxford University Press.

Tessler, Mark. 2002a. "Do Islamic Orientations Influence Attitudes toward Democracy in the Arab World? Evidence from Egypt, Jordan, Morocco, and Algeria." *International Journal of Comparative Sociology* 43 (3–5): 229–49. https://doi.org/10.1177/002071520204300302

Tessler, Mark. 2002b. "Islam and Democracy in the Middle East: The Impact of Religious Orientations on Attitudes toward Democracy in Four Arab Countries." *Comparative Politics* 34 (3): 337–54. https://doi.org/10.2307/4146957

Tessler, Mark. 2010. "Religion, Religiosity and the Place of Islam in Political Life: Insights from the Arab Barometer Surveys." *Middle East Law and Governance* 2 (2): 221–52. https://doi.org/10.1163/187633710X500748

Tessler, Mark, and Amaney A. Jamal. 2006. "Political Attitude Research in the Arab World: Emerging Opportunities." *PS: Political Science & Politics* 39 (3): 433–37. https://doi.org/10.1017/S1049096506060781

Tessler, Mark, Amaney A. Jamal, and Michael Robbins. 2012. "New Findings on Arabs and Democracy." *Journal of Democracy* 23 (4): 89–103.

Tezcür, Günes Murat. 2010. "The Moderation Theory Revisited." *Party Politics* 16 (1): 69–88. https://doi.org/10.1177/1354068809339536

Tobin, Sarah A. 2020. "Islamic Neoliberalism for Jordan's Islamic Action Front in Islamic Banking and Finance." *Politics and Religion* 13 (4): 768–95. https://doi.org/10.1017/S1755048320000073

van Hamme, Gilles, Alia Gana, and Maher Ben Rebbah. 2014. "Social and Socio-Territorial Electoral Base of Political Parties in Post-Revolutionary Tunisia." *Journal of North African Studies* 19 (5): 751–69. https://doi.org/10.1080/13629387.2014.974032

Wegner, Eva, and Francesco Cavatorta. 2019. "Revisiting the Islamist–Secular Divide: Parties and Voters in the Arab World." *International Political Science Review* 40 (4): 1–18. https://doi.org/10.1177/0192512118784225

Werner, Annika, Onawa Lacewell, and Andrea Volkens. 2015. *Manifesto Coding Instructions (5th Revised Edition)*. Berlin: Wissenschaftszentrum Berlin für Sozialforschung (WZB). https://manifestoproject.wzb.eu/down/papers/handbook_20 14_version_5.pdf

Zielinski, Jakub. 2002. "Translating Social Cleavages into Party Systems: The Significance of New Democracies." *World Politics* 54 (2): 184–211. https://doi.org/10 .1353/wp.2002.0005

Zuckerman, Alan. 1975. "Political Cleavage: A Conceptual and Theoretical Analysis." *British Journal of Political Science* 5 (2): 231–48. https://doi.org/10.1017/S00071 23400008140

CHAPTER 7

Lost in Translation?

Redemocratization and Mass–Elite Discrepancies in Indonesian Politics

Andreas Ufen

Party politics in Southeast Asian electoral democracies, that is, in countries such as the Philippines, Thailand (before and in between the last two military coups), East Timor, and Indonesia, is generally characterized by "money politics," clientelism, weak programmatic profiles, and a low degree of party and party-system institutionalization (Johnson Tan 2015; Aspinall et al. 2022; Ufen 2023b). Nevertheless, there are palpable differences. Indonesia's political parties are comparatively better socially rooted. The main reason for this is the establishment of large Islamic and nationalist organizations and parties during the colonial period and after independence, along with their reestablishment after democratization (Ufen 2008; Fossati 2022). The Indonesian party system was exceptional in the 1950s because a few big parties represented clearly definable social milieus. After 1998, and with the institution of free and fair elections since 1999, some cleavages reemerged, but parties are generally much less rooted in society than they used to be. Bread-and-butter issues are very important to voters, but it is almost impossible to link certain parties to specific economic policies. At the same time, Indonesia's populace is more devout than it was 10 or 20 years ago, and around a fifth of voters might vote for a decidedly Islamist party if given the option.

Today, religious issues divide and organize the ideological spectrum of Indonesian parties, but not in the way one might expect. According to Fossati (2020, 12), the religious cleavage "managed to survive almost 40 years of authoritarian rule, was a key driver of voting behaviour in 1999, and appears to be still influential as a driver of voting behaviour today" (see also Fossati 2019, 2022; Mujani et al. 2018, 199). Thus, a religious cleavage still structures the party system to an extent, but a substantial proportion of voters is only superficially represented by the existing Islamic parties (Pepinsky, Liddle, and Mujani 2018; Kompas 2019). The declining impact of political Islam in interparty relations has been paralleled by a growing radicalization of Islam in general because of global developments after September 11, but also because the democratization after the fall of Suharto opened up new avenues for organizing political activities. Because Islamic parties have moved to the political center since the early 2000s, many radical Muslims, who currently make up approximately 20 percent of the voters, see themselves as hardly represented by the existing political parties. These parties now have restricted capabilities to mobilize supporters, in contrast to religious mass organizations (Tomsa and Setijadi 2018; Nuraniyah 2020; Arifianto 2020).

Ahead of the gubernatorial elections in Jakarta in 2017 and during the presidential election campaigns in 2014 and 2019, conservative Islamic groups mobilized their supporters in large numbers against the Christian candidate in Jakarta and the supposedly more secular Joko Widodo, who has served as the Indonesian president since 2014 (Lim 2017; Tapsell 2020). All these cases were part of an illiberal turn in Indonesian politics (Bourchier 2019; Diprose, McRae, and Hadiz 2019; Power and Warburton 2020), and the discrepancy between a highly politicized civil society, on one side, and political parties and their candidates, on the other, was obvious. Demonstrations were not organized primarily by political parties, but by organizations such as the Front Pembela Islam (Islam Defenders Front), a radical and to some extent militant mass organization. Support for the Front Pembela Islam among Indonesian Muslims has hovered around 20 percent since 2004, reaching more than 22 percent in late 2016 (Mietzner and Muhtadi 2018, 487), resulting in a "mismatch between Indonesia's party system inhabited by moderate parties and the existence of a significant immoderate Muslim voting bloc" (Mietzner and Muhtadi 2018, 490).

This pattern is in line with the two-level survey results presented by Fossati et al. (2020) showing some striking discrepancies between voters and members of parliaments: 10 percent of the politicians think that sharia law should be implemented throughout Indonesia, in contrast to 39 percent of the voters; only 7 percent of politicians think that Islam should become Indonesia's only official religion, in contrast to 36 percent of the voters. Calculating the arithmetic mean of seven items capturing a pro-Islam orientation demonstrates that 46 percent of voters have such a tendency, in contrast to 35 percent of elites. Moreover, for all 10 compared parties, party supporters exhibited higher degrees of pro-Islam orientation than the parties they support (Fossati et al. 2020). Therefore, it can be said that the masses are more religious than elites and, at the same time, more divided.

This chapter sheds light on these dynamics and examines how key political dimensions are transformed during critical junctures. Indonesia is a particularly interesting case in this respect because, unlike in most other Southeast Asian countries, there are clearly detectable MEDs demonstrating strong variation over time for specific political dimensions.

The main arguments in this chapter are developed in three steps. First, this chapter briefly describes the Indonesian party system of the 1950s—the first critical juncture—and its unraveling and "simplification" under authoritarian regimes lasting until 1998. This part elucidates the unique rootedness of Indonesian political parties after national independence and the surprising ideological congruence of voters and politicians. MEDs were low against the backdrop of a politicized, mobilized electorate and political parties that to a large extent were able and willing to respond to voters' demands. The period of authoritarianism from 1957 to 1998 then served to stifle party and civil society activism.

Second, an analysis of party-system development from 1998, when Suharto stepped down, until the second parliamentary and first direct presidential elections in 2004, when the transition toward an electoral democracy ended, explains the path-determining effects of elite agency during this critical juncture. During this second critical juncture, increasing mass-level politicization on religious issues was neglected by elites, and a path toward patronage, or elite-dominated democracy, was chosen. Parties began to form grand coalitions with almost no effective opposition; they formed cartels built around the common interests of emaciating civil society's influence on party politics, decreasing accountability, and sharing in the spoils of office. Interparty competition was toned down until 2004, producing parties tending ideologically toward the center of the political spectrum. Arguably, the main dynamics of party politics were determined during the critical juncture from 1998 until 2004.

Third, since 2004 these dynamics have led to a further dealignment of political parties, also due to electoral reforms; the establishment of a new type of extremely personalized parties; and the growing commercialization of party politics. The 1998–2004 critical juncture has had self-reinforcing effects on intra-elite and mass–elite relations in line with the key path-dependency mechanisms specified in chapter 4.

7.1. Low Mass–Elite Discrepancy in the 1950s and the Subsequent Authoritarian Turn

In the 1950s, MEDs were much lower than today. We do not have survey data from the 1950s, and information on the institutionalization of political parties is scarce. But the literature (Feith 1962, 122–45; Hindley 1970; Mortimer 1982; Mietzner 2008) suggests that the party system ahead of and after the first national elections in 1955 was surprisingly strong in terms of the rootedness of political parties. Some even see parallels to the *verzuiling*, or pillarization, of political parties in the Netherlands. Not unlike parties in the Netherlands, Indonesian political parties were almost identical to, or were parts of, so-called *aliran*, or streams (or pillars) (Geertz 1963). Parties were divided by different degrees of religiosity and by their social bases with reference to a class cleavage. Of the four big parties, two were devoutly Islamic. The first was the traditionalist, rural-based Nahdatul Ulama (NU), which was simultaneously a religious organization that had been established in 1926 by religious scholars (*ulama*). These *ulama* were often owners or leaders, or both, of Islamic boarding schools (*pesantren*) that mainly existed in Javanese villages, meaning they had great influence in these religious rural milieus. The formation of the NU had been a reaction against the foundation of the modernist Muslim mass organization Muhammadiyah, which gave rise to the establishment of the second big Islamic party, Masyumi (Majelis Syuro Muslimin Indonesia, Consultative Council of Indonesian Muslims). Masyumi was strong in certain so-called Outer Islands (that is, beyond Java), and was more urban-based and dominated by the middle classes, meaning traders and professionals. In contrast to the NU and Masyumi, the two other big parties were either not very much interested in religion—the Communist Party of Indonesia (Partai Komunis Indonesia, PKI)—or stressed multireligiosity and tolerance—the Indonesian National Party (Partai Nasional Indonesia, PNI). A rather secularist (but not atheist) view was typical for the PNI, which was linked to the first Indonesian president, Sukarno.

The class cleavage particularly pitted the PKI against the NU and Masyumi, but also against the PNI, which had important followers within the powerful state bureaucracy. A strong bourgeoisie did not exist at that time. Even landholders usually owned small plots. Devout Muslims in Javanese villages voted for the NU; poor, nonorthodox Muslims for the PKI or PNI; better-off devout Muslims in the cities for Masyumi, and so forth. Although exact numbers are lacking, the existence of different social milieus and their direct connection to voters' choices is widely acknowledged (King

2003; Ufen 2008; Mietzner 2013). This does not mean that Indonesian parties were as strongly institutionalized as their European counterparts. They were rooted in milieus, but they were weak in terms of developing detailed policy proposals, diversifying party financing, building branches across the archipelago with active members at the grassroots, and in other areas. MEDs were low because the connection between voters and parties was quite strong. Attached to the four big parties was an array of peasant, labor, religious, women's, and other organizations, and ideologies such as nationalism, communism, socialism, and the notion of an Islamic state were very powerful (Feith 1962; Geertz 1963).

The rift between devout Muslims, on one hand, and nondevout Muslims as well as non-Muslims, on the other hand, came to a head in the late 1950s when in a constituent assembly the parties were unable to come to a consensus on the role of Islam to be enshrined in the constitution (Feith 1962). This led to the transition toward an authoritarian system under Sukarno, which lasted until the mid-1960s. After a military coup, a few hundred thousand people (communists or those alleged to be such) were killed by the military, with some support from orthodox Muslims (Hindley 1970). In parallel to the anticommunist massacres, the so-called New Order (1966–98), the military regime under General Suharto, was instituted. The party system consisted of the regime party Golkar (Golongan Karya, Functional Groups) and two smaller, at best half-opposition parties: the PDI (Partai Demokrasi Indonesia, Indonesian Democratic Party), which was to an extent the successor of the PNI and some Christian parties, and the PPP (Partai Persatuan Pembanguan, United Development Party), which represented, if not in name, the Islamic parties of the 1950s. Not just leftist and liberal democratic ideas, but also Islamism in its different versions was suppressed.[1] As specified in chapter 5, the authoritarian turn in Indonesia exemplifies how the process of political cleavage institutionalization often stalls in new democracies. Specifically, high levels of mass–elite congruence in both the economic and religious dimensions disappeared as a result of top-down repression during Indonesia's authoritarian periods.

7.2. Redemocratization and the Increased Mass–Elite Discrepancy: 1998–2004

7.2.1. The New Party System and the Religious–Secular Political Dimension

After the fall of Suharto in May 1998, a "protracted transition" (Malley 2000) toward electoral democracy began. It ended with the second parliamentary election (the first one was in June 1999) and first direct presidential election, both in 2004. In 2004, the military no longer enjoyed reserved seats in the national parliament, the People's Representative Council of the Republic of Indonesia (DPR) (see table 7.1), and most constitutional reforms were completed. During this critical juncture from 1998 until 2004, political parties abstained from offering strong programmatic incentives to voters and slowly agreed to build an informal cartel including moderate reformers and conservatives. Programmatic weakness and cartelization are still major characteristics of the Indonesian party system today.

From May 1998 until early 1999 approximately 200 new parties were established that had to connect themselves to the available political ideas at that time. One of the easiest ways to mobilize supporters was a revitalization of old legacies. Yet the major dynamics of the *aliran*-based or cleavage-based system of the first Indonesian democracy surfaced (Mujani, Liddle, and Ambardi 2018, 36–37). The annihilation of the political left during the New Order, the persistence of a deep suspicion toward leftist ideas even after the fall of Suharto, the fragmentation of the trade union movement, and the domination of most parties by New Order elites led to an under-representation of lower-class groups. Only a few very small labor parties lacking roots within the working class emerged, and they had no success in the 1999 elections.

In recent years, the discrepancy between existing social inequalities and the lack of political articulation has been due to the incapability of the myriad of trade unions to translate grievances into party politics. The labor movement has had an impact on certain policies (Caraway and Ford 2019) and has been at times quite active, but it is fragmented and lacks close links to political parties (Lane 2019). Since the class cleavage has been blurred or almost annihilated, what has been left is the politicization of religious identities.

Religion is still a kind of overarching cleavage, whereas economic and social dimensions are relatively weak (Mietzner 2013; Fossati 2019; Fossati et al. 2020). In the 1950s, two major parties (NU and Masyumi) campaigned on an Islamist platform, and the downfall of the first democracy in Indonesia was also due to the stalemate in the Constitutional Assembly (Konstituante) of the mid-1950s that pitted Islamists against secularists. The suppression of Islamism during the New Order in combination with a general taming of political Islam effected the rise of a range of Islamic parties that refrained from radically politicizing religious issues. Though voting patterns still indicated the perseverance of certain voter milieus connected to specific regions and ethnic and religious groups, the deep-seated division of these milieus along *aliran* had been substituted by weaker allegiances of voters to parties. The elections in 1999 indicated a continuity of *aliran* politics, though in a significantly altered way. Comparing election results from 1955 and 1999, King (2003) found substantial continuities.

Yet most major parties did not politicize religious issues. Although a majority of Indonesians were Muslims, it is striking that the biggest parties in Indonesia were by name and with regard to their platforms rather secular in 1998–99. They were still religious but referred primarily to the "state philosophy" of Pancasila[2] and tended to respect the peaceful coexistence of different religions in the country. The PDI-P (Partai Demokrasi Indonesia Perjuangan, Indonesian Democratic Party of Struggle) was the successor of the PNI, and its chairwoman, Megawati Sukarnoputri, the daughter of Sukarno, was the towering figure in the party. The PDI-P had many non-Muslims among its cadres and supporters and was the most obvious propagator of the Pancasila. Golkar, the somewhat reformed successor of the New Order regime party, also adhered to the Pancasila, but in terms of its orientation was less rooted in specific milieus or ideological traditions.

Political parties that existed during the New Order and profited from name recognition were most successful in 1999 (see table 7.1). Together, Golkar, the PDI-P, and the PPP gained 67 percent of the votes. Golkar and the PPP were perceived as rather conservative (together with the military faction that was given 38 seats in the DPR without taking part in the parliamentary elections). Islamic parties could have revived the legacies of political Islam in the 1950s. But major Muslim leaders decided to establish moderate—to an extent even secular—parties such as the PKB (Partai Kebangkitan Bangsa, National Awakening Party) and the PAN (Partai Amanat Nasional, National Mandate Party).

The PKB and the PAN were still linked to religious mass organizations (NU and Muhammadiyah, respectively). However, the respective names of the PKB and the PAN referred to a "national awakening" and a "national mandate"; in this way, they abstained from using the symbols and narratives of political Islam. Both the towering figure within the PKB, Abdurrahman Wahid, who belonged to the most prominent *ulama* family within the NU and was Indonesian president from 1999 to 2001, and Amien Rais, the former chairman of Muhammadiyah and then a major leader of the PAN, pursued a strategy of orientation toward a Pancasila-based religious tolerance. Wahid was a so-called neomodernist who had long promoted a prodemocratic, inclusive Islam. Amien Rais was a modernist Muslim who in 1998–99 was also among the prodemocratic Muslims. Thus, the PKB and the PAN, together with the NU and Muhammadiyah, were instrumental in bridging divides between political Islam and secularists.

Table 7.1. Results of Parliamentary Elections since 1999

Party	1999 Votes (%)	1999 Seats	2004 Votes (%)	2004 Seats	2009 Votes (%)	2009 Seats	2014 Votes (%)	2014 Seats	2019 Votes (%)	2019 Seats
PDI-P	33.8	153	18.5	109	14.0	95	18.9	109	19.3	128
Golkar	22.5	120	21.6	128	14.4	107	14.7	91	12.3	85
Gerindra	—	—	—	—	4.5	26	11.8	73	12.6	78
PKB	12.6	51	10.6	52	4.9	27	9.0	49	9.7	58
NasDem	—	—	—	—	—	—	6.7	39	9.1	58
PD	—	—	7.5	57	20.8	150	10.2	61	7.8	54
PK/PKS	1.4	7	7.3	45	7.9	57	6.8	40	8.2	50
PAN	7.1	34	6.4	52	6.0	43	7.6	47	6.8	44
PPP	10.7	58	8.2	58	5.3	37	6.5	35	4.5	19
Total		500		550		560		560		575

Source: Data from Election Commission.
Note: Only parties represented until 2019. In 1999, 38 seats were reserved for the military. Party acronyms are as follows:
PDI-P = Partai Demokrasi Indonesia—Perjuangan (Indonesian Democratic Party—Struggle)
Golkar = Partai Golongan Karya (Party of Functional Groups)
Gerindra = Partai Gerakan Indonesia Raya (Great Indonesia Movement Party)
PKB = Partai Kebangkitan Bangsa (National Awakening Party)
NasDem = Partai Nasional Demokrat (National Democratic Party)
PD = Partai Demokrat (Democratic Party)
PK/PKS = Partai Keadilan Sejahtera (Prosperous Justice Party); 1999: PK = Partai Keadilan (Justice Party)
PAN = Partai Amanat Nasional (National Mandate Party)
PPP = Partai Persatuan Pembangunan (United Development Party)

To be sure, some less moderate Islamic parties also arose. In the first few years after the 1999 elections until around 2004, the PPP, the direct successor of the New Order party of the same name, and the PBB (Partai Bulan Bintang, Crescent Star Party), which defined itself as the successor of Masyumi, were perceived as Islamist (Slater 2004, 308). The PPP and the PBB advocated for the inclusion of the so-called Jakarta Charter in the constitution. This is a short passage demanding the introduction of Islamic law, which means in this case a sharia-based penal code. Debates about the Jakarta Charter had been ongoing since 1945, but in 2002 a great majority of members of the MPR (Majelis Permusyawaratan Rakyat, People's Consultative Assembly) voted against its inclusion, and since then the issue has been mostly considered settled. The PBB was not able to enter Parliament after the introduction of a minimum threshold, that is, 2 percent, and the PPP has since become a more moderate party.

The PK (Partai Keadilan [Justice Party]; since 2004, Partai Keadilan Sejahtera [Prosperous Justice Party, PKS]), founded by Islamist students previously belonging to a grassroots opposition movement under the New Order, became an example of a party directly representing a new urban middle class and conservative or even reactionary Muslim clientele. But over the years the PKS has become part of the cartel and moved toward the center of the political spectrum (Tomsa 2012, 2019).

All in all, the moderation of the religious–secular political dimension in party politics has been evident. To a certain extent, this can be attributed to the fragmentation of political Islam due to traditional rivalries and decades-long enfeebling by New Order authoritarianism. But, more fundamentally, it had to do with the decisions made by major Muslim leaders not to stress exclusivism. The subsequent section expounds on how key political actors in Indonesia decided to mute the mass-level politicization demand on religious issues during its redemocratization period.

7.2.2. The Transition and the Formation of a Cartel

Critical junctures can be characterized "by the adoption of a particular institutional arrangement from among two or more alternatives. These junctures are 'critical' because once a particular option is selected it becomes progressively more difficult to return to the initial point when multiple alternatives were still available" (Mahoney 2000, 513). The contingent historical events are followed by path-dependent sequences and "cannot be explained on the basis of prior historical conditions" (Mahoney 2000, 507). The end of an authoritarian system and the rapid installation of an electoral democracy is such a critical juncture, during which political actors dispose of a range of viable options not fully determined structurally (Lipset and Rokkan 1967, 54; Peters, Pierre, and King 2005, 1276).

Reflecting the top-down democratization process often observed in new democracies (see Bornschier in this volume, chapter 5), in Indonesia the transition was pacted and based on compromises from the beginning. A pact is defined as "an explicit, but not always publicly explicated or justified, agreement among a select set of actors which seeks to define (or, better, to redefine) rules governing the exercise of power on the basis of mutual guarantees for the 'vital interests' of those entering into it" (O'Donnell and Schmitter 1986, 37). The pacted transition in Indonesia was helpful in avoiding a sudden breakdown of social order, preventing nationwide violence, and not deepening existing social and religious cleavages within the emerging party system. In this sense, similar to the Tunisian case described in the previous chapter, the pacification of the religious–secular political dimension by Indonesian party elites can be understood as an attempt to stabilize the political order in the middle of an uncertain political landscape. But O'Donnell and Schmitter (1986, 43) warn that pacts are typically negotiated by "established and often highly oligarchical" groups seeking to "limit accountability to wider publics" (see also Karl 1990 and Hagopian 1996). And, indeed, the transition in Indonesia was to a large extent steered "from above": "The groups which were strongest organizationally were those which had flourished by working within or around the New Order's rules. They tended to be the most risk-averse, the most likely to accept compromise with the regime, and the least likely to have clear democratic goals and ideology. Groups that possessed clear democratic goals, and were prepared to mobilize their followers to realize them, were fragmented, suppressed, and marginalized" (Aspinall 2005, 240).

Therefore, civil society did not play a large role after the fall of Suharto, and old elites cooperated with new emerging elites to bring about a smooth, but not radical democratization (Ufen 2023c). Arguably, those promoting much more fundamental democratic reforms soon realized that they had to be part of the cartel in order to succeed. Only some minor parties without the organizational, financial, and name-recognition advantages of older parties had clearer platforms.

Rather than competing with clear policy alternatives over issues resonating with voter demand, party elites took the path of forming a political cartel—a state of interparty collusion in which key parties utilize state resources to maintain their position within the political system (Katz and Mair 1995). An elite cartel came into existence step by step. In November 1998, long before the foundational elections in June 1999, the main opposition party leaders Megawati Sukarnoputri, Abdurrahman Wahid, and Amien Rais (as well as the sultan of Yogyakarta), pressured by student activists, issued the moderate reformist "Ciganjur Declaration" (Horowitz 2013, 46–48). In general, they supported President B. J. Habibie, but shied away from radical Reformasi demands directed against Suharto, the generals, and their cronies. The military under Wiranto successfully mediated between Habibie and the Ciganjur group. The next step, after rather conservative or moderate parties had succeeded in the June 1999 parliamentary elections, was the creation of a very broad coalition in favor of Abdurrahman Wahid in October 1999. After the parliamentary elections, there were no clear majorities and it turned out to be very difficult to forge coalitions. There was a rivalry between traditionalist and modernist Islam (Abdurrahman Wahid from the NU versus Amien Rais from Muhammadiyah), and between conservatives and reformers, but also between supporters of a stronger role for political

Islam and secularists (in Indonesian parlance also often denoted as "nationalists"). The complex power negotiations in 1999 that led to Abdurrahman Wahid being elected the Indonesian president finally gave rise to an oversized coalition incorporating as many forces as possible. The seemingly only solution to the problem of the lack of a clear majority was to create a broad coalition in the DPR and MPR that also included status quo forces such as Golkar and the military factions. Slater (2014, 306) concludes: "Ironically, strenuous party-led mobilization along the regime and religious cleavages in the 1999 national election and MPR session had produced a ruling coalition utterly devoid of clear convictions, or even leanings, on either the regime or religious divide."

In 1998–99, most MPs were soft-liners leaning toward reforming the New Order and manufacturing a form of democracy, but not one that would radically change Indonesia. Therefore, they tried to restrain trade unions, radical reformers within civil society, and Islamists from influencing politics. And, indeed, after the 1999 elections, the new political elite had nothing to fear from the radical student movement and, in general, an opposition that had been able to play a decisive role in 1998 in bringing down the Suharto regime. Planned reforms of the military, initially strongly pushed by Abdurrahman Wahid, were watered down. Widespread corruption, which even intensified after the breakdown of the closed authoritarian New Order, was not forcefully fought against, and the bureaucracy with all its inbuilt conservatism remained more or less the same as under Suharto.

After 1998, all presidents were directly involved in party politics; they needed strong partisan support in order to be elected by the MPR (Abdurrahman Wahid and Megawati) or to be selected as a presidential candidate by coalitions of parties (since 2004). Indonesia exhibited a strange form of presidentialism. Under the New Order, Suharto was elected by the MPR, that is, indirectly, but because the DPR was almost powerless, the system was similar to a form of super-presidentialism. After 1998, the DPR and the MPR gained enormous power, whereas the role of the president was not well defined. Actually, the first president who was elected by the new MPR in 1999, Abdurrahman Wahid, perceived his role as that of a strong president, but in reality he was accountable on a yearly basis to the MPR (Horowitz 2013, 99–108). Wahid's own party, the traditionalist Muslim PKB, had only 51 out of 500 seats in the DPR. Moreover, his role and his power as president were ill defined by the constitution. This as well as his at times stubborn behavior (and his downsized second cabinet from 35 to 26 minister positions in August 2000) enraged a great majority of MPs who viewed the cartel as being in danger. This led to Wahid's ouster by the MPR in 2001.

His successor, Megawati Sukarnoputri from the PDI-P, was aware of her precarious position and also established a rainbow coalition. Megawati needed a broad coalition because her rather secular party had to hedge against an Islamic coalition that could potentially form to oppose her at a time when a president was not constitutionally secured against impeachment. During these years, a specific pattern of coalition-building was established. The ensuing cartel has been characterized by the openness of every significant party to share power with every other one "even when those parties have profound ideological differences" (Slater 2018, 29). The whole cartelization process vindicates the observation that "the salience of particular dimensions of competition are shaped not only by competition *between* parties, but also by ongoing processes of coalition formation and maintenance that dictate processes *internal* to parties and *among* party elites, which can be significantly shaped by historical patterns of party formation and original coalition construction" (Riedl 2016, 230).

Slater points to informal norms that arose within a "small and familiar handful of party and military elites" settling "their respective fractions' recurrent distributional disputes entirely in opaque rather than transparent settings" (Slater 2004, 73) in order to reduce "pressure on the government to respond to societal pressures." This "promiscuous power-sharing primarily arose from 1999 to 2004 because parliamentary parties had the power to demand it; it has persisted since 2004, even while evolving and abating, because strengthened presidents have had a strategic interest in maintaining it" (Slater 2018, 32).

From 1998 until 2004, party elites were able to centralize decision-making and to build elite-centered party apparatuses with weak links to civil society (at least much weaker than in the 1950s). However, was the political cartelization bound to happen? By no means. Critical junctures are not deterministic but open a window of opportunity for political agents. During the 1998–2004 critical juncture, other options were available to political elites in Indonesia. Specifically, if civil society activists and politicians, for example the Ciganjur Four, had worked closely together, their influence on the transition would have been much stronger. If Abdurrahman Wahid had been more accommodating as president, there would not have been an impeachment, and a different relationship between government and the opposition might have been institutionalized. Furthermore, even with a pacted democratization driven by elites, the MED observed on the religious–secular dimension was not destined to occur. Another Muslim-majority Southeast Asian country, Malaysia, can serve as a counterfactual in this case. In the 1970s, the National Front (Barisan Nasional), a multiethnic and multireligious coalition of political parties led by the United Malays National Organization, included many former opposition parties and tried to subdue religious and ethnic conflicts after so-called racial riots in 1969. But in contrast to Indonesia, this led more and more to a politicization of religion and ethnicity in party politics, especially when the Islamist Parti Islam Se-Malaysia (PAS, Islamic Party of Malaysia) decided to leave the National Front after a few years (Ufen 2009). The National Front obviously did not have the capability to set in motion self-reinforcing processes to bind together the coalition member parties for a long time.

Despite other alternative choices, Indonesian elites decided upon a car-telized coalition, and party elites learned to overcome internal ideological divisions. The supposedly reactionary Golkar stressed its democratic creden-tials as did the PKB and the PAN. But the coalition-building brought all these parties closer to each other, and the existing ideological differences, which were already not very strong, weakened even more. When the pro-democratic party elites realized that radical reforms led to strong resistance by conservatives, they moderated their stances. In the same vein, their opposition to introducing the Jakarta Charter, combined with their need to become part of the coalitions at different levels in order to get patronage, led parties such as the PPP and the PKS to tone down their Islamist platforms (Buehler 2013; Tomsa 2012, 2019). The result was a centripetal party sys-tem in contrast to the centrifugal one of the 1950s (Mietzner 2008).

The path of forming rainbow coalitions and of moderating party plat-forms has been pursued ever since. In 2004, the Partai Demokrat imme-diately won 7.5 percent of the popular votes (see table 7.1). When Susilo Bambang Yudhoyono won the direct presidential elections against Megawati a few weeks later, he again resorted to extensive power-sharing, thus cement-ing the party cartel. In the following years, the PDI-P turned into a hesitant opposition party, although Susilo tried to bring the party into the cabinet. Yet this PDI-P opposition was modest and mostly based on Megawati's dis-appointment in Susilo, whom she perceived as a traitor because he had left her cabinet in order to become a presidential candidate.

7.3. The Glaring Islamism MED in Recent Years

MED persisted even after the critical juncture period in Indonesia. Here, I will explain the reinforcement path of the cartelized political dynamic, which increasingly has become intertwined with a personalistic, oligarchic, and commercialized form of politics.

The protracted transition in Indonesia guaranteed the lasting impact of old elites such as the military, the bureaucracy, big business, and New Order politicians (Malley 2000; Aspinall 2005; Buente and Ufen 2009; Horowitz 2013, 89–92). These old elites were strong enough to stave off radical civil society demands. Yet they also realized that the system of government was still imperfect, and in 2002 they voted for a much more candidate-centered electoral system. Thus, since 2004, presidents have been elected directly, and impeachment has been made very difficult. Since 2005, mayors, district heads, and governors have also been elected directly.[3] The regime elite had to institute reforms after the standoff between Wahid and the political parties and parliaments in 2001. The constitutional amendments and the introduction of a full presidential system were a reaction to the highly problematic and undefined relation between president and parliament, but also to the growing MEDs (Horowitz 2013, 108–22).

The first directly elected president, Susilo Bambang Yudhoyono, was highly popular and easily won a second term in 2009. The second directly elected president, Joko Widodo (Jokowi), was, arguably, even more popular. But did his presidency help to decrease MEDs? It did so with reference to voters who felt better represented by somebody who was not a member of the old New Order elites (such as Habibie, Wahid, Megawati, Susilo, and so forth), but had a lower-middle-class background and spoke the language of ordinary Indonesians (Mietzner 2015; Bland 2020). Still, Jokowi's party, the PDI-P, supported him, but he was not very closely linked to party elites. Thus, presidentialism links voters to the president, but not necessarily to political parties. However, presidents cannot be completely detached from the influence of parties. For instance, the selection of presidential candidates has guaranteed the enduring hold of political parties on this process. Under the 2008 Presidential Election Law, a candidate pair must be nominated by a party or coalition that won at least 25 percent of the popular vote or 20 percent of seats in the DPR. In 2004 there were five pairs of candidates for the direct presidential elections (with two left in the second round), and in 2009 there were three pairs (with Susilo Bambang Yudhoyono winning outright in the first round); today, the number of candidate pairs is usually reduced to two contenders (Prabowo Subianto and Jokowi in 2014 and 2019).

Reflecting the influence of parties, minimum winning coalitions have not been viable choices for presidents. Before Joko Widodo won the 2014 presidential elections, he announced he would end the tradition of horse-trading and large coalitions, but after his victory he included some controversial former generals in his cabinet and inner circle. In 2016 he reshuffled his cabinet and widened his coalition. After his victory in 2019, again against Prabowo Subianto (Gerindra), the Partai Demokrat made overtures to be included in his new cabinet; and even with Gerindra and Prabowo, his staunch and populist adversary only weeks before, he started to negotiate about power-sharing agreements. Prabowo attended the PDI-P congress in August 2019 together with Jokowi and Megawati in a peaceful atmosphere, and a new power-sharing agreement was possible.

The path of cartelization, very weak opposition, and patronage sharing was somewhat shaken by full presidentialism, which enabled a connection between voters and a directly elected president. Yet political actors immediately conformed to new electoral circumstances (Ufen 2023a) and muted the potential MED-decreasing effect of the new electoral rules. Adaptations encompassed the formation of a new type of personalistic, oligarchic, and programmatically shallow party. What have emerged are these presidential vehicles with vague platforms that are totally dependent on powerful, usually rich, men at the top. These vehicle parties are also outgrowths of the general dealignment of political parties (Fossati 2020; Gethin and Thanasak 2021). The Partai Demokrat was established ahead of the 2004 elections in order to give Susilo Bambang Yudhoyono the opportunity to take part in the presidential polls. Other such parties are Partai NasDem under media mogul Surya Paloh, Hanura under former general Wiranto, and Gerindra under Prabowo Subianto.

Direct elections and elections of MPs via open candidate lists, a system that was fully established in 2009, together with the rise of pollsters, have dramatically increased costs (Mietzner 2013, 207–33). Different forms of patronage and vote-buying have become obvious (Shin 2015; Aspinall and Sukmajati 2016; Aspinall and Berenschot 2019). Every third Indonesian was personally exposed to vote-buying in 2014, whereas this practice did not play a palpable role in 1999 (Muhtadi 2019). After often difficult negotiations, parties are paid *mahar politik*, or a "political dowry," by candidates who want to be nominated. Legislators can intervene in tendering processes and can impact budgets, and in some cases they may use so-called aspiration funds to deliver pork-barrel projects to voters in their constituencies. Patronage goods and services such as welfare programs "remain largely outside the control of political parties, but are instead distributed at the discretion of bureaucrats, community-level elected officials, or by politicians whose party links are weak" (Aspinall and Berenschot 2019, 13). The growing commercialization and dealignment is well reflected by weakened party identification, which was measured at a rate of almost 90 percent in 1999, fell to approximately 30 percent two to three years later, climbed to 50–60 percent in 2004, and fell to less than 20 percent in 2014. In addition, party membership has declined from about 10 percent to around 5 percent in recent years (Kenny 2018, 39).

During the aforementioned elite-level lock-in process, the three elite-level lock-in mechanisms analyzed by Shim (chapter 4) were all present: the pre-election deliberate selection of candidates, who were forced to play by the rules of the cartel because they needed money to finance their candidacies and campaigns; postelection socialization within a culture of decision-making behind closed doors, avoiding open conflict, excluding civil society activists, and finding compromises to further encapsulate the elite; and the marginalization of opponents within political parties and society at large—whistleblowers and fundamental reformers are isolated, and electoral reforms result in the reduction of the number of political parties.

7.4. Concluding Remarks

During Indonesia's first critical juncture—in the 1950s—religious MEDs were low because the NU and Masyumi directly translated traditionalist and modernist ideas and sentiments into their party systems. Although they were also partners in coalitions with non-Muslim partners, each clung to its platform and both parties advocated for the Jakarta Charter in the constituent assembly in the mid-1950s. Therefore, it seems reasonable to state that discrepancies between party leaders and the grassroots, and between parties and voters, were low at that time. After redemocratization, MEDs between voters and political parties in the parliamentary elections were not low like in the 1950s. Because some major Islamic parties started to stress their Islamic credentials much less, catch-all parties like Golkar had emerged, and the linkages between parties and voters via mass organizations were much looser than in 1955. Subsequently, the rise of a new type of vehicle party, the commercialization of party politics, clientelism, and vote-buying contributed to dealignment and increasing MEDs.

Political parties represent certain social milieus, but coalition-building is determined by power-sharing and (from the perspective of the president) by the attempt to preclude the emergence of a very strong opposition that could derail the government. This does not mean that political parties do not differ in terms of ideology, especially with respect to religious issues, but this plays a role only from time to time, leaving many orthodox and conservative Muslim voters disillusioned. There is a conspicuous and growing MED related to radical Islam. Particularly in recent years, this has had a marked influence on the outcome of direct local and presidential elections. These Islamists have an impact via street demonstrations on direct elections—and to an extent also on party politics—but the cleavage between a more moderate and a radical Islam is only tentatively translated into party politics. This was not the result of a "natural" process. The comparison with parties in the 1950s shows that rooted parties with close links to civil society existed before.

During the second critical juncture of transition and the formation of the new party system from 1998 until 2004, a cartel was built based on the willingness to share patronage. The early formation of a cartel-like pact has set in motion self-reinforcing sequences, as oligarchs have taken power within political parties (Robison and Hadiz 2004; Winters 2013). Oligarchs were able to do so not only because they had the money, but because political parties adapted to the clientelistic, money-driven, and cartelized environment. Once a cartel has been formed, actors develop an interest in pursuing this path. Although at times partisan opposition in parliament arose, this was only temporary or was rather shallow; examples include the personal rivalries between Megawati and Yudhoyono, or the period before Jokowi reshuffled his cabinet from 2014 until 2016.

Especially with the introduction of direct elections at the local level and of a presidential system with direct presidential elections, but also due to other factors, a dealignment has progressed. It has led to much stronger MEDs between voters and parliamentary elites than before. Direct elections at all levels have led to rising costs. This again has elevated the role of the oligarchs. The direct elections also triggered a much more central role for surveys and have forced politicians to directly respond to voter demands ahead of and after elections using clientelistic means. In Indonesia, party cartelization is still predominant and has a deleterious effect on vertical accountability. Even after the highly polarized presidential elections in 2019, President Jokowi offered to share power with Prabowo, who had been his greatest adversary. Meanwhile, Joko Widodo further broadened his grand coalition. With the entry of PAN, the coalition expanded its majority from 74.3 percent, or 427 seats, to 81.9 percent, or 471 seats in the DPR (Supriatma 2021). The cartelized political elite had no difficulties in rushing the controversial Job Creation Act, or Omnibus Law 2020, through parliament without adequately consulting the public. It contains revisions to 79 existing laws and has sparked unprecedented nationwide protests (Lane 2021). In this case, the cartel was again firmly united, civil society was marginalized, and protesters were ruthlessly silenced.

Notes

1. Islamism is defined here as the attempt to establish an Islamic state, including a penal code based on sharia law. This is in contrast to Islamic parties that take a much more moderate approach.

2. The Pancasila ("Five Pillars") were devised by Sukarno and respect several religions that are defined as monotheistic and equal. Even today, Indonesia is not an Islamic state, but it is also not secular. Atheism and adherence to unrecognized religions are banned.

3. Moreover, the introduction of electoral thresholds has reduced the number of parties in parliament from 21 in 1999 to 9 in 2019.

References

Ambardi, Kuskridho. 2008. "The Making of the Indonesian Multiparty System: A Cartelized Party System and Its Origin." PhD diss., Ohio State University.

Arifianto, Alexander. 2020. "Rising Islamism and the Struggle for Islamic Authority in Post-Reformasi Indonesia." *TRaNS: Trans-Regional and National Studies of Southeast Asia* 8 (1): 37–50.

Aspinall, Edward. 2005. *Opposing Suharto: Compromise, Resistance, and Regime Change in Indonesia*. Stanford: Stanford University Press.

Aspinall, Edward, and Ward Berenschot. 2019. *Democracy for Sale: Elections, Clientelism, and the State in Indonesia*. Ithaca: Cornell University Press.

Aspinall, Edward, and Mada Sukmajati, ed. 2016. *Electoral Dynamics in Indonesia: Money Politics, Patronage and Clientelism at the Grassroots*. Singapore: NUS Press.

Aspinall, Edward, Meredith L. Weiss, Allen Hicken, and Paul D. Hutchcroft, eds. 2022. *Mobilizing for Elections: Patronage and Political Machines in Southeast Asia*. Cambridge: Cambridge University Press.

Bland, Ben. 2020. *Man of Contradictions: Joko Widodo and the Struggle to Remake Indonesia*. Melbourne: Penguin Books.

Bourchier, David M. 2019. "Two Decades of Ideological Contestation in Indonesia: From Democratic Cosmopolitanism to Religious Nationalism." *Journal of Contemporary Asia* 49 (5): 713–33.

Buehler, Michael. 2013. "Revisiting the Inclusion-Moderation Thesis in the Context of Decentralized Institutions: The Behavior of Indonesia's Prosperous Justice Party in National and Local Politics." *Party Politics* 19 (2): 210–29.

Buente, Marco, and Andreas Ufen. 2009. "The New Order and Its Legacy: Reflections on Democratization in Indonesia." In *Democratization in Post-Suharto Indonesia*, edited by Marco Buente and Andreas Ufen, 3–30. London: Routledge.

Caraway, Teri, and Michele Ford. 2019. "Indonesia's Labor Movement and Democratization: Activists in Transition." In *Activists in Transition: Progressive Politics in Democratic Indonesia*, edited by Thushara Dibley and Michele Ford, 61–78. Ithaca: Cornell University Press.

Diprose, Rachael, David McRae, and Vedi R. Hadiz. 2019. "Two Decades of Reformasi in Indonesia: Its Illiberal Turn." *Journal of Contemporary Asia* 49 (5): 691–712.

Feith, Herbert. 1962. *The Decline of Constitutional Democracy in Indonesia*. Ithaca: Cornell University Press.

Fossati, Diego. 2019. "The Resurgence of Ideology in Indonesia: Political Islam, *Aliran* and Political Behaviour." *Journal of Current Southeast Asian Affairs* 38 (2): 1–30.

Fossati, Diego. 2020. "Electoral Reform and Partisan Dealignment in Indonesia." *International Political Science Review* 41 (3): 349–364.

Fossati, Diego. 2022. *Unity through Division: Political Islam, Representation and Democracy in Indonesia*. Cambridge: Cambridge University Press.

Fossati, Diego, Edward Aspinall, Burhanuddin Muhtadi, and Eve Warburton. 2020. "Ideological Representation in Clientelistic Democracies: The Indonesian Case." *Electoral Studies* 63 (February). https://doi.org/10.1016/j.electstud.2019.102111

Geertz, Clifford. 1963. *Peddlers and Princes*. Chicago: University of Chicago Press.

Gethin, Amory, and Jenmana Thanasak. 2021. "Democratization and the Construction of Class Cleavages in Thailand, the Philippines, Malaysia, and Indonesia, 1992–2019." In *Political Cleavages and Social Inequalities: A Study of Fifty Democracies, 1948–2020*, edited by Amory Gethin, Clara Martínez-Toledano, and Thomas Piketty, 375–404. Cambridge, MA: Harvard University Press.

Hagopian, Frances. 1996. *Traditional Politics and Regime Change in Brazil*. New York: Cambridge University Press.

Hindley, Donald. 1970. "Alirans and the Fall of the Old Order." *Indonesia* 9: 23–66.

Horowitz, Donald L. 2013. *Constitutional Change and Democracy in Indonesia*. Cambridge: Cambridge University Press.

Johnson Tan, Paige. 2015. "Explaining Party System Institutionalization in Indonesia." In *Party System Institutionalization in Asia: Democracies, Autocracies, and the Shadows of the Past*, edited by Allen Hicken and Erik M. Kuhonta, 236–59. New York: Cambridge University Press.

Karl, Terry L. 1990. "Dilemmas of Democratization in Latin America." *Comparative Politics* 23 (1): 1–21.

Katz, Richard S., and Peter Mair. 1995. "Changing Models of Party Organization and Party Democracy: The Emergence of the Cartel Party." *Party Politics* 1 (1): 5–28.

Kenny, Paul D. 2018. *Populism in Southeast Asia*. Cambridge: Cambridge University Press.

King, Dwight Y. 2003. *Half-Hearted Reform: Electoral Institutions and the Struggle for Democracy in Indonesia*. Westport, CT: Praeger.

Kompas. 2019. Survei LSI: Mayoritas pemilih lebih pertimbangkan nama caleg daripada parpol [LSI Survey: Majority of voters considers names of candidates rather than of political parties], https://nasional.kompas.com/read/2019/04/05/16205491/survei-lsi-mayoritas-pemilih-lebih-pertimbangkan-nama-caleg-daripada-parpol

Lane, Max. 2019. *An Introduction to the Politics of the Indonesian Union Movement*. Singapore: ISEAS Publishing.

Lane, Max. 2021. *Widodo's Employment Creation Law, 2020: What Its Journey Tells Us about Indonesian Politics*. Singapore: ISEAS Publishing, https://doi.org/10.1355/9789814951944

Lim, Merlyna. 2017. "Freedom to Hate: Social Media, Algorithmic Enclaves, and the Rise of Tribal Nationalism in Indonesia." *Critical Asian Studies* 49 (3): 411–27.

Lipset, Seymour M., and Stein Rokkan. 1967. "Cleavage Structures, Party Systems, and Voter Alignments: An Introduction." In *Party Systems and Voter Alignments: Cross-National Perspectives*, edited by Seymour M. Lipset and Stein Rokkan, 1–64. New York: Free Press.

Mahoney, James. 2000. "Path Dependence in Historical Sociology." *Theory and Society* 29 (4): 507–48.

Malley, Michael. 2000. "Beyond Democratic Elections: Indonesia Embarks on a Protracted Transition." *Democratization* 7 (3): 153–80.

Mietzner, Marcus. 2008. "Comparing Indonesia's Party Systems of the 1950s and the Post-Suharto Era: From Centrifugal to Centripetal Inter-Party Competition." *Journal of Southeast Asian Studies* 39 (3): 431–53.

Mietzner, Marcus. 2013. *Money, Power, and Ideology: Political Parties in Post-Authoritarian Indonesia*. Singapore: NUS Press.

Mietzner, Marcus. 2015. *Reinventing Asian Populism: Jokowi's Rise, Democracy, and Political Contestation in Indonesia*. Policy Studies 72. Honolulu: East-West Center.

Mietzner, Marcus. 2018. "Fighting Illiberalism with Illiberalism: Islamist Populism and Democratic Deconsolidation in Indonesia." *Pacific Affairs* 91 (2): 261–82.

Mietzner, Marcus, and Burhanuddin Muhtadi. 2018. "Explaining the 2016 Islamist Mobilisation in Indonesia: Religious Intolerance, Militant Groups and the Politics of Accommodation." *Asian Studies Review* 42 (3): 479–97.

Mortimer, Rex. 1982. "Class, Social Cleavage and Indonesian Communism." In *Interpreting Indonesian Politics: Thirteen Contributions to the Debate*, edited by Benedict Anderson and Audrey Kahin, 54–68. Ithaca: Cornell University Press.

Muhtadi, Burhanuddin. 2019. *Vote Buying in Indonesia: The Mechanics of Electoral Bribery*. Basingstoke: Palgrave Macmillan.

Mujani, Saiful, R. William Liddle, and Kuskridho Ambardi. 2018. *Voting Behavior in Indonesia since Democratization: Critical Democrats*. New York: Cambridge University Press.

Nastiti, Aulia, and Sari Ratri. 2018. "Emotive Politics: Islamic Organizations and Religious Mobilization in Indonesia." *Contemporary Southeast Asia: A Journal of International and Strategic Affairs* 40 (2): 196–221.

Nuraniyah, Nava. 2020. "Divided Muslims: Militant Pluralism, Polarisation and Democratic Backsliding." In *Democracy in Indonesia: From Stagnation to Regression?*, edited by Thomas Power and Eve Warburton, 81–100. Singapore: ISEAS Publishing.

O'Donnell, Guillermo, and Philippe Schmitter. 1986. *Tentative Conclusions about Uncertain Democracies*. Baltimore: Johns Hopkins University Press.

Pepinsky, Thomas B., R. William Liddle, and Saiful Mujani. 2018. *Piety and Public Opinion: Understanding Indonesian Islam*. New York: Oxford University Press.

Peters, B. Guy, Jon Pierre, and Desmond S. King. 2005. "The Politics of Path Dependency: Political Conflict in Historical Institutionalism." *Journal of Politics* 67 (4): 1275–1300.

Power, Thomas P. 2018. "Jokowi's Authoritarian Turn and Indonesia's Democratic Decline." *Bulletin of Indonesian Economic Studies* 54 (3): 307–38.

Power, Thomas, and Eve Warburton, ed. 2020. *Democracy in Indonesia: From Stagnation to Regression?* Singapore: ISEAS Publishing.

Riedl, Rachel. 2016. "Political Parties, Regimes, and Social Cleavages." In *The Oxford Handbook of Historical Institutionalism*, edited by Orfeo Fioretos, Tulia G. Falleti, and Adam Sheingate, 223–38. Oxford: Oxford University Press.

Robison, Richard, and Vedi R. Hadiz. 2004. *Reorganizing Power in Indonesia: The Politics of Oligarchy in an Age of Markets*. London: Routledge.

Shim, Jaemin. 2019. *Global Analysis of Mass–Elite Discrepancy (GMED): Conceptual, Methodological, and Theoretical Innovations*. Project background paper.

Shim, Jaemin, and Mahmoud Farag. 2022. "Blind Spots in the Study of Political Representation: Actors and Political Dimensions." Paper presented at the Annual Meeting of the 2022 Swiss Political Science Association.

Shin, Jae Hyeok. 2015. "Voter Demands for Patronage: Evidence from Indonesia." *Journal of East Asian Studies* 15 (1): 127–51.

Slater, Dan. 2004. "Indonesia's Accountability Trap: Party Cartels and Presidential Power after Democratic Transition." *Indonesia* 78: 61–92.

Slater, Dan. 2014. "Unbuilding Blocs: Indonesia's Accountability Deficit in Historical Perspective." *Critical Asian Studies* 46 (2): 287–315.

Slater, Dan. 2018. "Party Cartelization, Indonesian Style: Presidential Power-Sharing and the Contingency of Democratic Opposition." *Journal of East Asian Studies* 18: 23–46.

Supriatma, Made. 2021. "Jokowi's Shrinking Opposition: Smoothening the Path to Constitutional Amendments." *Fulcrum*, October 6. https://fulcrum.sg/jokowis-sh rinking-opposition-smoothening-the-path-to-constitutional-amendments/

Tapsell, Ross. 2017. *Media Power in Indonesia: Oligarchs, Citizens and the Digital Revolution*. London: Rowman and Littlefield International.

Tapsell, Ross. 2020. "The Media and Democratic Decline." In *Democracy in Indonesia: From Stagnation to Regression?*, edited by Thomas Power and Eve Warburton, 210–27. Singapore: ISEAS Publishing.

Tomsa, Dirk. 2012. "Moderating Islamism in Indonesia: Tracing Patterns of Party Change in the Prosperous Justice Party." *Political Research Quarterly* 65 (3): 486–98.

Tomsa, Dirk. 2019. "Islamism and Party Politics in Indonesia." In *The Oxford Encyclopedia of Politics and Religion*, edited by Paul A. Djupe, Mark J. Rozell, and Ted G. Jelen. Oxford: Oxford University Press. http://dx.doi.org/10.1093/acrefore/97 80190228637.013.1157

Tomsa, Dirk, and Charlotte Setijadi. 2018. "New Forms of Political Activism in Indonesia: Redefining the Nexus between Electoral and Movement Politics." *Asian Survey* 58 (3): 557–81.

Ufen, Andreas. 2008. "From Aliran to Dealignment: Political Parties in Post-Suharto Indonesia." *South East Asia Research* 1: 5–41.

Ufen, Andreas. 2009. "Mobilising Political Islam: Indonesia and Malaysia Compared." *Commonwealth & Comparative Politics* 47 (3): 308–333.

Ufen, Andreas. 2023a. "Tales of Presidentialization in Indonesia." In *Presidentialism and Democracy in East and Southeast Asia*, edited by Marco Bünte and Mark Thompson, 86–104. London: Routledge.

Ufen, Andreas. 2023b. "Political Parties in Southeast Asia." In *The Routledge Handbook of Political Parties*, edited by Neil Carter, Dan Keith, Gyda Sindre, and Sofia Vasilopoulou, 371–81. London: Routledge.

Ufen, Andreas. 2023c. "Civil Society and Efforts at Regime Change in Southeast Asia." In *The Routledge Handbook of Civil and Uncivil Society in Southeast Asia*, edited by Eva Hansson and Meredith Weiss, 101–17. London: Routledge.

Winters, Jeffrey A. 2013. "Oligarchy and Democracy in Indonesia." *Indonesia* 96: 11–34.

CHAPTER 8

Mass–Elite Discrepancy over Foreign Policy

Constitutional Revision in Japan

Kenneth McElwain

Japan experienced competitive, multiparty elections in the early twentieth century, but full democracy—including universal suffrage and constitutional guarantees of civil and political rights—only began after its defeat in World War II. The first decade after 1945 was a tumultuous period. Citizens contended with economic insecurity, particularly food and job shortages due to the destruction of industrial capital and mass displacement during the war. Many established elites were purged from political office for war culpability. Hanging over these uncertainties was the American-led Allied Occupation. The onset of the Cold War stimulated public debates about the future shape of Japanese foreign and security policy. However, elites had no choice but to accept constitutional constraints on military capabilities and a security alliance with the United States. These were seen as necessary concessions to end the Occupation and restore national sovereignty—goals that were achieved with the 1952 San Francisco Peace Treaty.

Once freed of these external constraints, political competition in the 1950s began to center on two issues. The first was clientelistic, redistributive politics. The rapid concentration of labor and capital in cities enabled rapid postwar reindustrialization, but it also created wealth inequalities between urban and rural regions. Legislators used fiscal transfers, agricultural subsidies, and public works projects to compensate for economic inequalities and demonstrate their political acumen. By contrast, structural cleavages that can be observed elsewhere, such as ethnicity, religion, and language, had limited salience in the comparatively homogenous Japanese society.[1] Strong economic growth through the 1980s also curtailed the development of class-based party attachments (Richardson 1997).

The second was the "normal nation" vs. "peace state" cleavage, particularly disagreements about whether to amend Article 9, or the "Peace Clause," of the Constitution of Japan, which bans Japan from possessing war potential (McElwain 2021). In practice, Japan has well-funded Self-Defense Forces, but Article 9 places restrictions on sending troops overseas on combat missions, developing offensive weaponry, or forming military alliances. Progressive political parties have called for the defense of the "peace constitution," as it epitomizes the pacifist turn of the nation after Japanese imperialism in the early twentieth century. Conservative parties have countered that the constitution unnecessarily constrains the foreign policy autonomy of the government, and that Japan must become a "normal nation" with a full-fledged military.

The elite-level politicization of these two political dimensions has shifted over time. The urban–rural dimension dominated political debate through the 1980s, but constitutional revision has become increasingly important since the 1990s. This chapter argues that this shift can be attributed to elite strategy in response to two critical junctures. The first was a decade after the end of the Allied Occupation. Conservative governments in the early 1950s were in favor of amending Article 9. However, they faced fierce public backlash when the US-Japan Mutual Security Treaty, which locked Japan into an alliance with the United States, was extended in 1960. In response, the conservative Liberal Democratic Party (LDP) chose to depoliticize foreign and security policy in favor of economic revitalization. This strategy proved prescient: economic growth burnished the party's reputation for macroeconomic competence, and the LDP remained in power continuously between 1955 and 1993. Conservative actors periodically raised the necessity of revisiting constitutional revision in the 1970s and 1980s, but the party did not make it a prominent element of their electoral campaigns. In other words, while there had been a clear positional difference between left- and right-leaning parties on this cleavage, it was not sufficiently politicized because the LDP deliberately kept its saliency low. (As noted in chapter 4, this volume defines a political dimension as "politicized" only if it is highly salient and, at the same time, polarized).

By contrast, the LDP chose to politicize constitutional politics during the second critical juncture, composed of three interlinked events in the early 1990s. The first event was a change in the geopolitical environment. Bipolar competition between the United States and the Soviet Union, which had kept a lid on historical animosities between East Asian nations, unraveled with the end of the Cold War. This caused tensions between Japan and its neighbors to come to the fore. It also led elites to reevaluate the wisdom of relying on the American nuclear umbrella as the lynchpin of national defense, given the growing economic importance of China to the United States and the risk of being entrapped in American military adventurism in the Middle East.

The second event was the bursting of the economic "bubble." Despite rapid postwar growth, the Japanese economy was showing cracks in the 1980s, including anemic consumer spending and excessive speculative investments, which produced a stock market and real estate bubble. The bursting of this asset bubble began what came to be called the "Lost Decades" of low economic growth, persistent deflation, and growing job insecurity. The hit to its reputation for macroeconomic competence incentivized the LDP to focus on nonvalence issues.

The third factor was institutional. The electoral system for the House of Representatives (the lower house) was overhauled in 1994, replacing the multimember district, single nontransferable vote (MMD-SNTV) system with a mixed-member majoritarian (MMM) system. This nudged political parties to emphasize programmatic competition over clientelistic redistribution. One manifestation of this ideological turn was the LDP's growing focus on foreign and security policy (Catalinac 2016) and constitutional revision (McElwain 2021) as part of the "normal nation" vs. "peace state" debate.

The combination of these three factors provided a window of opportunity to reshape postwar party cleavages, and governing elites took advantage of it. From the mid-1990s, the LDP politicized the normal nation vs. peace state dimension by increasing its saliency. However, a mass–elite representation gap only became obvious two decades later when the level of politicization reached a new level with the LDP's proposal of a constitutional overhaul. Amending the constitution requires two-thirds assent in parliament, followed by a simple majority in a national referendum. The political timing only became ripe when parties favoring revision combined to win the requisite two-thirds in the House of Representatives (in 2014) and the House of Councillors (in 2016). As a result of increased politicization, the elites' stance favoring constitutional revision became more apparent compared to that of the masses.

This disconnect between "elite" and "mass" opinion can be bridged if elites successfully persuade the masses to shift their views. The ruling elites in Japan have tried but not succeeded due to two factors: message consistency and partisan credibility. On the first point, while constitutional revision began to gain prominence in public debates and election manifestos in the 1990s, individual LDP elites have not consistently seen it as a priority. Elite surveys show that while almost all LDP politicians are in favor of constitutional amendments, less than 10 percent list it as one of their top three issues. This disconnect between issue position and priority is connected to strategic electoral concerns. Because most voters place greater electoral weight on valence issues, such as economic growth and socioeconomic redistribution, candidates lack strong incentives to emphasize constitutional reform in their own campaigns, which in turn reduces the LDP's ability to convert voters to their side.

On the second point, the LDP has less credibility on constitutional matters than on valence issues. Postwar Japanese education has long emphasized the perils of militarism and the importance of the "Peace Constitution." Changing this status quo belief is not easy, especially in the absence of clear and present geopolitical dangers. While the LDP has argued that Article 9 is no longer suited to Japan's geopolitical environment, its postwar deemphasis of this issue has meant that voters do not automatically believe the party's claims.

This chapter uses the case of constitutional revision to explore the discrepancy between elite (legislative) and mass (public) sentiment in Japan and reexamine the salience of foreign policy cleavages more generally. While much of the analysis focuses on strategic decisions by the LDP, which has dominated postwar Japanese politics, the data analysis will cover opposition parties and legislators as well. The first section explores the formation of political cleavages in postwar Japan, focusing on the role of elite agency during two critical junctures in the 1950s and 1990s. The second section looks more closely at mass–elite discrepancies in the "normal nation" vs. "peace state" cleavage since the 2000s. Using survey data, I show two distinctive patterns. On the one hand, elites express greater average support for constitutional amendment than do voters. On the other hand, elites are more polarized on the issue of amending the constitution, suggesting a lack of consensus on the future shape of the supreme law. Although the politicization of the foreign policy cleavage started in the 1990s, the data show that the politicization level peaked in the 2010s when the parties favoring amendments reached the necessary legislative threshold and made political attempts to revise the constitution. The third section explores the reasons for the continuing mass–elite divergence. One factor is message consistency: while the LDP as a party has strengthened its focus on amendments, individual politicians are less eager, largely because the topic lacks resonance with most voters. A second factor is credibility, which affects the persuasiveness of LDP messaging. Using data from a survey experiment, I show that support for a given amendment is higher when it is framed as a neutral, rather than an LDP-backed, proposal. These results suggest that the best path forward for the LDP is to *not* take an overly strident position on amendment and, instead, build up cross-partisan support.

8.1. Political Cleavages and Party Competition in Postwar Japan

8.1.1. Origin of Two Political Cleavages in Japan and the Role of the First Critical Juncture

Japan's first political parties date back to the late nineteenth century (Kawato 1992). The creation of the modern nation-state began with the Meiji Restoration of 1868, but party politics only took form with the creation of the Imperial Diet (parliament) in 1889. While universal male suffrage was established in 1925, the state was fundamentally autocratic: sovereignty resided with the emperor, and human rights were subordinate to public welfare and social order. Nonetheless, divisions among the Meiji oligarchs prompted factions to establish political parties in the elected lower house (House of Representatives), not to promote democracy per se but to strengthen their position through popular legitimacy (Ramseyer and Rosenbluth 1995). Prewar parties exercised their influence in the Diet by blocking legislation and toppling cabinets, but their institutionalization was sidelined by the country's descent into militarism in the 1930s.

After its defeat in World War II, Japanese governance came under the control of the Allied Occupation, whose goal was to transform Japan into a stable democracy and a bulwark against communism in Asia. One of its immediate goals was to establish a new Constitution of Japan, which was duly ratified in 1946 and implemented in 1947. The constitution's origins exemplify the ability of international elites to shape domestic politics in non-Western settings, as noted in chapter 2. Occupation officers drafted the constitution in nine days, placing strong emphasis on the three pillars of popular sovereignty, pacifism, and fundamental human rights (Hellegers 2001). The Diet, not the emperor or oligarchs, would select the prime minister, and both houses of parliament became elected bodies. Suffrage was extended to women, and new protections for the rights to assembly and association gave voice to underrepresented, poorer voters. Labor unions mobilized urban voters against wealthy landowners and privileged business conglomerates (*zaibatsu*), and their support became the base of left-wing parties, whose electoral power grew rapidly as discontent mounted with postwar food shortages and rising unemployment.

The political cleavages of party competition began to take shape during this period. One dimension was fiscal redistribution to offset economic inequality. Classical models of political ideology divide parties on a left–right spectrum based on class conflict, with the former prioritizing income transfers in alliance with labor unions, and the latter promoting lower taxation in collaboration with capital owners (Lipset and Rokkan 1967; Przeworski and Sprague 1986). This manifested in Japan as divisions between urban and rural interests. Conservative parties based their support on rural farmers, who provided votes, and urban industrialists, who provided campaign funds. Progressives, in contrast, relied on their ties to public and private sector labor unions, and much of their vote came from the rapidly industrializing cities. Because the fiscal structure of the Japanese government has been highly centralized—the national government decides two-thirds of public expenditures—local governments, particularly poorer ones, depended heavily on fiscal transfers to fund social and infrastructural projects (DeWit and Steinmo 2002; Scheiner 2006).

The second dimension has been foreign policy, specifically the constitution's Article 9 "Peace Clause," which proscribes a military, and the US-Japan Mutual Security Treaty, which permits American bases on Japanese territory. Both were established during the Allied Occupation of Japan, and their acceptance was a precondition for the return of Japanese sovereignty. Conservative legislators favored a strong security alliance with the United States, given the threat of the Soviet Union just to the north, although there were disagreements about the wisdom of demilitarization. Progressives, many of whom had opposed Japan's rising militarism in the 1930s and early 1940s, strongly supported the Peace Clause but were wary of the Security Treaty, which limited policy autonomy in building stronger ties with China and North Korea. The positional division between left- and right-leaning politicians crystallized during this period and has persisted ever since.

Through the 1980s, the primary political linkage between legislators and voters rested on the first dimension of fiscal redistribution. The contributing factors were the electoral system, postwar urbanization, and elite strategy. Between 1947 and 1993, lower house elections were held under the multimember district, single nontransferable vote (MMD-SNTV) system. The country was divided into electoral districts with an average magnitude (M) of four seats, with the top-M vote-getters in a district awarded seats. Given strategic entry by legislators (no-hope candidates choosing not to run) and strategic voting (voters abandoning fringe candidates), the theoretical, equilibrium number of competitive candidates per district is M+1. In the Japanese case, this translated into a five-party system (Reed 1990). The preeminent party was the center-right Liberal Democratic Party, which was established in 1955 and held a stable single-party majority until 1993. Progressives were more divided, with the leftist Japan Socialist Party (JSP) and Japan Communist Party (JCP) and the centrist Komeito and Democratic Socialist Party (DSP) splitting votes in urban districts.

Separate from the shape of the party system, the electoral system also encouraged clientelistic relationships between the elites and the masses. With an average district magnitude of four, majority-seeking parties, particularly the LDP, ran multiple candidates per district. Because co-partisans competed against each other for the same pool of votes, they sought to differentiate themselves by highlighting their clientelistic competence in securing pork-barrel projects and patronage for their districts (Curtis 1971; Ramseyer and Rosenbluth 1993; Kohno 1997). As a result, the personal characteristics of individual candidates were a better predictor of victory than party affiliation (Scheiner 2006). At the party system level, Shim (2020) uses bill-sponsorship data to show that left- and right-wing parties have been more divided on their enthusiasm for particularistic redistribution than on conventional social welfare policies.

Rapid urbanization in the postwar period also inhibited the development of strong party identification, as voters were given different party options when they moved around the country. Rapid urbanization also distorted the representation of urban versus rural districts in favor of the latter, because the ruling LDP impeded the periodic reapportionment of seats (McElwain 2008). Rural districts retained most of their seat allocations despite having fewer eligible voters over time, meaning that the value of one vote was greater in rural than urban areas. This produced a sizable boon to the rurally oriented LDP, which used fiscal distribution to solidify support among farmers.

Lastly, the LDP made a conscious decision to emphasize valence or competence issues over ideological differences. The party's founding charter from 1955 included the revision of Article 9 as one of its core goals. However, constitutional amendments face a high procedural hurdle, requiring two-thirds approval in both houses of the Diet, followed by a simple majority in a national voter referendum. The semiproportional nature of the MMD-SNTV electoral system made it unlikely that the LDP would obtain the requisite two-thirds in the Diet unilaterally. At the same time, the LDP government faced mass demonstrations in 1960 when it pushed through an extension of the US-Japan Mutual Security Treaty, forcing Prime Minister Nobusuke Kishi to step down. His successor, Hayato Ikeda, reversed course and introduced the "Income Doubling Plan." Its purpose was to shift national discourse away from sensitive foreign policy issues and instead focus on rapid economic development (Kapur 2018). The plan's success, including double-digit GDP growth in the 1960s and early 1970s, burnished the LDP's reputation as an effective manager of the macroeconomy. In fact, Miyake, Kohno, and Nishizawa (2001) find that the LDP's support during this period rested largely on retrospective pocketbook voting.

This is not to say that tensions over security policy were absent in the postwar period. As American commitment to Asia deepened with the Korean War, rising tensions between China and Taiwan, and the Vietnam War, its demands for increased burden-sharing became more pronounced. In particular, the Japanese government's decision not to deploy Self-Defense Forces troops to the Gulf War (1990–91) and only send financial aid came under international criticism.

At heart were dueling concerns in Japan between American abandonment versus entrapment (Samuels 2007). The LDP called for Japan to become more involved in international military and peace-keeping operations, if only to ensure that the US did not abandon its security commitment to Japan. Progressive parties, by contrast, defended the importance of abiding by Article 9, noting the alternate risks of being too closely aligned with the US and being forced to participate in missions with low relevance to Japan. As noted in chapter 2, its deep connection to Japan's geopolitical decision-making makes debates about revising Article 9 sit more comfortably in the foreign relations, not the sociocultural, policy domain.

8.1.2. The Second Critical Juncture and Elite-Level Politicization of the Peace State vs. Normal Nation Cleavage

The status quo began to shift in the late 1980s due to changes in the political environment, and then more decisively in 1994 with electoral reform.[2] On the economic side, postwar industrialization shrank the LDP's electoral base of farmers, to the point that it needed to adopt policies that were also attractive to urban residents. In addition, the bursting of the asset bubble in the early 1990s, which eventually manifested as the "Lost Decades" of the 1990s and 2000s, dimmed public trust in the LDP's macroeconomic competence. On the ideological dimension, the fall of the Soviet Union marked a crucial turning point. The communist threat had justified Japan's reliance on the American security umbrella, which itself had seemed reliable because the United States benefited from stationing military bases in Japan. With the end of the Cold War, however, it remained uncertain whether the US would retain its commitment to Japan.

The LDP's decision to increase its emphasis on the "normal nation" vs. "peace state" cleavage was reinforced by electoral reform in 1994. The LDP was ousted from power in the 1993 election, due to the combination of economic slowdown and the revelation of high-profile political scandals (Reed and Thies 2001). Institutional reformers sought to replace the clientelistic MMD-SNTV electoral system with a more programmatic, Westminster-style single-member-plurality system. The eventual compromise established a mixed-member majoritarian system for the lower house, combining two electoral tiers: 300 single-member districts with plurality winners (now 289 districts) and 200 proportional representation seats, divided among 11 regional blocks (now 176 seats).

Because the single-member district tier comprises most of the seats, victory in these districts has become critical to winning parliamentary majorities. While candidates under the previous system could win a seat with 15–25 percent of the votes, they now needed to win 50 percent to guarantee victory. As a result, they have shifted their focus from cornering particularistic, sectoral interests to becoming policy generalists (Krauss and Pekkanen 2011). Elections have "nationalized": local factors such as candidate quality and district characteristics have become weaker predictors of election outcomes than national-level swings in party popularity (McElwain 2012). Noble (2010), analyzing the composition of the budget, shows that pork-barreling has given way to a greater emphasis on national public goods, such as education and social insurance.

This change in mass–elite linkages has also elevated the salience of foreign policy debates over becoming a "normal nation" or remaining a "peace state." This increasing politicization is captured by Catalinac (2016), who demonstrates that the proportion of candidate pledges that discuss foreign and security policies has increased substantially since the 1990s. However, as noted in multiple chapters in this volume, critical junctures may increase the likelihood that actors attempt to change the focal point of political competition, but they do not determine any specific path. In the case of Japan, partisan discourse shifted to the constitutional dimension for three reasons. First, this issue had divided elites in the conservative and liberal camps since the 1950s, and so it had ideological resonance. Second, there were no immediate, alternative policy dimensions to anchor political debate, whether that be immigration, which remained restricted until the 2010s (cf. Strausz 2019), or structural socioeconomic inequalities, which did not become apparent until the late 1990s/early 2000s. Third, because the LDP held the reins of government for all but three years after it returned to power in 1994, it could shape the national political agenda in a way that suited its long-standing ideological goal for Japan to adopt a more muscular foreign policy stance.

To summarize, the increased political salience of the normal nation versus peace state dimension was a conscious choice of conservative political elites. It set in motion significant foreign policy changes in Japan and began to focus the national debate on constitutional amendment, particularly the Article 9 "Peace Clause." The full realization of this shift only occurred in the 2010s, two decades after the second critical juncture, in part because of mass–elite discrepancies on issue position, as well as intra-elite divisions on the strategic merits of emphasizing constitutionalism. In the next section, I turn to a discussion of the evolution of constitutional discourse.

8.2. Mass–Elite Discrepancy on the Normal Nation vs. Peace State Cleavage

Elites play a critical role in structuring policy debates, but attempts to do so for strategic electoral gain are not always successful. Deegan-Krause and Enyedi (2010) point to a number of complicating factors, such as deep social divisions (e.g., ethnicity and religion), that make voters resistant to elite cues. They also warn that altering voters' prioritization of issues may be easier than persuading them to change their positions. As earlier sections explored, the LDP has changed the salience of the urban–rural vs. normal–peace state cleavage at critical junctures, so that it can focus voters' attention on advantageous topics—what Deegan-Krause and Enyedi (2010) term "agency over time." These were achieved through consistent party messaging over multiple election cycles. These successes do not necessarily imply, however, that all such attempts at altering saliency will work, much less that the LDP can sway voters to their side on contentious ideological debates.

This section examines the LDP's attempts to raise the electoral salience of constitutional revision. First, I briefly review the contemporary agenda on constitutional politics, including the LDP's tactics to increase the visibility of amendments. Next, I explore important differences in elite and mass opinion, focusing on positional disagreements about whether and how to change the constitution.

8.2.1. Contemporary Agenda over Constitutional Revision

The Constitution of Japan is built on the three pillars of popular sovereignty (Article 1), pacifism (Article 9), and fundamental human rights (Article 11). These have also been the focal point of amendment debates over the last 70 years (Winkler 2011). Domestic opposition to the constitution, mostly by conservative politicians, intellectuals, and media, has rested on both the origins and content of the constitution. Drafted by Occupation officers and ratified while sovereignty was limited, Japanese critics have decried the constitution for lacking democratic legitimacy. Its contents, too, have been seen as Western-inspired, particularly the defanging of the emperor and the elevation of individual rights over collective duties. However, the heart of national debate has centered on Article 9, which states (underlines added by the author):

> Article 9.1. Aspiring sincerely to an international peace based on justice and order, the Japanese people <u>forever renounce war as a sovereign right of the nation</u> and the threat or use of force as a means of settling international disputes.
> Article 9.2. In order to accomplish the aim of the preceding paragraph, <u>land, sea, and air forces, as well as other war potential, will never be maintained</u>. The right of belligerency of the state will not be recognized.

Conservatives have criticized Article 9 for depriving Japan of the right of a "normal nation" to self-defense, which is granted under the United Nations Charter. In practice, since 1954, Japan has possessed Self-Defense Forces that include land, air, and maritime capabilities. As of 2022, it has the tenth-largest military budget in the world but has refrained from investments in offensive capabilities, limiting itself to coastal protection and defense against foreign invasions. This constraint has been feasible largely because of the US-Japan Mutual Security Treaty, which mandates that the former come to the latter's defense in case of a military attack.

Since the 2000s, the LDP has tried to increase the electoral salience of constitutional revision in two ways. First, it published comprehensive proposals for a new constitution in 2005 and 2012.[3] These drafts included changes—some cosmetic, some substantial—to virtually every article, but public debate centered on revisions to Article 9. The 2012 LDP draft, which I will focus on for the remainder of the chapter, proposed the establishment of a National Defense Army, charged with defending the territory, resources, and people of Japan. The most consequential change was to allow the deployment of Japanese forces on international missions, including for collective self-defense. The Self-Defense Forces had already participated in UN-sanctioned peacekeeping operations, but they cannot engage in combat missions. In practice, new legislation in 2015 reinterpreted Article 9 to grant limited collective self-defense authority, notably to fight in defense of allies even without a direct threat to the homeland (Liff 2017). However, progressive parties have argued that this law violates Article 9's principles, and the matter remains divisive in political discourse.

Second, the LDP has given greater attention to constitutional amendment in its election manifestos. For example, its 2017 lower house election manifesto identified four priorities, including adding a third clause to Article 9 that explicitly acknowledges the right to self-defense.[4] The growing salience of constitutional amendment is reflected in the fact that every political party in that election took a clear stance on constitutional revision. Komeito, the LDP's coalition partner, did not commit to Article 9 revision but agreed with the addition of national emergency provisions. The Constitutional Democratic Party (CDP)—the largest opposition party as of 2021—urged the enumeration of government transparency but opposed changes to Article 9. The Japan Communist Party and the Social Democratic Party opposed any revision whatsoever to the constitution.

8.2.2. Mass–Elite Discrepancies

Despite the increasing significance of changing Article 9, there continues to be a substantial discrepancy in the preferences of legislators and that of voters. This discrepancy can be defined in two ways: means and distributions.

The first type is differences in average attitudes. Overall, elites are more pro-normal nation and pro-constitutional revision than are voters. The University of Tokyo–*Asahi* Survey (UTAS) has asked election candidates and voters for their positions on a common set of political questions since 2005 (McElwain 2020).[5] Table 8.1 shows the percentage of candidates and voters who supported constitutional change in the 2012, 2014, and 2017 lower house elections, all of which the LDP won by large margins.[6] In the full sample, the proportion of all candidates (row 1) who were in favor of some type of amendment ranged between 55.8 and 63.1 percent. That for winning candidates (row 2) was significantly higher, between 81.9 and 88.9 percent,

Table 8.1. Mass-Elite Discrepancies in Constitutional Revision Preferences

CANDIDATES	2012	2014	2017
All (1)	58.8	55.8	63.1
Winners (2)	88.9	84.5	81.9
LDP Winner (3)	98.6	97.1	97.4
DPJ/CDP Winner (4)	58.9	61.6	24.5
VOTERS			
All (5)	49.5	33.4	41.5
LDP (6)	57.3	45.5	61.6
DPJ/CDP Voters (7)	30.5	19.4	16.9

Source: Data from University of Tokyo-*Asahi* Surveys (UTAS 2012, 2014, 2017).

Note: Original responses were given on a five-point Likert scale with a "no answer" option. Percentages in this table were calculated after dichotomizing the responses into support ("agree," "somewhat agree") for amending the constitution, and nonsupport (all other options). DPJ = Democratic Party of Japan; CDP = Constitutional Democratic Party of Japan.

reflecting the electoral success of the LDP during this period. There was, however, less ardor among voters (row 5), with support ranging between 33.4 and 49.5 percent.

Breakdowns by partisanship reveal the extent to which positions on amendment have become more polarized. Among LDP election winners (row 3), support for constitutional change has remained virtually unanimous at greater than 97 percent in all years. Among the victors of the main opposition party (row 4: the Democratic Party of Japan in 2012 and 2014, and the Constitutional Democratic Party in 2017), however, support fell significantly, dropping from 61.6 percent in 2014 to 24.5 percent in 2017. The Constitutional Democratic Party, which emerged after the Democratic Party of Japan itself splintered into different groups, was explicitly against amending Article 9 under the LDP administration. Voter positions reflect this divide. Voters who cast their proportional representation ballot for the LDP (row 6) have broadly backed constitutional change, including 61.6 percent in 2017.[7] By contrast, the views of progressive voters (row 7) have trended lower, with only 16.9 percent in favor that same year. Although there is a divide at both the mass and elite levels, the extent of the divide appears greater among elites. While the difference between LDP and opposition voters ranges between 26 and 45 percent during the period of observation, the equivalent gap ranges from 35 to 73 percent for elites.

A similar picture of mass–elite divergence emerges when we look at how voters evaluate the positions of parties. Using data from the Web Survey on

Table 8.2. Mass-Elite Discrepancy in Intensity of Constitutional Revision Preferences

		Agree	Somewhat Agree	Somewhat Disagree	Disagree
2012	Elite	44.9%	18.0%	4.4%	32.6%
	Mass	36.5%	37.0%	13.0%	13.5%
2014	Elite	42.2%	17.2%	5.2%	35.4%
	Mass	24.1%	28.5%	22.8%	24.6%
2017	Elite	48.2%	16.5%	4.6%	30.8%
	Mass	27.7%	32.3%	23.9%	16.1%

Source: Data from University of Tokyo-*Asahi* Surveys (UTAS 2012, 2014, 2017).
Note: "Elite" refers to all election candidates, while "mass" refers to all social survey respondents, including nonvoters. Original responses were given on a five-point Likert scale with a "no answer" option. Percentages in this table were calculated after first omitting "neutral" and "no answer" options.

Locality and Civic Life (2014), Jou, Endo, and Takaneka (2017) compare respondents' personal views on various policy issues with their subjective perceptions of the government's position. The topic with the greatest discrepancy was constitutional amendment: mean perceptions of the government's stance were significantly more pro-revision than respondents' own positions. Other controversial foreign policy topics, such as visits by prime ministers to the Yasukuni Shrine, which is a nationalist symbol, and permitting collective defense ranked third and fourth, respectively. In other words, voters themselves believe on average that the government's position on the "normal nation" vs. "peace state" issue diverges greatly from their own.

Another way to gauge the level of opinion polarization is to examine the intensity of agreement or disagreement on constitutional revision. To capture this, table 8.2 disaggregates the UTAS data in table 8.1 and shows response distributions across four answer categories—agree, somewhat agree, somewhat disagree, disagree—between all candidates and all voters. While UTAS also includes a middle, "neutral" response category, this is omitted from the denominator here to preserve consistency with other empirical chapters in this volume.[8]

A comparison of the masses and elites clearly shows that the latter are more polarized. On the one hand, elites have a markedly higher percentage sum of fully "agree" and "disagree" answer categories, reaching almost 80 percent across all three periods. On the other hand, masses tend to be more moderate. Roughly 50–55 percent of respondents answered either "somewhat agree" or "somewhat disagree" during the period of observation.

To summarize, these survey data point to patterns in mass–elite divergence. First, legislators are significantly more favorable toward constitutional revision than are voters. This is largely because of the disproportionality of the electoral system, which magnifies the seat share of the largest vote-getting party, that is, the LDP. However, even when comparing LDP legislators to LDP voters, we can see that elites espouse stronger support for the "normal nation" view of foreign policy. Second, legislators are markedly more polarized on the issue of constitutional revision than voters, with clearer positions either for or against amendment. Put differently, the masses are more moderate than elites, speaking to the limitations of elite cues in changing the preferences of citizens.

8.3. Elite Failure and the Persistence of Mass–Elite Discrepancy in Japan

Why are voters more lukewarm toward constitutional revision and the "normal nation" position on foreign policy than candidates are? One important factor is political socialization. Jou and Endo (2016) argue that younger and older voters differ in how they understand and prioritize ideological issues, due to exposure to different political conflicts during their formative years. Older voters, who came of age during or immediately after World War II, may have stronger views in favor of or against amending Article 9. However, younger voters who grew up after the bursting of the economic bubble may worry more about their job prospects and economic well-being. Given that Japanese politicians are, on average, older than voters, it may not be surprising that the former place greater weight on constitutional matters.

However, this does not mean that the LDP cannot *change* voters' minds. Socialization is not destiny, and elites have agency over which issues are given prominence in the electoral and legislative agenda. Indeed, UTAS data suggests that the LDP's emphasis on the "normal nation" vs. "peace state" cleavage, and on constitutional revision more specifically, has increased their salience among voters. In its survey for the 2014 lower house election, 13 percent chose foreign and security policy as the policy domain to which they paid the most attention, ranking it third out of 15 topics. The salience of constitutionalism was lower, at 5 percent, or ninth place. By 2017, however, both topics had clearly become more relevant. Foreign and security policy was the top-rated policy issue, at 24 percent prioritization, while constitutional revision had risen to third place, at 13 percent.

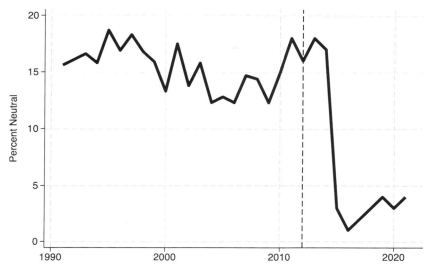

Fig. 8.1. Proportion of "Don't Know" or "Neutral" on Constitutional Revision

A related piece of evidence demonstrating the LDP's successful politicization of constitutional revision is the reduction in the number of voters who have no opinion on the matter. *Yomiuri Shimbun*, Japan's largest daily newspaper, has run annual surveys on attitudes toward constitutional revision since the early 1990s. Figure 8.1 tracks the proportion of voters who answered "do not know" or "neutral" on the merits of constitutional revision. While the trend held steady at roughly 15 percent between 1991 and 2014, this has plummeted to 3 percent between 2015 and 2020. Notably, this decline coincides with the publication of the LDP's 2012 constitutional revision proposal (dashed line), suggesting that its attempts to raise the profile of this issue have pushed voters to take a concrete position as well.

Taken together, the evidence here suggests that the political salience of the "normal nation" vs. "peace state" cleavage saw a substantial increase due to elite-level political initiatives in the 2010s, two decades after the second critical juncture noted earlier. The question is whether the ruling LDP can successfully change voter's *positions* as well and, as a result, close the mass–elite opinion divergence gap. Without it, any attempt to revise the constitution will likely fail in the national referendum required of amendments. On this matter, I argue that the answer is likely "no," due to two reasons: message consistency and partisan credibility.

8.3.1. Message Consistency

For parties to persuade voters to change policy positions, they need to transmit a consistent message. It is not enough for parties to simply state their position once—they must repeat it in legislative debates and electoral campaigns, ideally over multiple cycles. Prior research suggests that when voters lack knowledge of or experience with policy issues, partisan cues can have a powerful effect on their issue positions and prioritization (Hobolt 2007; Hobolt and Brouard 2010). However, Lupia (1994) warns that the value of elite cues as information heuristics depends on the credibility of the messenger. For voters to see signals as credible, they must believe that elites are being truthful, accurate, and transparent about their own preferences.

However, the LDP has not engaged in this type of message discipline. At the party level, changes to Article 9 were laid out in its 2012 constitutional revision proposal, and the topic was included in its 2012 and 2017 manifestos. However, it was ignored in the LDP's 2014 manifesto, on the heels of a bruising fight over reinterpreting Article 9 to permit collective self-defense. This is echoed at the candidate level. UTAS's candidate surveys include an item on policy priorities, separate from individual questions about preferred policy positions. Among all LDP candidates (not just winners), *none* chose constitutional revision as their first priority in 2014, although 2 percent listed it among their top three issues. In 2017, these rates barely budged to 1 percent and 8 percent of LDP candidates, respectively. McElwain (2020) attributes this pattern to strategic electoral incentives. First, ideological centrists and nonpartisans, who comprise the bulk of the electorate, have tended to place greater weight on bread-and-butter socioeconomic issues, such as pensions, health care, and employment. Second, left-wing voters express a greater desire to protect the constitutional status quo than right-wing voters do to change it. As such, LDP candidates, particularly those running in competitive districts, prefer to stay away from constitutional amendment. Doing so would not attract the all-important independent voters and possibly mobilize leftist opponents more than their own supporters, a point echoed by Maeda (2023).

One take-away point is the importance of carefully distinguishing the party's official position, which can be studied using election manifestos or leaders' speeches, from the preferences of the party's individual legislators, which require additional data to parse. Strategies that are electorally beneficial for the party as a whole may not guarantee victory for every legislator, given that candidates represent districts that vary in ideological makeup and socioeconomic needs. This distinction is particularly important in national contexts where the party leadership's control of electoral or political resources is weak, and legislators have greater agency to act independently.

8.3.2. Partisan Credibility and Persuasiveness

Even if LDP candidates become more consistently vocal in their support for the "normal nation" vision of foreign and security policy, including constitutional revision, their ability to convert voters depends on the persuasiveness of their message. Two pieces of evidence suggest that voters may not be receptive to the LDP's cues. First, many voters already have strong opinions on the merits of constitutional revision, as discussed in figure 8.1. They are also evenly split. In the 2020 *Yomiuri* survey, 49 percent of respondents favored amendment, while 48 percent were opposed, reflecting the parity in sentiment that has held true since 2014. Second, while voters have entrusted the LDP with macroeconomic policy, they may be more apprehensive about the party's conservative positions on ideological issues, including Article 9. The Constitution of Japan has long enjoyed public support for its contribution to postwar peace and prosperity. In fact, school textbooks identify Article 9's "Peace Clause" as one of the three core principles of the constitution, along with popular sovereignty and respect for fundamental human rights. Attempts to change it, absent a clear and present danger, may be seen as an unnecessary turn toward the "normal nation" vision of foreign and security policy. Put differently, voters may shy away from amendments that they see as excessively partisan.

I test this thesis using data from McElwain, Eshima, and Winkler (2021), who estimate the effects of partisan framing through an original survey experiment. The experiment's key innovation is the information treatment, which varies the identity of the proposer on 14 different amendment topics. Control group respondents were told that the amendment was being proposed by the Liberal Democratic Party, while treatment group respondents were told that the proposal was made by a "panel of neutral experts." Here, I focus on three issues that varied in ideological focus and salience in 2017:

(1) Amend Article 9 to specify that Japan can "possess a Defense Army." {Conservative, High Salience}
(2) Add national emergency provisions, during when "the House of Representatives cannot be dissolved, and legislators' terms are extended." {Conservative, Low Salience}

(3) Add environment rights, wherein "the State, in cooperation with citizens, must preserve a good environment for citizens."
{Progressive, Low Salience}

As discussed earlier in this chapter, conservative elites have long advocated for changes to Article 9 and the addition of national emergency provisions, but the former has drawn much more attention. It has been at the center of constitutional debates since the constitution's ratification, and it also pertains to foreign and security policy issues, which have gained importance since the early 1990s. As Sakaiya (2017) argues, for many citizens, questions about constitutional amendment essentially equate to the merits of changing Article 9. This suggests that people are more likely to have strong priors about amending Article 9. By implication, partisan framing may have less effect on public opinion toward Article 9 than on national emergency issues.

Environmental rights, by contrast, is a progressive priority. It was included in the LDP's 2012 revision draft as a way to attract moderates, but it has not been high on the party's agenda, and it has not been given much attention in the LDP's recent election manifestos. Here again, I expect partisan framing to have a bigger effect, especially among progressive voters who are more likely to support non-LDP proposals.

The estimated quantity of interest is the average treatment effect (ATE), or the average difference in the evaluation of an amendment proposal between those who were informed it was drafted by a neutral panel of experts (treatment) and those who were informed it was by the LDP (control). In this chapter, I estimate the ATE using an OLS regression. While treatment assignment is balanced on key demographic variables, I include controls for gender, age, and education in the models. Table 8.3 shows the average treatment effect (first column), as well as the conditional average treatment effect by whether the respondent is a supporter of the LDP (second column) or not (third column). Positive values denote greater support for amendment when it is described as a "neutral" proposal," relative to its description as an "LDP proposal."

In the full sample model, the "neutral proposal" treatment increases support for adding national emergency provisions (15.8 percentage points) and environmental rights (11.3 percentage points), but it has no statistically significant effect on amending Article 9. In other words, partisan framing matters principally for lower-salience issues, not high-salience ones. Disaggregating average treatment effects by partisanship shows that their primary impact is on the constitutional assessment of non-LDP supporters. Among LDP partisans, the treatment is not statistically significant, except

Table 8.3. Survey Experiment Results

	ATE	ATE | LDP=1	ATE | LDP=0
Article 9—Defense Army	0.044	0.104	–0.031
	(0.065)	(0.092)	(0.078)
National Emergency	0.158***	0.083	0.159**
	(0.059)	(0.101)	(0.067)
Environment Rights	0.113***	–0.129*	0.212***
	(0.041)	(0.066)	(0.050)

Note: positive = neutral framing (treatment) preferred over LDP framing (control).
* $p < 0.1$, ** $p < 0.05$, *** $p < 0.01$. Standard errors in parentheses.

for on environmental rights, where support actually falls by 12.9 percentage points. Among non-LDP supporters, however, the story is quite different. The "neutral proposal" framing increases support for national emergency provisions by 15.9 percentage points, and for environmental rights by 21.2 percentage points.

The results support the hypothesis that an issue's saliency and its partisan framing both matter. On issues that have been in the limelight for many years, like Article 9, most respondents do not need additional cues to make judgments, as they have already formed strong opinions. On those that have lower salience, however, framing matters more, particularly for those opposed to the LDP. Respondents use the identity of the proposer as a heuristic to make judgments about the merits of constitutional revision. If debates over Article 9 have saturated society sufficiently, such that preferences have hardened, then it is not surprising that we do not observe a treatment effect on this issue.

8.4. Discussion and Conclusion

Foreign policy, particularly whether to remain a "peace state" or become a "normal nation," is a key ideological cleavage in Japan. It was highly politicized in the first decade after World War II, but its salience faded due to the peace brought by the American nuclear umbrella and the electoral system's emphasis on clientelistic, not programmatic, linkages. Two main changes have resurrected the political salience of this cleavage. The first is the end of the Cold War, which reanimated historical animosities and rivalries between Japan and its geopolitical neighbors. The second is electoral reform, which established a more majoritarian electoral system that encouraged parties to focus on programmatic issues.

The politics of constitutional revision, particularly to Article 9's "Peace Clause," lies at the intersection of these two changes. At the elite level, the dominant LDP has long pressed for constitutional amendment, but the issue gained prominence after 2012, with the party's publication of a new constitutional draft. At the mass level, this chapter's analysis suggests that partisan framing matters, but in a way that discourages elite politicization. Japanese citizens prefer revisions whose provenance is perceived to be neutral rather than partisan. This effect is stronger for topics that have received less attention historically, such as adding environmental rights or national emergency provisions, than for those whose purpose and effects have been discussed extensively, especially Article 9.

Let me end by discussing the broader implications of these findings. In terms of the normal nation–peace state cleavage in Japan, the LDP is caught in a catch-22. If the LDP wants to revise the constitution, then it must persuade the public that this is not a partisan project. That said, developing an amendment jointly with an opposition party is difficult, precisely because it deals with a major political cleavage; the priorities of conservative and progressive parties clearly differ, particularly on Article 9. The LDP may continue to dangle constitutional amendment as a carrot to conservative voters, but the pursuit of controversial proposals risks turning off independent voters, threatening the electoral survival of LDP candidates in marginal districts.[9]

In terms of comparative implications, the Japanese case illuminates the importance of not only distinguishing elites from the masses, but also of separating a party's position from that of its legislators. These distinctions matter for understanding the position (preference) and salience (prioritization) of actors (Shim and Gherghina 2020). For example, the LDP increasingly emphasized the normal nation–peace state cleavage over the urban–rural dimension after the 1990s. As discussed in this chapter, this can be seen in the growing space that the LDP devoted to constitutional revision in its election manifestos. However, candidate-level surveys reveal that legislators were divided on how to amend the supreme law, and that they continued to prioritize fiscal redistribution in their own campaigns. As a result, voters received mixed messages: while the party's pro-amendment position was clear, that was not what they were hearing from their candidates. The result of this inconsistency is that voters, particularly left- and right-wing partisans, began to take greater interest in constitutional revision, but not enough that they backed the priorities of their preferred parties' elites.

Similar differences likely exist elsewhere. However, it is difficult to contrast parties from candidates from voters in the absence of high-quality candidate surveys. While manifesto analysis and voter surveys have become commonplace in most countries, these do not allow us to estimate the extent to which legislators differ among one another, even within the same party. This points to the importance of developing research projects that explicitly analyze the positions and priorities of individual elites, as well as the utility of using Japan, where this type of data exists, to study mass–elite divergence.

The findings in this chapter complement the key patterns observed in other chapters: mass–elite discrepancies persist because the established parties benefit from the status quo. But the Japanese example demonstrates that mass–elite discrepancies can persist even when elites want to change the status quo to achieve their ideological goals. Two reasons pointed out in this chapter—elite consistency and persuasiveness—hint at the importance of elite competence in closing mass–elite gaps. In other words, having the choice to politicize issues versus doing so tactfully to change people's preferences are distinct matters.

Notes

1. This is not to say that Japan is a homogenous society, particularly with the gradual liberalization of immigration laws in recent years (cf. Strausz 2019). However, many Japanese citizens consider ethno-cultural homogeneity to be a key criterion of "Japanese-ness" (Woo 2022).

2. See Winkler (2017) for a discussion of how the end of the Cold War, the bursting of the asset bubble, and electoral reform combined to shape the LDP's party manifestos, and how these compare to conservative parties in other nations.

3. The year 2012 marked the sixtieth anniversary of the San Francisco Peace Treaty, which ended the Allied Occupation and returned sovereignty to the Japanese government. The 2005 draft coincided with the sixtieth anniversary of the end of World War II. For a comparison of the 2005 and 2012 versions, see McElwain and Winkler (2015).

4. The other three topics are (1) expanding the right to free education beyond the ninth grade/junior high school; (2) adding "state of emergency" provisions, with a particular focus on allowing the postponement of House of Representatives' elections during states of emergency; and (3) permitting each prefecture to have at least one seat in the House of Councillors (upper house). The rest of this chapter will focus on debates over Article 9, which are at the heart of the "normal nation" vs. "peace state" cleavage. A further discussion of the other topics can be found in McElwain (2018), and its continuing salience in the 2021 election can be found in McElwain (2023).

5. The University of Tokyo–*Asahi* Survey, conducted by Masaki Taniguchi of the University of Tokyo and the *Asahi* newspaper, polled all election candidates (preelection) and the Japanese electorate (postelection mail survey) on a variety of policies, ideologies, and constitutional matters. The full UTAS data, which received responses

from 97 percent of all candidates, can be found at http://www.masaki.j.u-tokyo.ac.jp/utas/utasindex_en.html

6. Originally responses in UTAS were recorded on a five-point Likert scale. Table 8.1 collapses these into a dichotomous measure, where respondents are coded as being in support if they "agreed" or "somewhat agreed" with the constitutional amendment.

7. The proportional representation ballot is a better measure of "sincere" preferences than the single-member districts with plurality winners ballot, which is subject to strategic voting incentives.

8. In general, neutral responses are more common among voters (31.1% in 2012, 36.7% in 2014, and 33.4% in 2017) than candidates (6.5%, 6.1%, and 6.7%, respectively). The lower level of neutrality among candidates speaks to the issue's greater saliency and polarization among elites, as discussed in McElwain (2020).

9. Furthermore, Liff and Maeda (2019) argue that the LDP is already constrained in its ability to promote major changes to Article 9 by its electoral dependence and political coalition with the Komeito, whose supporters oppose any movement toward (possible) militarization. While Komeito politicians are not reflexively against amendments, the party's 2017 manifesto listed priorities that are of less interest to the LDP, such as stronger local governments and the addition of environmental rights.

References

Catalinac, Amy. 2016. *Electoral Reform and National Security in Japan: From Pork to Foreign Policy*. New York: Cambridge University Press.

Curtis, Gerald L. 1971. *Election Campaigning Japanese Style*. Tokyo: Kodansha International.

Deegan-Krause, Kevin, and Zsolt Enyedi. 2010. "Agency and the Structure of Party Competition: Alignment, Stability and the Role of Political Elites." *West European Politics* 33 (3): 686–710.

DeWit, Andrew, and Sven Steinmo. 2002. "The Political Economy of Taxes and Redistribution in Japan." *Social Science Japan Journal* 5 (2):159–78.

Hellegers, Dale M. 2001. *We the People: World War II and the Origins of the Japanese Constitution*. Stanford: Stanford University Press.

Hobolt, Sara Binzer. 2007. "Taking Cues on Europe? Voter Competence and Party Endorsements in Referendums on European Integration." *European Journal of Political Research* 46 (2): 151–82.

Hobolt, Sara Binzer, and Sylvain Brouard. 2010. "Contesting the European Union? Why the Dutch and the French Rejected the European Constitution." *Political Research Quarterly* 64 (2): 309–22.

Jou, Willy, and Masahisa Endo. 2016. *Generational Gap in Japanese Politics: A Longitudinal Study of Political Attitudes and Behaviour*. New York; Palgrave Macmillan.

Kapur, Nick. 2018. *Japan at the Crossroads: Conflict and Compromise after Anpo*. Cambridge, MA: Harvard University Press.

Kawato, Sadafumi. 1992. *Nihon no seito seiji, 1890–1937-nen: Gikai bunseki to senkyo no suryo bunseki*. Tokyo: Tokyo Daigaku Shuppankai.

Kohno, Masaru. 1997. *Japan's Postwar Party Politics*. Princeton: Princeton University Press.

Krauss, Ellis S., and Robert J. Pekkanen. 2011. *The Rise and Fall of Japan's LDP: Political Party Organizations as Historical Institutions.* Ithaca: Cornell University Press.

Liff, Adam P. 2017. "Policy by Other Means: Collective Self-Defense and the Politics of Japan's Postwar Constitutional Reinterpretations." *Asia Policy* 24 (1): 139–72.

Liff, Adam P., and Ko Maeda. 2019. "Electoral Incentives, Policy Compromise, and Coalition Durability: Japan's LDP–Komeito Government in a Mixed Electoral System." *Japanese Journal of Political Science* 20 (1): 53–73.

Lipset, Seymour M., and Stein Rokkan, eds. 1967. *Party Systems and Voter Alignments.* New York: Free Press.

Lupia, Arthur. 1994. "Shortcuts versus Encyclopedias: Information and Voting Behavior in California Insurance Reform Elections." *American Political Science Review* 88 (1): 63–76.

Maeda, Ko. 2023. "Wedge Issue Politics in Japan: Why Not Revising the Constitution Is Helping the Pro-Revision Ruling Party." *Journal of East Asian Studies* 23 (2): 1–15.

McElwain, Kenneth Mori. 2008. "Manipulating Electoral Rules to Manufacture Single Party Dominance." *American Journal of Political Science* 52 (1): 32–47.

McElwain, Kenneth Mori. 2012. "The Nationalization of Japanese Elections." *Journal of East Asian Studies* 12 (3): 323–50.

McElwain, Kenneth Mori. 2014. "Party System Institutionalization in Japan." In *Party System Institutionalization in Asia: Democracies, Autocracies, and Shadows of the Past,* edited by Allen Hicken and Erik Martinez Kuhonta, 74–107. Cambridge: Cambridge University Press.

McElwain, Kenneth Mori. 2018. "Constitutional Revision in the 2017 Election." In *Japan Decides 2017: The Japanese General Election,* edited by Robert J. Pekkanen, Steven R. Reed, Ethan Scheiner, and Daniel M. Smith, 297–312. London: Palgrave Macmillan.

McElwain, Kenneth Mori. 2020. "When Candidates Are More Polarised Than Voters: Constitutional Revision in Japan." *European Political Science* 19 (3): 528–39.

McElwain, Kenneth Mori. 2021. "The Japanese Constitution." In *The Oxford Handbook of Japanese Politics,* edited by Robert J. Pekkanen and Saadia M. Pekkanen, 22–40. Oxford: Oxford University Press.

McElwain, Kenneth Mori. 2023. "Constitutional Revision in the 2021 Election." In *Japan Decides 2021: The Japanese General Election,* edited by Robert J. Pekkanen, Steven R. Reed, and Daniel M. Smith, 319–31. New York: Palgrave Macmillan.

McElwain, Kenneth Mori, Shusei Eshima, and Christian G. Winkler. 2021. "The Proposer or the Proposal? An Experimental Analysis of Constitutional Beliefs." *Japanese Journal of Political Science* 22 (1): 15–39.

McElwain, Kenneth Mori, and Christian G. Winkler. 2015. "What's Unique about Japan's Constitution? A Comparative and Historical Analysis." *Journal of Japanese Studies* 41 (2): 249–80.

Miyake, Ichiro, Yoshitaka Nishizawa, and Masaru Kohno. 2001. *55-Nen taisei-ka no seiji to keizai: Jiji Yoron-Chousa data no bunseki.* Tokyo: Bokutaku-sha.

Noble, Gregory W. 2010. "The Decline of Particularism in Japanese Politics." *Journal of East Asian Studies* 10 (2): 239–73.

Pierson, Paul. 2011. *Politics in Time: History, Institutions, and Social Analysis.* Princeton: Princeton University Press.

Przeworski, Adam, and John Sprague. 1986. *Paper Stones: A History of Electoral Socialism*. Chicago: University of Chicago Press.

Ramseyer, J. Mark, and Frances McCall Rosenbluth. 1993. *Japan's Political Marketplace*. Cambridge, MA: Harvard University Press.

Ramseyer, Mark, and Frances M. Rosenbluth. 1995. *The Politics of Oligarchy: Institutional Choice in Imperial Japan*. Cambridge: Cambridge University Press.

Reed, Steven R. 1990. "Structure and Behavior: Extending Duverger's Law to the Japanese Case." *British Journal of Political Science* 20 (3): 335–56.

Reed, Steven R., and Michael F. Thies. 2001. "The Causes of Electoral Reform in Japan." In *Mixed-Member Electoral Systems: The Best of Both Worlds?*, edited by M. S. Shugart and M. P. Wattenberg, 152–72. New York: Oxford University Press.

Richardson, Bradley M. 1997. *Japanese Democracy: Power, Coordination, and Performance*. New Haven: Yale University Press.

Sakaiya, Shiro. 2017. *Kenpō to yoron: Sengo Nihonjin wa kenpō to dō mukiatte kitanoka*. Tokyo: Chikuma Shobou.

Samuels, Richard J. 2007. *Securing Japan: Tokyo's Grand Strategy and the Future of East Asia*. Ithaca: Cornell University Press.

Scheiner, Ethan. 2006. *Democracy without Competition in Japan: Opposition Failure in a One-Party Dominant State*. Cambridge: Cambridge University Press.

Shim, Jaemin. 2020. "Left Is Right and Right Is Left? Partisan Difference on Social Welfare and Particularistic Benefits in Japan, South Korea and Taiwan." *Journal of International and Comparative Social Policy* 36 (1): 25–41.

Shim, Jaemin, and Sergiu Gherghina. 2020. "Measuring the Mass-Elite Preference Congruence: Findings from a Meta-Analysis and Introduction to the Symposium." *European Political Science* 19 (4): 509–27.

Strausz, Michael. 2019. *Help (Not) Wanted: Immigration Politics in Japan*. Albany: State University of New York Press.

Taniguchi, Masaki, and Asahi Shimbun. 2012, 2014, 2017. University of Tokyo–Asahi Survey. http://www.masaki.j.u-tokyo.ac.jp/utas/utasindex_en.html

Winkler, Christian G. 2011. *The Quest for Japan's New Constitution: An Analysis of Visions and Constitutional Reform Proposals (1980–2009)*. London: Routledge.

Winkler, Christian G. 2017. "Right On? The LDP's Drift to the Right and the Persistence of Particularism." *Social Science Japan Journal* 20 (2): 203–24.

Woo, Yujin. 2022. "Homogenous Japan? An Empirical Examination on Public Perceptions of Citizenship." *Social Science Japan Journal* 25 (2): 209–28.

CHAPTER 9

Domesticizing Foreign Policy?

The Opportunistic Engagement of Bulgarian Elites with Mass Attitudes on EU Integration

Petar Bankov and Sergiu Gherghina

The European Union (EU) plays a crucial role in the domestic politics of many of its member states. For example, the national experiences during the Great Recession of the 2010s demonstrate the significant impact and influence of the EU on domestic policy and on the mass–elite congruence of opinion within each of its member states. The EU is also influential in policy areas that remain the domain of national governments. For instance, foreign policy remains a policy area in which, despite significant integration, especially in defense and security matters, the EU-27 can nevertheless speak with distinct voices. Examples of such situations are the invasion of Iraq, the annexation of Crimea, and the Syrian Civil War.

Despite these examples, very little exploration has been done on the mass–elite congruence of opinion about the EU and its relation to the geopolitical orientation of a country. The studies that have covered the topic have focused on the congruence among candidate countries where the European orientation is a prerequisite for accession. Understanding how this European orientation is maintained in an EU member state is important due to the gradual shift in the geopolitical balance of power in recent years, which is marked by increasing challenges to the leadership role of the US, the declining international clout of the EU, and the growing importance of other geopolitical players such as the BRICS countries (Brazil, Russia, India, China, and South Africa).

As noted with global examples by Shim (see chapter 2), changing geopolitical dynamics are particularly important in shaping key domestic political cleavages in new democracies. New democracies in Central and Eastern Europe are particularly vulnerable to such geopolitical changes. Positioned between Western Europe and Russia, and close to the MENA region, countries in Central and Eastern Europe often developed their external relations in accordance with these circumstances. The end of the authoritarian regimes in Central and Eastern Europe in the late 1980s caused a significant change in their foreign policy since most of these countries looked toward the West. Given that 11 postcommunist countries have now completed the EU accession process, this seems to confirm the overall mass–elite consensus about the EU. Yet several postaccession developments reflect adversarial attitudes, such as the recent democratic backsliding in several Eastern European member states, the questioning of EU policy-making and decision-making processes, the rather uncritical attitude toward China, and intensifying links with Russia. Since 2022, following the Russian invasion of Ukraine, most of these countries have reconsidered their relations with Russia: while some of them, such as Poland and the Baltic states, favor further Western integration, others, such as Bulgaria and Serbia, strive for a more balanced position despite declaring their public support for Ukrainian defense. All these developments raise two questions: Is there any significant preference mismatch between the preferences of the masses and the preferences of the parliamentary elites toward EU integration? If so, what explains it?

This chapter addresses this question by focusing on the particular case of Bulgaria. Bulgaria successfully consolidated its democracy by the late 2000s, becoming a member of the European Union in 2007, a step underpinned by widespread public and political consensus. Yet recent developments in the country seem to challenge this consensus, as is evident in the electoral rise of antipolitical establishment parties, the regular eruption of mass antigovernment protests, government instability, and continuous monitoring by the EU of the country's efforts to tackle corruption. In this context, the main aspects of the preaccession mass–elite congruence of attitudes that are being challenged in Bulgaria concern questions of foreign policy, among other issues. The time frame of this chapter is 2013–17, which includes several electoral periods and the period when the EU integration issues became politicized.

In order to understand the mass–elite discrepancy on EU integration issues since 2013, the empirical evidence largely focuses on the actions of the main political parties in Bulgaria. This includes four parties that together achieved continuous parliamentary representation for the entirety of the studied time frame: Citizens for European Development of Bulgaria (GERB), the Bulgarian Socialist Party (BSP), the Movement for Rights and Freedoms (DPS), and Attack (Ataka).

The next section provides a detailed background of Bulgarian foreign policy and the role of the EU within it. The second section then sets out a detailed overview of the methodological approach of measuring mass–elite congruence of opinion within the time frame before presenting the research results. The key insight from this is the general lack of mass–elite congruence in this period, with the Bulgarian public staying pro-European, while the Bulgarian elites became gradually more divided on foreign policy matters. The third section discusses the main findings and offers explanations for them. The divergence of opinion stems from the efforts of the Bulgarian elite to recover some of its internal legitimacy by politicizing the EU political dimension, while being reluctant to reform the domestic political system to address growing public disillusionment. The fourth section concludes the chapter, drawing more general lessons from the Bulgarian case that are mainly related to the central role of elites not just in maintaining but also in distorting the mass–elite congruence of opinion in key policy areas, such as foreign policy and European integration.

9.1. Foreign Policy in Bulgaria: The Euro-Atlantic vs. Russia

The choice of foreign policy reflects the particularities of political competition in Central and Eastern Europe in general, and in Bulgaria in particular. Like most countries in the region, by the mid-2000s Bulgaria had completed its transition to democracy and a market economy through its accession to the EU and the North Atlantic Treaty Organization (NATO). From that perspective, it seems that the country has clearly oriented itself toward more intensive political and social relations with the West based on shared values. However, this was not without its challenges. Bulgaria joined NATO in 2004 and the EU in 2007, yet it could not completely enjoy the benefits of these memberships. Economically, the country still lags behind the EU average, while it also remains subject to close monitoring by the EU regarding its efforts at judicial reform and in tackling corruption. In such circumstances, foreign policy is one of the most contested topics among both the Bulgarian national elite and the wider society.

In Bulgaria, foreign policy is not limited to the country's place within the Western system of international relations, but also encompasses its relations with other major geopolitical actors, particularly Russia. During the communist period, Bulgaria was the closest European ally of the Soviet Union; this relationship developed not only because of the close historical and cultural links between the two countries, but also as a pragmatic strategy on the part of Bulgaria to integrate itself into the postwar system of international relations (Baeva and Kalinova 2011). Following the collapse of the authoritarian communist regime in Bulgaria, the country could no longer rely on Russia as its main economic and political partner, necessitating a reorientation of its foreign policy. This reorientation was closely entwined with the process of regime change. Essentially, during the 1990s, the Bulgarian elite was divided between two main positions. On the one hand, the main representatives of the former democratic opposition, the Union of Democratic Forces on the center-right, argued that Bulgaria needed to completely sever its links with the former Soviet successor states, and instead orient itself toward the West and seek membership in the EU and NATO to consolidate its fragile system of liberal democracy and its market economy. On the other hand, the former communist party, by then transformed into the center-left Bulgarian Socialist Party, maintained the idea that the country should aim for neutrality in its foreign policy in order to establish a stable political and economic system that reflected the social demands in the country. In this respect, while the BSP actively supported the Bulgarian candidacy for EU membership, it was reluctant to pursue NATO membership, advocating for the similar Russian position that the end of the Cold War required the abolition of this defense organization (Karasimeonov 2010). Yet the party reversed this position in the late 1990s, allowing for the country to successfully resolve this foreign policy debate.

Between 2008 and 2013 this consensus remained, as the overwhelming majority of the parliamentary parties openly supported the Euro-Atlantic orientation of the country. Yet it should be noted that there were some important nuances encompassed within this stance. Following the demise of the Union of Democratic Forces in the early 2000s, the Bulgarian right has been represented by two main currents: the liberal right, represented by the Union of Democratic Forces remnants, has taken an unquestionably pro-Western position, while the center-right populist Citizens for European Development of Bulgaria has maintained a balancing position advocating for continuous Euro-Atlantic integration, but also for productive relations with Russia. The centrist Movement for Rights and Freedoms, representative of the large Turkish minority in Bulgaria, was also pro-Western, but following the change in leadership of its leader, Lyutvi Mestan, in 2013 it took a balancing stance similar to GERB's. Until 2013 the Bulgarian Socialist Party had also maintained pro-Western positions, but it also made noticeable pro-Russian moves. For example, when the party was in power (2005–9), it delayed taking a position on the Russian invasion of Georgia in 2008 and aimed to accelerate links with Russia by signing a series of contracts on energy projects, the main one being the building of the Belene nuclear power plant with Russian technology and investment. In contrast to the other three parties, the populist radical right Attack (Ataka) has maintained a firm anti-Western stance, claiming that EU and NATO membership has transformed Bulgaria into a US colony.

During the same period between 2008 and 2013, Bulgarian society also shared the general pro-European attitude of the elite but was generally quite warm toward Russia as well. According to Eurobarometer, support for EU membership remained strong, ranging between 49.6 percent (2013) and 63 percent (2009). At the same time, however, favorable opinions on Russia experienced a similar trend. In 2007, the year of Bulgaria's EU accession, 78 percent of Bulgarian society had a favorable attitude toward Russia (Pew Research Center 2007, 73). This was confirmed in 2009 in a survey revealing that 45 percent thought that Russian influence had a positive effect on Bulgaria (Pew Research Center 2009, 61). Prior to 2013 there was an overall mass–elite congruence of opinion in support of the EU, coupled with strong potential for a similar congruence on supporting Russia too, given the pro-Russian positions of BSP and Ataka and the generally positive attitudes of Bulgarian society toward Russia.

These kinds of political dynamics are not unusual for countries in Central and Eastern Europe. What makes the Bulgarian case distinct are two main features. First, the divide between pro-European and pro-Russian attitudes in Bulgaria exists in the absence of a major structural dimension that underpins it. The country does not have a sizable Russian-speaking minority, such as those in the Baltic countries or Ukraine, so the geopolitical debate lacks firm links to existing ethnolinguistic divisions within the country. This is important, because the absence of this structural element places the debate clearly within the foreign policy dimension and leaves aside the complexities of the roles that identity, ethnicity, and language may bring to such a debate.

Second, the pro-Russian positions in Bulgaria remain less tarnished than in most Central European countries, and thus carry strong mobilization potential. This is because in contrast to some Central and Eastern European countries, Bulgaria has never formally been part of Russia, so the public perception of Russia in Bulgaria has constantly been that of a foreign country that has influenced and shaped Bulgarian politics externally. Furthermore, the historical relations between Bulgaria and Russia lack defining events around which Bulgarian society and elites could agree. For example, the period of communist rule has not been perceived as imposed from abroad in the same way as it is viewed in Poland, Czechia, Slovakia, or Hungary due to the absence of Soviet troops on Bulgarian territory and the lack of traumatic events enshrined in the collective memory, such as the Soviet crackdowns on mass public protests supporting democracy and liberty (e.g., the invasions of Hungary in 1956 and Czechoslovakia in 1968). The closest Bulgaria came to this sort of traumatic event with strong underpinnings in the Bulgarian collective memory is perhaps the period of the communist takeover of power in 1944, which occurred during the Soviet invasion and occupation of Bulgaria, when Bulgarian communists violently persecuted and removed any rival elites, especially those associated with the past regime. Nevertheless, this event remains a point of heavy debate in Bulgarian society, as it is also entangled with domestic social divides in Bulgaria. In other words, there is a relative distance between Russia and some of the more traumatic events in Bulgarian history, which cannot necessarily be said for the experiences of other countries in Central and Eastern Europe.

Given this context, we can learn two main things from the Bulgarian case. First, we can understand the dynamics shaping mass–elite congruence on European integration as a geopolitical choice. In this respect, the debate is not necessarily only between different visions of European integration or its pace, but also involves a third perspective that challenges the need for European integration at all, and which proposes the potential pursuit of alternative pathways. From the Western European perspective, as noted in chapters 2 and 3, the core tension of the EU lies between keeping national sovereignty and entrusting more power to a supranational institution, which resembles the center vs. periphery conflict. In contrast, in Bulgaria, the EU dimension often boils down to the competing orientation between two different centers, and thus can be summed up as a center A vs. center B conflict. This may be valuable for studies on mass–elite congruence in countries such as those from the western Balkans that are pursuing EU membership while also remaining open to influences from other major geopolitical players like Russia and China. Certainly, the Russian invasion of Ukraine substantially reduced the public wish among those countries to have closer relations with Russia, although elite economic interests can still push forward such linkages. Also, the Bulgarian case provides insights into the potential ways the EU could reaffirm its role in the domestic politics of its members when faced with a geopolitical challenge. Second, Bulgaria is an illuminating case for any small country debating a balance between the major geopolitical powers. This is particularly relevant for countries from the Global South that find themselves in similar situations: while not sharing a border with influential political actors in the international arena, the development of these countries very much depends on the domestic debate and consensus between society and elites on relations with major global actors.

9.2. The Level of Mass–Elite Congruence on the EU Integration Dimension: 2013–2017

9.2.1. Previous Scholarship and Its Limitations

The study of the mass–elite congruence of opinions about the EU takes a variety of forms. Existing research has explored the dynamics of party competition (Dolný and Baboš 2015), debates on particular politics (Rosset and Stecker 2019), and the different forms of politicization of key questions (Leconte 2015), looking at these topics at both pan-European (Thomassen and Schmitt 1999; Schmitt and Thomassen 2000) and national levels (Holmberg 1997; Andeweg 2011). What we know so far is that mass and elite opinions on the EU influence each other (Hooghe 2003; Steenbergen, Edwards, and de Vries 2007; Sanders and Toka 2013), and that the EU question has multiple subdimensions (Hooghe, Marks and Wilson, 2002; Mattila and Raunio 2006, 2012; chapter 3, this vol.). For example, an important dimension is the trust that societies and elites have in the EU to address particular challenges, such as resolving the financial and economic crisis within the union (Serricchio, Tsakatika, and Quaglia 2013), the challenges related to the migrant waves moving toward its member states (Bertelsmann Stiftung 2016), and its long-standing democratic deficit (Norris 1997; Rohrschneider 2002).

In this context, the question of European integration as a geopolitical matter has not received significant attention. The topic has, however, been addressed in works focused on EU-related referenda held in current or candidate member states (Mikkel and Pridham 2004; Tverdova and Anderson 2004; Hobolt and Brouard 2011). These works highlight the prevalent dynamics between masses and elites in the debate about pursuing EU integration or following an independent path shaped by national interests, as well as the nature of the relations between the country in question and the EU. Bulgaria's mass–elite congruence of opinion on the EU as a geopolitical matter has attracted very little prior academic attention. Existing works involving the Bulgarian case are mainly comparative, focusing on the mass–elite congruence on EU integration rather than the foreign policy element of it from a geopolitical perspective (Lengyel and Szabó 2019); and even when researchers do touch upon it, they focus on the role of certain parts of the elite that challenge the congruence (Sygkelos 2015). More importantly, these works have not looked at relations with Russia and how they shape the mass–elite congruence of opinion on the EU within the country. These relations, and the role of Russia in the geopolitical orientation of Bulgaria, remain firmly a matter for international relations studies (Veleva-Eftimova 2017). Nevertheless, the role of the mass–elite congruence of opinion has been highlighted there as well. Most recently, for example, Dimitar Bechev argued that despite the general Russophilia of Bulgarian society, the Bulgarian and Russian political elites continue to pursue a rather pragmatic approach in which both countries engage based on their own rational interests (Bechev 2017). The same work notes that this pragmatism is a product of, among other factors, the declining strength of this widespread public Russophilia among Bulgarians.

Beyond the limited focus on the mass–elite congruence of opinion on the EU as a geopolitical matter, its study also faces some key methodological and data availability challenges. The current literature relies predominantly on either quantitative (Real-Dato 2017; Mattila and Raunio 2012) or qualitative studies (Ray 2007; Helbling and Tresch 2011; Leconte 2015), which rarely make use of each other's insights. Furthermore, the measurement of mass–elite congruence remains unclear and faces three main issues. First, there is a predominant focus on political developments in election years (e.g., Ibenskas and Polk 2022). However, this approach leaves out more frequent measurements of continuing fluctuations in mass–elite congruence. The latter is needed in the Bulgarian case, as the discussion centers around dynamic domestic and international developments between 2013 and 2017, which could not be grasped if only election years are focused upon.

Second, existing studies examining Bulgaria rely on the dichotomy of "congruent" and "incongruent" mass–elite relations, thus neglecting any potential nuances (e.g., Savkova 2010). In this respect, the present chapter grounds its assessments on the available data in an attempt to establish whether and to what extent mass–elite opinion has been "congruent" or "incongruent." As will be detailed, the level of congruence examined here focuses not only on the congruence of opinion between masses and elites but also on the internal consensus within each of these two sides. In doing so, it takes into account the distribution aspects of opinion congruence that are noted in chapters 2 and 4 of this book.

Third, data gathering remains a costly challenge for the study of mass–elite congruence in new democracies. While mass opinion can be gauged by surveys, elite opinion remains hard to distill, and is usually gathered by elite surveys, expert surveys, roll call votes, party manifestos, legislative speeches, newspaper descriptions, public speeches, or elite interviews. As has been discussed in more detail elsewhere (Bankov and Gherghina 2020), all these sources have issues relating to validity, comprehensiveness, and with being longitudinal. Among them, the two most reliable sources that allow elite opinion to be gauged are elite surveys and the public speeches of members of the political elite (Bankov and Gherghina 2020). In this respect, however, very few elite surveys have been done in Bulgaria, so the only remaining option is public speeches. These carry the benefits of being available in ample quantity for analysis, as elites regularly share their views on the questions of the day, while also being accessible directly.

9.2.2. Utilizing Public Speeches and the Eurobarometer

The time frame of this analysis is 2013–17, which captures a period of significant political instability in Bulgaria marked by three early parliamentary elections (2013, 2014, 2017) and two major waves of antigovernment protests against both right-leaning and left-leaning governments (2013 and 2013–14). The same period also covers important international events that illuminate the underlying political tensions between pro-EU and pro-Russian positions in Bulgaria, including the 2013 Euromaidan protests in Ukraine, the 2014 annexation of Crimea by Russia, the conflict between Ukraine and secessionist forces in the Donbas and Luhansk Oblasts, the migration wave since the eruption of the Syrian Civil War in 2011, and the Russian involvement in the Syrian Civil War since 2015. When all of these are combined, the mid-2010s can be defined as a critical juncture for the EU dimension in Bulgaria, during which both masses and elites revisited and reconsidered Bulgaria's relationship with the European Union, and as a result, elite agency for politicization increased.

The data for mass opinions analyzed here comes from the Eurobarometer (EB) surveys. This is an international survey that uses representative probability samples at the national level and asks the same questions in all EU member states and in a few candidate countries. The standard version of the questionnaire is collected twice a year, once in the spring and once in the fall. For this analysis, we used the November version because it allowed us to capture the attitudes formed throughout the year. The Eurobarometer surveys analyzed have the following numbers: 80.1, 82.3, 84.3, 86.2, and 88.3.

The EB does not regularly gauge opinion on Russia, but it does on the

EU, so we used one key question included in all surveys to establish the extent to which Bulgarian society was affiliated with the EU during that period. This is a straightforward question of support for the EU's direction: "At the present time, would you say that, in general, things are going in the right direction or in the wrong direction, in the European Union?" After combining the total number of respondents, we calculated the proportion of those who said that the EU is on the right track, that is, Right direction/ (Right direction + Wrong direction).

For the elite attitudes, we analyzed the public speeches of the party presidents of the four main political parties that were either in government or which formed the main opposition in Bulgaria: Attack (Ataka), the Bulgarian Socialist Party, the Movement for Rights and Freedoms, and Citizens for European Development of Bulgaria. Data on their speeches came from media sources representing the broad ideological and pro-/antigovernment palette of views, including the websites of 24 Chasa, Trud, Sega, Dnevnik, and Duma. Through the search functions of these websites, we looked for articles for the period between January 1, 2013 and December 31, 2017 that included as keywords the name of the particular party leader, the full name or abbreviation of their party, and the words "Europe," "European," or "EU" in Bulgarian.

Following a manual screening process to identify whether a particular article was relevant for the purposes of the research, we relied on a general content analysis assessing the overall attitude of a given party on a particular matter related to the EU in the given year. We sought to include the assessments by the political parties on the relations between Bulgaria with the EU if statements were presented in a given year. For example, an article reporting that in 2015 Boyko Borisov, the GERB leader, was critical of the sanctions imposed by the EU on Russia was coded as referring to GERB; relating to the EU; taking a negative view on the EU; and being supportive of Russia. For the sake of simplicity, we did not consider the salience or strength of position of each party on the EU. In our overall assessment for the given year, we coded the party position at the end of the year. This means that if we had evidence that a party's latest opinion on the EU in a given year was positive, then we coded it as positive overall. Where a party had expressed both positive and negative views on the EU, we acknowledged this in the analysis.

Aggregating the elite-level position adopted by parties allowed us to establish the extent to which political elites were congruent within themselves and to then compare this internal elite congruence with the level of public consensus on the EB question described above. The overall proportion of elites on the EU issue—either for or against—in a given year was coded based on the combined seat proportion for each side. For the purpose of building a more comprehensive description of the elite-level EU position within the legislature, beyond the aforementioned four major parties, five other parties and alliances with more than 10 parliamentary seats were included for a mass–elite discrepancy comparison. These were the Alternative for Bulgarian Revival, Reformist Block, Patriotic Front, Bulgaria without Censorship, and Volya. The calculation of their positions was based on their known pro- or anti-EU sentiment, for instance, by noting whether they belonged to Europhile or Eurosceptic party groups at the European Parliament level.

9.2.3. Results: State of Mass–Elite Discrepancy

Data analysis was sequential, establishing the internal congruence with each side and then the overall congruence of opinion between mass and elite on the EU year by year. The results of our data analysis are shown on table 9.1. Based on examining the mass side, it is quite clear that Bulgarians were clearly Europhile during the period of observation. Roughly 77–80 percent were in favor of the direction in which the EU was heading until 2014, and then, presumably as a result of the rising saliency of the migration crisis, they turned a bit more skeptical in 2015–16. To offer some context for this decline, the country experienced a migrant influx (Kolarova and Spirova 2014), culminating with the building of a wall on sections of the southern border with Turkey and Greece, and the rise of local antimigrant vigilantes (Barker 2016; Brunwasser 2016). As was revealed in an opinion poll from 2015, while Bulgarians were in favor of providing help to the migrants entering the country, they also supported improved border security (Club Z 2015).

In this context, the declining belief that the EU is going in the right direction reflects the widespread disillusionment of Bulgarian society with EU migration policy, and particularly with the Dublin Regulation that stipulates that the first member state where an asylum seeker is registered is responsible for their claim. This affected Bulgaria in particular because it was often among the first EU countries that migrants entered. Following the relative resolution of this crisis by late 2015 (Kolarova and Spirova 2016), public perceptions on the future of the EU recovered, reflecting the general trend of pro-European attitudes among Bulgarian society. Overall, it can be said that the Bulgarian public was largely in favor of the EU in spite of a short divisive period during the height of the migration crisis in 2016.

Table 9.1. The Distribution of Elite and Mass Attitudes toward the EU (%)

	Mass opinion				
	2013	2014	2015	2016	2017
Right direction of the EU	76.9%	80.1%	72.8%	58.4%	63.5%
	Elite opinion				
	2013	2014	2015	2016	2017
Europhile parties	GERB, BSP (government), DPS	GERB, DPS, Reform-ist Block, Alternative for Bulgarian Revival	GERB, DPS, Reform-ist Block, Alternative for Bulgarian Revival	GERB, DPS, Reform-ist Block, Alternative for Bulgarian Revival	GERB, DPS
Eurosceptic parties	BSP (opposi-tion), Ataka	BSP, Patriotic Front, Bul-garia without Censorship, Ataka	BSP, Patriotic Front, Bul-garia without Censorship, Ataka	BSP, Patriotic Front, Bul-garia without Censorship, Ataka	BSP, United Patriots, Volya
Pro-EU parties' seat %	71.92%**a**	65.00%	65.00%	65.00%	50.42%

a For 2013, the proportion was calculated based on averaging the pro-EU party proportion before and after the parliamentary election held in May. Prior to the election the BSP was Eurosceptic, but it then turned Europhile after the election when it formed a minority government.

In contrast to the clearly pro-European attitudes of Bulgarian society, the Bulgarian elite became more skeptical and divided on the EU and more open to alternative geopolitical orientations. This trend is clearly demonstrated by the proportion of pro-European parties since 2013. In 2013 the elites were largely Europhile, with only a 5 percent gap with the masses. Then, after 2014, the proportion of elites with Eurosceptic opinions grew and reached almost 50 percent in 2017. The only year when a brief moment of mass–elite congruence was observed was in 2016 owing to the refugee crisis in the previous years. However, unlike the masses, whose Europhile orientation bounced back, the Eurosceptic force grew even stronger in 2017. The next section includes some context regarding the elites' growing Euroscepticism over the period of observation.

9.2.4. Elite-Level Politicization: Contexts behind Growing Euroscepticism

Eurosceptic forces in Bulgaria began to be visible by 2014–15 when the question of the EU was related to the potential impact of further European integration on the country. There were two reasons for this growing skepticism. First, the series of mass protests since 2013 empowered a Eurosceptic discourse, framing the mounting social and economic challenges in Bulgaria as a result of its European integration. For example, Mihail Mikov, the BSP leader between 2014 and 2016, explained these challenges as an outcome of the EU's policies of austerity and neoliberalism (Mikov 2016); whereas Volen Siderov, the Ataka leader, called upon Bulgaria to leave the EU and join the Russia-led Eurasian Union as a reaction to the "colonization" of Central and Eastern Europe by the EU (Dnevnik.bg 2014b). In these circumstances, Eurosceptics saw the future direction of the EU as enforcing and perpetuating the existing domestic challenges of Bulgaria.

Second, the Europhiles failed to respond to this Eurosceptic discourse. Unfamiliar with being on the defensive side of the debate, they remained rather vague and ambiguous, regularly pledging allegiance to the European integration of Bulgaria without providing a clear vision on its purpose. For example, the GERB electoral manifesto from 2014 subordinated the future development of Europe to their own policies, stating that "Europe is following a successful path and solves its issues thanks to right-wing solutions and the politics we started together since 2009" (GERB 2014, 2–3). The clearest message in favor of European integration came from the DPS leader, Lyutvi Mestan, between 2013 and 2015. Mestan declared that the Euro-Atlantic orientation of the country constituted a "civilizational choice," fundamental to Bulgarian democracy (Parliament.bg 2014).

Furthermore, a section of the Bulgarian political elite has gradually become less attached to the EU. Anti-EU positions were particularly evident at the height of the Ukrainian crisis between 2013 and 2015. On the one hand, Eurosceptic party leaders such as Mikov and Siderov criticized the EU sanctions on Russia as damaging to Bulgarian business and against the Bulgarian national interest (Mikov 2016), and as "an anti-Russian offensive of . . . overseas [US] strategists" (Dnevnik.bg 2014b). In contrast, Europhile politicians held rather ambivalent positions. For example, while expressing opposition to the sanctions (Dnevnik.bg 2014a), the Bulgarian prime minister and leader of GERB, Boyko Borisov, also acted on them in 2015 by withdrawing Bulgaria from the Russian-led gas pipeline project "South Stream" (Dnevnik.bg 2015a). Such ambivalence enabled the Eurosceptics to reinterpret the European identity of the Bulgarian elite by relating an anti-EU, yet still European, identity with pro-Russian positions. This was particularly visible in the actions of the BSP, which embarked upon a protest campaign, called "With Europe, never against Russia," against the EU sanctions (Dnevnik.bg 2015b).

More importantly, the Bulgarian elite became increasingly nationalist, especially since 2015. Two factors explain this development. First, the growing authoritarian turn in Turkey during the period under study here enabled the Bulgarian elite to emphasize the close ties between Bulgarian identity and Europe. The pro-European yet somewhat nationalist discourse of DPS, the representative of the Turkish minority in Bulgaria, was particularly telling in this respect. Facing a major challenge to maintain its voter base in the early 2017 elections from a small party affiliated with Turkish government circles, DPS emphasized its democratic credentials for ethnic peace in Bulgaria and highlighted the need for further EU integration to avoid ethnic tensions (DPS 2017). Second, and more importantly, the refugee crisis amplified the nationalist rhetoric of the Bulgarian elite. After 2015, the radical right electoral alliance United Patriots (which included Ataka) gained momentum as its 2016 presidential candidate came in third on a platform opposing "the immigrant invasion" and demanding "a reform in the EU . . . that breaks with ultraliberalism and preserves the age-old Christian spirit of the Union" (VMRO 2016). A year later, similar rhetoric enabled this alliance to form a coalition government with GERB.

More noticeably, the center-left BSP adopted similar nationalist rhetoric. Led by Korneliya Ninova since 2016, the party pursued a highly nationalist electoral campaign in 2017, calling Bulgarian supporters of the EU–Canada Comprehensive Economic and Trade Agreement "national traitors" (Dnevnik.bg 2017b) and declaring that "the democracy took away a lot from us" (Dnevnik.bg 2017a), thus making clear reference to the country's authoritarian past. In such circumstances, antinationalist political voices in the country remained rather marginal. After the 2017 elections, DPS and GERB were the only pro-European parties left in the Bulgarian parliament. A relative normalization of the migration flow through Bulgaria in 2016 and 2017 then coincided with growing pro-European attitudes among Bulgarians. However, paradoxically, the country ended up with a coalition government that included both the pro-European GERB and the staunch Eurosceptic United Patriots alliance (including Ataka). In these circumstances, it therefore seems that the dynamics within the Bulgarian political elite failed to reflect public attitudes, further contributing to the overall failure of the Bulgarian political elite to achieve a congruence of opinion on key policy matters, including the country's Euro-Atlantic orientation.

Overall, we can observe a general mass–elite incongruence of opinion in Bulgaria on the question of the EU as a foreign policy matter throughout the 2013–17 period. While Bulgarian citizens have generally remained pro-European with the exception of 2016, the Bulgarian political elite has grown increasingly Eurosceptic with the development of two camps—one pro-European and committed to the EU and the Euro-Atlantic orientation of Bulgaria, and the other Eurosceptic and openly toying with alternative geopolitical orientations. Only in 2016 can a somewhat fragile congruence of opinion set around a shared skepticism of the EU's handling of the migration crisis be observed.

9.3. Critical Junctures and Elite Agency: Politicizing EU Issues for Domestic Purposes

9.3.1. A Critical Juncture for the EU Dimension in Bulgaria: 2013–2015

Looking at the data above, two main questions arise: Why did the divergence occur exactly in the period of our study? And, what explains the continuous divergence between the Bulgarian public and the elites? The answer to the first question relates to the context within which the divergence occurs. In Bulgaria, the divergence became clearly visible when the window of opportunity presented itself, allowing the elites to politicize EU issues. As noted in chapter 4, such moments are commonly known as critical junctures; they highlight a break with the old status quo and offer the potential to carve out a new path. In the Bulgarian case explored here, this new path is characterized both by a continuous pro-European attitude in Bulgarian society and a rising Euroscepticism among the Bulgarian elite. We identify two main reasons for this having occurred at that moment of time, in the mid-2010s. First, the internal situation exerted pressure on the existing status quo, including on the question of Bulgaria's EU membership and its geopolitical orientation. Since 2009, two years into its EU membership, the country has been governed by a center-right populist party, GERB, which came to power with promises of improving Bulgaria's ability to gain EU funding and resolving its long-term issues with corruption. By the end of its government term in 2013, however, GERB had already lost much of its initial popularity following its implementation of a strict austerity program, coupled both with a general failure to address the issue of corruption and multiple policy failures. At the same time, by 2013, a general realization had developed within Bulgarian society that the promised rapid development after entering the EU would not occur, thus sowing the seeds for voices from the political elite questioning the Bulgarian commitment to the EU.

Second, the critical juncture occurred at a moment of increasing international uncertainty, particularly within the Black Sea region to which Bulgaria belongs. Two particular developments enabled this change. First and foremost, in 2014 and 2015, the Ukrainian crisis, caused by the annexation of Crimea by Russia and the insurgency war in eastern Ukraine, required Bulgaria to take a clear stand. As has been demonstrated in the previous sections, these matters had the potential to open up significant social divisions in the country. Bulgaria generally abided by the general EU policy, supporting the sanctions against Russia as well as the Minsk protocols, but the internal process through which it took those decisions allowed for more critical voices to make themselves heard. Generally, beyond some parliamentary discussions and declarations, the Bulgarian position on these matters was decided by the government, prompting critics to voice concern over the transparency of these decisions. In other words, this was yet another crisis that the political opposition used for internal purposes. Second, the migration crisis related to the ongoing civil war in Syria created another layer of potential opposition to Bulgaria's geopolitical orientation. In this respect, as seen above, the critics of the current foreign policy status quo took advantage of the general public anxiety regarding the migration wave, by taking proactive steps to oppose the resettlement of refugees in the country. Bulgaria's geographical position, specifically its border with Turkey, made the country a key transit area for the migrant wave and a country highly affected by the Dublin Regulation. In these circumstances, the pro-European political elites in Bulgaria failed to provide a coherent message about supporting the refugees or the relevant EU policies and responses, thus allowing xenophobic messages to drive a further wedge between public attitudes and the dominating political elites.

9.3.2. Causes behind the Mass–Elite Discrepancy on EU Issues: Elite-Level Politicization of Domestic Politics

Here we seek an explanation for the divergence of mass–elite opinion from what the political elites did through the critical juncture period. The existing literature on mass–elite congruence of opinion emphasizes the central role of elites in shaping the topic of European integration (Franklin, Marsh, and McLaren 1994; Ray 2003; De Vries and Edwards 2009). In the Bulgarian case, the elites clearly played a key role by politicizing EU issues during the critical juncture period. Consequently, as demonstrated in the previous section, the elites became more Eurosceptic and more divided than the masses. This raises the question of why we see asymmetric politicization between the masses and the elites. We argue that the discrepancy arose because EU issue politicization has worked mainly to support the domestic political interests of the Eurosceptic segments of the Bulgarian elite. This politicization followed two main dynamics, related to two key strategic political aims.

First, in the government-opposition dynamic, parties may develop a strategy that aims to sway public opinion in their favor and thus gain support from swing and peripheral supporters. This is an external strategic gain as it refers to the abilities of political parties to expand their social clout. The literature reveals that foreign policy issues can be used as a part of such a dynamic (Sitter 2001), and the Bulgarian case confirms this expectation. This dynamic, which is mainly between the dominating parties in the Bulgarian party system—the center-right GERB and the center-left BSP—enabled the politicization of the EU question to mount pressure on the opposing side. In that way, the BSP politicized the development of a nuclear power plant with Russian technology, while subsequently challenging the government's decision to endorse the Transatlantic Trade and Investment Partnership and EU–Canada Comprehensive Economic and Trade Agreement. Similarly, GERB applied pressure on the BSP-DPS coalition to take a decisively pro-European position on the events in Ukraine in 2014. Interestingly, as already indicated, there was a noticeable continuity in the political behavior of the two sides when in government, as both GERB and BSP sought to take a balancing, yet EU-leaning position on foreign policy matters related to Russia during the studied period. Only when they were in opposition did the two sides become much more vocal and consistent in their views. In this context, it seems that both parties were reluctant to politicize the matter to an extent that would cause a significant public backlash, since both of their governments had already faced noticeable pressures due to their domestic policies. This reluctance, however, left room for Eurosceptic voices to further politicize the issue in order to strengthen their political influence.

Second, the politicization of the geopolitical orientation of Bulgaria also allowed parties to mobilize their core supporters. This mobilization refers to the pursuit of internal strategic gains where parties aim to strengthen their abilities to bring their own voter base to the ballot box. Hence, parties may choose to take positions that do not necessarily sway public opinion overall, but which appeal to their own electoral constituency. This scenario is particularly valid for BSP, as well as the two minor parties studied here—DPS and Ataka. In the case of BSP, party leaders used foreign policy to distance themselves from their predecessors in an effort to bring back disillusioned voters. After 2014, following the end of Sergey Stanishev's 12-year leadership of the party, his successors, Mihail Mikov (2014–16) and Korneliya Ninova (2016 onward), increasingly toyed with Eurosceptic discourses as revealed above, partially to demonstrate to socialist voters that the party had ended its soft pro-Europeanism under Stanishev. An added effect of this decision, however, was the growing divergence of opinion between Bulgarian elites and the wider society.

The politicization of the EU question served a similar purpose for Ataka and DPS. Ataka was already polling well below the 4 percent electoral threshold for parliamentary entry in 2013 since its supporters had become disillusioned with the party's tacit backing of a GERB minority government. The 2013 winter protests and Ataka's heightened activism around them, through which it linked its staunch opposition to the EU with openly pro-Russian positions, allowed the party to bring back some of those disillusioned supporters and keep its place in the parliament. For DPS, the EU question was less visible on its public agenda, but it nevertheless made use of it for its own purposes, particularly during the campaign for the early 2017 elections, when DPS faced a challenge for its core electorate among the Turkish minority in Bulgaria. As its challenger had an allegedly strong association with the Turkish state, DPS emphasized its commitment to Bulgaria and its Euro-Atlantic orientation as a counterpoint. Hence, we can observe how the majority of the main parties in the Bulgarian political system made use of the EU question mainly to serve their own domestic (and even internal party) goals.

The 2013–17 period studied here contains some evidence in support of the weak legitimacy of the Bulgarian elite. At that time, Bulgaria held three national referendums that addressed various policy issues ranging from the development of a new nuclear power plant (2013) to major reforms to the electoral code such as the introduction of machine voting (2015) and even a change to its electoral system from proportional representation to a two-round majoritarian system (2016). All these proposals found substantial public support but failed to pass the turnout threshold required to make them binding. Nevertheless, the 2015 and 2016 electoral code referenda had to be discussed in the Bulgarian parliament, something that the parliamentary parties reluctantly did in the first case, and completely refrained from doing in the second case until 2021. These experiences demonstrate a strong reluctance on the part of the Bulgarian political elite to reflect public attitudes that were in favor of major reforms to the political system. In view of this, it can be said that the primary motivation behind the elite-level politicization of EU issues was the elites' search for sources of political legitimacy. As has been traced above, the politicization of the EU question among the political elite was mainly used for strategic political gains rather than to address any actual public attitudes and demands. In such circumstances, we can understand the divergence as an attempt by the Bulgarian political elite to forge a new relationship with society by promoting a new social divide that diverged from the status quo, but which also essentially preserved the elites' influence. In other words, the politicization of the matter helped the Bulgarian elite to reinvent itself in the face of declining legitimacy and social clout.

The literature on mass–elite convergence of opinion points out that an incongruence over time should be the product of changing public attitudes rather than the elites' actions. This is because the elites are inclined to maintain their existing behavior if doing so benefits them (Pierson 2010). However, the situation was reversed in the Bulgarian case during the studied period, as it was the elite that shifted their attitudes away from supporting Bulgaria's Euro-Atlantic orientation, rather than the public that changed its views. Hence, the discrepancy indeed stems from the elites' activities we have discussed above. This pattern clearly contributes to the core argument of this volume, that mass–elite discrepancy can be a result of either mass- or elite-level changes.

9.4. Conclusion

This chapter has studied the mass–elite congruence of opinion about the EU and foreign policy in Bulgaria between 2013 and 2017. This was a period of ongoing political crises, marked by mass public protests, government instability, and three snap parliamentary elections. The findings revealed a significant divergence of opinion between Bulgarian society and its elites in these circumstances. The former has largely stayed pro-European, while the latter were increasingly divided on their attitude toward the EU. This chapter established that this divergence mainly stemmed from the declining political legitimacy of the Bulgarian elites. In the absence of a concrete response to public calls for a substantial reform of the political system, the parties instead politicized the EU as a foreign policy matter in order to pursue their own strategic political gains.

The mass–elite opinion divergence on EU issues deepened after 2017. The political elite became increasingly Eurosceptic, with the center right–radical right government between GERB and the United Patriots (including Ataka) taking an uncompromising stance on the potential EU accession of North Macedonia, while simultaneously being very critical of their European partners in NATO for their low financial contributions to the alliance. In contrast to the deepening Euroscepticism of the Bulgarian elite, Bulgarian society generally retained its pro-European attitudes. Nevertheless, in recent years these attitudes have been less pronounced than in the pro-Europeanism of the 2013–17 period. Symbolic of this trend are the 2020 mass antigovernment protests that refrained from making open calls to EU institutions to intervene, as had been done during the 2013–14 protest wave. In fact, the Bulgarian public has openly questioned the continued support of the EU among the Bulgarian elites despite numerous cases of high-level corruption. Nevertheless, there is also no indication that Russia presents an attractive alternative for Bulgarian foreign policy, even though the potential still remains: in December 2022 an EU-wide public survey showed that the Bulgarian public expresses much lower levels of support for Ukraine (48%) than the EU average (74%) (bTV Novinite 2022).

The Bulgarian case teaches us three important lessons. First, the experiences of the 2013–17 period confirm the key role of the elite in the mass–elite convergence of opinion about the EU. Political elites may not necessarily seek a convergence of opinion with the public, but they can use polarization to strengthen their own legitimacy. In this respect, future studies may need to consider the strategic political gains political elites may achieve from a potential divergence of opinion. Second, the legitimacy of the political elite is an important factor in explaining the level of mass–elite convergence of opinion on a particular topic. Generally, a divergence of opinion between the masses and elites may be a sign of the low public legitimacy of the latter. Hence, the elites' actions may not have a substantial impact if they lack strong public legitimacy—and the Bulgarian case demonstrates precisely that. Third, despite its growing Euroscepticism and overall divide on foreign policy matters, the Bulgarian political elite largely failed to drive a noticeable wedge in Bulgarian society on foreign policy, as Bulgarians remain generally pro-European. Hence, future studies on mass–elite opinion may seek to look into the relationship between political legitimacy and congruence in order to explain the impact of the elites' actions on the masses.

References

Andeweg, Rudy. 2011. "Approaching Perfect Policy Congruence: Measurement, Development, and Relevance for Political Representation." In *How Democracy Works: Political Representation and Policy Congruence in Modern Societies*, edited by Martn Rosema, Bas Denters, and Kees Aarts, 39–53. Amsterdam: Pallas Publications.

Baeva, Iskra, and Evgenia Kalinova. 2011. *Balgarskite prehodi, 1939–2010* [The Bulgarian transitions, 1939–2010]. Sofia: Paradigma.

Bankov, Petar, and Sergiu Gherghina. 2020. "Post-Accession Congruence in Bulgaria and Romania: Measuring Mass-Elite Congruence of Opinions on European Integration through Mixed Methods." *European Political Science* 19 (4): 562–72. https://doi.org/10.1057/s41304-020-00271-0

Barker, Neave. 2016. "Petar Nizamov: Vigilante 'Migrant Hunter' of Bulgaria." *Al Jazeera*, November. https://www.aljazeera.com/news/2016/11/petar-nizamov-vigilante-migrant-hunter-bulgaria-161105110101596.html

Bechev, Dimitar. 2017. *Rival Power: Russia's Influence in Southeast Europe*. New Haven: Yale University Press.

Bertelsmann Stiftung. 2016. *From Refugees to Workers: Mapping Labour Market Integration Support Measures for Asylum-Seekers and Refugees in EU Member States. Volume II: Literature Review and Country Case Studies*. Gutersloh: Bertelsmann Stiftung.

Brunwasser, Matthew. 2016. "Bulgaria's Vigilante Migrant 'Hunter.'" *BBC News*, March 30. https://www.bbc.co.uk/news/magazine-35919068

bTV Novinite. 2022. "Prouchvane: Bulgaria e s nay-slaba podkrepa za resheniyata Na ES za voynata v Ukrayna" [Survey: Bulgaria has the weakest support for the EU decisions on the war in Ukraine]. *Btvnovinite.Bg*, December 14. https://btvnovinite.bg/svetut/prouchvane.html

Club Z. 2015. "Bulgarite: I pomosht za bezhantsite, i poveche ohrana na granitsite" [The Bulgarians: Both in favor of help for the refugees and for securing the borders]. September 28. https://clubz.bg/28345-bylgarite_i_pomosht_za_bejancite_i_poveche_ohrana_na_granicite

Dnevnik.bg. 2014a. "Borisov se obyavi sreshtu evropeiski sanktsii za Rusia" [Borisov declared himself in opposition to European sanctions against Russia]. April 2. https://www.dnevnik.bg/bulgaria/2014/04/02/2273598_borisov_se_obiavi_sreshtu_evropeiski_sankcii_za_rusiia/

Dnevnik.bg. 2014b. "Edno naum: Siderov iska Bulgaria da izleze ot NATO i ES" [Being alert: Siderov wants Bulgaria to Leave NATO and EU]. December 5. https://www.dnevnik.bg/bulgaria/2014/12/05/2432866_edno_naum_siderov_iska_bulgariia_da_izleze_ot_nato_i_es/

Dnevnik.bg. 2015a. "Borisov: I Putin Razbra Zashto Spryahme 'Yuzhen Potok'" [Borisov: Putin also understood why we terminated 'South Stream']. December 17. https://www.dnevnik.bg/biznes/companii/2015/12/17/2672084_borisov_i_putin_razbra_zashto_spriahme_jujen_potok/

Dnevnik.bg. 2015b. "BSP svikva dnes protest pod mototo 'S Evropa, no nikoga sreshtu Rusia'" [BSP call for a protest today under the slogan 'With Europe, but Never against Russia']. February 10. https://www.dnevnik.bg/bulgaria/2015/02/10/2469189_bsp_svikva_dnes_protest_pod_mototo_s_evropa_no_nikoga/

Dnevnik.bg. 2017a. "Korneliya Ninova: Demokratsiyata ni otne mnogo" [Korneliya Ninova: Democracy took away a lot from us]. March 19. http://www.dnevnik.bg/politika/2017/03/19/2937751_korneliia_ninova_demokraciiata_ni_otne_mnogo/

Dnevnik.bg. 2017b. "Ninova opredeli kato natsionalni predateli glasuvalite 'za' CETA" [Ninova declared the voters 'in Favour' of CETA as national traitors]. February 15. http://www.dnevnik.bg/bulgaria/2017/02/15/2918841_ninova_opredeli_kato_nacionalni_predateli_glasuvalite/

De Vries, Catherine E., and Erica E. Edwards. 2009. "Taking Europe to Its Extremes: Extremist Parties and Public Euroscepticism." *Party Politics* 15 (1): 5–28.

Dolný, Branislav, and Pavol Baboš. 2015. "Voter–Representative Congruence in Europe: A Loss of Institutional Influence?" *West European Politics* 38 (6): 1274–1304.

DPS. 2017. "Programna deklaratsia na DPS" [DPS program declaration]. https://dps .bg/izbori/izbori-2017/predizborna-programa.html

Franklin, Mark N., Michael Marsh, and Lauren McLaren. 1994. "Uncorking the Bottle: Popular Opposition to European Unification in the Wake of Maastricht." *Journal of Common Market Studies* 32 (4): 455–72.

GERB. 2014. *Stabilna Bulgaria: Programa za reformi* [Stable Bulgaria: A reform program]. Sofia: Citizens for European Development of Bulgaria.

Helbling, Marc, and Anke Tresch. 2011. "Measuring Party Positions and Issue Salience from Media Coverage: Discussing and Cross-Validating New Indicators." *Electoral Studies* 30 (1): 174–83.

Hobolt, Sara B., and Sylvain Brouard. 2011. "Contesting the European Union? Why the Dutch and the French Rejected the European Constitution." *Political Research Quarterly* 64 (2): 309–22.

Holmberg, Sören. 1997. "Dynamic Opinion Representation." *Scandinavian Political Studies* 20 (3): 265–83.

Hooghe, Liesbet. 2003. "Europe Divided? Elites vs. Public Opinion on European Integration." *European Union Politics* 4 (3): 281–304.

Hooghe, Liesbet, Gary Marks, and Carole J. Wilson. 2002. "Does Left/Right Structure Party Positions on European Integration?" *Comparative Political Studies* 35 (8): 965–89.

Ibenskas, Raimondas, and Jonathan Polk. 2022. "Congruence and Party Responsiveness in Western Europe in the 21st Century." *West European Politics* 45 (2): 201–22.

Karasimeonov, Georgi. 2010. *Partiynata sistema v Bulgaria* [The party system in Bulgaria]. 3rd ed. Sofia: Friedrich Ebert Stiftung Bulgaria.

Kolarova, Rumyana, and Maria Spirova. 2014. "Bulgaria." *European Journal of Political Research Political Data Yearbook* 53 (1): 45–56.

Kolarova, Rumyana, and Maria Spirova. 2016. "Bulgaria." *European Journal of Political Research Political Data Yearbook* 55 (1): 36–41.

Leconte, Cécile. 2015. "From Pathology to Mainstream Phenomenon: Reviewing the Euroscepticism Debate in Research and Theory." *International Political Science Review* 36 (3): 250–63.

Lengyel, György, and Laura Szabó. 2019. "The Political Elite and Trust in EU Institutions after the Crisis: A Comparative Analysis of the Hungarian Case." In *Elites and People: Challenges to Democracy*, edited by Fredrik Engelstad, Trygve Gulbrandsen, Marte Mangset, and Mari Teigen, 91–111. Bingley, UK: Emerald Publishing.

Mattila, Mikko, and Tapio Raunio. 2006. "Cautious Voters–Supportive Parties: Opinion Congruence between Voters and Parties on the EU Dimension." *European Union Politics* 7 (4): 427–49.

Mattila, Mikko, and Tapio Raunio. 2012. "Drifting Further Apart: National Parties and Their Electorates on the EU Dimension." *West European Politics* 35 (3): 589–606.

Mikkel, Evald, and Geoffrey Pridham. 2004. "Clinching the 'Return to Europe': The

Referendums on EU Accession in Estonia and Latvia." *West European Politics* 27 (4): 716–48.

Mikov, Mihail. 2016. *Bulgaria dnes i zadachite na Bulgarskata Sotsialisticheska Partiya. Politicheski doklad* [Bulgaria today and the tasks for the Bulgarian Socialist Party: A political report]. Sofia: Bulgarian Socialist Party.

Norris, Pippa. 1997. "Representation and the Democratic Deficit." *European Journal of Political Research* 32 (2): 273–82.

Parliament.bg. 2014. "Verbatim, First Session, 27 October 2014." https://www.parlia ment.bg/bg/plenaryst/ns/51/ID/5305

Pew Research Center. 2007. "Rising Environmental Concern in 47-Nation Survey: Global Unease with Major World Powers." June 27. Washington, DC. https://www.pewresearch.org/wp-content/uploads/sites/2/pdf/2007-Pew-Global-Attitud es-Report-June-27.pdf

Pew Research Center. 2009. "Two Decades after the Wall's Fall: End of Communism Cheered but Now with More Reservations." November 2. Washington, DC. https://www.pewresearch.org/global/wp-content/uploads/sites/2/2009/11/Pew -Research-Center_Two-Decades-After-the-Walls-Fall-End-of-Communism-Chee red-But-Now-With-More-Reservations_2009.pdf

Pierson, Paul. 2010. *Dismantling the Welfare State? Reagan, Thatcher and the Politics of Retrenchment.* Cambridge: Cambridge University Press.

Ray, Leonard. 2003. "When Parties Matter: The Conditional Influence of Party Positions on Voter Opinions about European Integration." *Journal of Politics* 65 (4): 978–94.

Ray, Leonard. 2007. "Validity of Measured Party Positions on European Integration: Assumptions, Approaches, and a Comparison of Alternative Measures." *Electoral Studies* 26 (1): 11–22.

Real-Dato, José. 2017. "Citizens-Representatives Congruence concerning the European Union: Evolution during the Eurozone Crisis." *Corvinus Journal of Sociology and Social Policy* 8 (3S): 85–112.

Rohrschneider, Robert. 2002. "The Democracy Deficit and Mass Support for an EU-Wide Government." *American Journal of Political Science* 46 (2): 463–75.

Rosset, Jan, and Christian Stecker. 2019. "How Well Are Citizens Represented by Their Governments? Issue Congruence and Inequality in Europe." *European Political Science Review* 11 (2): 145–60.

Sanders, David, and Gabor Toka. 2013. "Is Anyone Listening? Mass and Elite Opinion Cueing in the EU." *Electoral Studies* 32 (1): 13–25.

Savkova, Lyubka G. 2010. "Mass-Elite Dimensions of Support for the EU in Bulgaria." University of Sussex.

Schmitt, Hermann, and Jacques J. A. Thomassen. 2000. "Dynamic Representation: The Case of European Integration." *European Union Politics* 1 (3): 318–39.

Serricchio, Fabio, Myrto Tsakatika, and Lucia Quaglia. 2013. "Euroscepticism and the Global Financial Crisis." *Journal of Common Market Studies* 51 (1): 51–64.

Sitter, Nick. 2001. "The Politics of Opposition and European Integration in Scandinavia: Is Euro-Scepticism a Government-Opposition Dynamic?" *West European Politics* 24 (4): 22–39.

Steenbergen, Marco R., Erica E. Edwards, and Catherine E. de Vries. 2007. "Who's

Cueing Whom? Mass-Elite Linkages and the Future of European Integration." *European Union Politics* 8 (1): 13–35.

Sygkelos, Yannis. 2015. "Nationalism versus European Integration: The Case of ATA-KA." *East European Quarterly* 43 (2–3): 163–88.

Thomassen, Jacques, and Hermann Schmitt. 1999. "Issue Congruence." In *Political Representation and Legitimacy in the European Union*, edited by Hermann Schmitt and Jacques Thomassen, 186–208. Oxford: Oxford University Press.

Tverdova, Yulia V., and Christopher J. Anderson. 2004. "Choosing the West? Referendum Choices on EU Membership in East-Central Europe." *Electoral Studies* 23 (2): 185–208.

Veleva-Eftimova, Mirela. 2017. "Bulgaria's Return to Europe: Under the Shadow of the Russophile Tradition." *Sotsiologicheski Problemi* 49 (1–2): 186–207.

VMRO (Bulgarian National Movement). 2016. "Bulgarskata platforma—Programa na Obedinenite Patrioti [The Bulgarian platform—program of the United Patriots]." https://bit.ly/3oxHhRo

Conclusion

CHAPTER 10

Conclusion

What the Book Does and What Further Research Might Follow from It

Stephen Whitefield and Robert Rohrschneider

This book starts with the vital point that democracy relies on political elites representing the views of citizens, and that if they do not, then democracies may face profound challenges. But we know—and the book has presented ample empirical evidence—that gaps between the stances taken by elites and the views of citizens are not only widespread in democracies but can be long-lasting. How and why do such gaps develop? That is the focus of attention of the collective authors of this book, which provides a comprehensive overview of existing research on mass–elite representation and summarizes the current understanding of its causes. But it also advances numerous novel and theoretically interesting and challenging arguments to explain the mass–elite gap, backed up with wide-ranging empirical evidence in support. Taken together, the chapters present a remarkably focused and consistent engagement with the subject.

In what follows, we will attempt first briefly to sum up the book's main theoretical arguments and the ways in which the empirical chapters speak most directly to these claims. We will then suggest some additional ways in which mass–elite gaps may be relevant and where further research that may draw on the insights of this book can be fruitful.

Summarizing the Main Findings

There are four significant ways in which the book contributes to our understanding of mass–elite gaps. First, the theoretical chapters are developed to deal with a global set of cases, so that insights from the mainly Western European literature to date can be placed alongside such diverse polities as Japan, Indonesia, Tunisia, and Bulgaria, such that the representation gap can be understood in a common framework. Second, because politics are contested in democracies over very different kinds of political cleavage structures and with varied elite-voter linkages, the book explicitly studies representation gaps from a multidimensional perspective. Third, because representation gaps in some contexts remain persistent, the book pays close attention to the historical circumstances in which masses and elites come to diverge and to what sustains these differences. Finally, the center of attention is placed firmly on elite choices in explaining gaps, while showing appropriate awareness of the circumstances in which elites are constrained in diverging from public sentiment and over what issues.

The core explanatory concept deployed by the book and empirically operationalized in the country studies is that of critical junctures. Quoting from Giovanni Capoccia's seminal work on this subject:

> Critical junctures are cast as moments in which uncertainty as to the future of an institutional arrangement allows for political agency and choice to play a decisive causal role in setting an institution on a certain path of development, a path that then persists over a long period of time. (Capoccia 2016, 148)

The core argument of the book follows then from the possibilities for mass–elite representation gaps to emerge at precisely the critical juncture when elites have incentives and capacities to do so. As Jaemin Shim argues in chapter 4:

> The asymmetric politicization process during the critical juncture is a result of deliberate action or inaction by elites. Put differently, elites intentionally politicize specific issues without much general public demand, or depoliticize issues with high public demand. The representation gap is an elite-level choice because elites have the agency to take other paths and can prevent the representation gap from emerging or continuing.

Table 10.1. Representation Gap Types and Observed Frequency

	Mass undivided	**Mass divided**
Elites undivided	mass centrist–elite centrist gap: rare	mass polarization–elite centrist gap: frequent
Elites divided	mass centrist–elite polarization gap: frequent	mass polarization–elite polarization gap: none

The choices that elites make at critical junctures on policy issues and their salience will vary as to their proximity to citizens' preferences, and it is this proximity that determines the nature and size of the representation gap. Theoretically, the book outlines a matrix of possible configurations depending on the interaction of citizens' and elites' stances and divisions on issues. Empirically, where citizens and elites are similarly divided—or undivided—representation gaps rarely emerge or do not emerge. However, it is when elites divide and citizens do not—or vice versa—that gaps frequently appear. While the book does not explicitly label each of these configurations, we might characterize them as in table 10.1.

We will discuss further below the factors that might lead elites to make choices to open or curtail the gaps that the table describes along with consideration of the consequences of each type of representation gap for democratic politics. However, the book focuses strongly on the circumstances in which gaps once opened will remain so. The premise that gaps mainly open during critical junctures implies that if democracies start off with a clear mapping of elite stances onto citizens' preferences, then there may be little incentive for elites to change and often clear incentives to continue to represent. So why would gaps that do open at critical junctures not close over time? A democratic theorist might expect that in this respect democracies should be self-correcting because, so long as the democracy is open to challengers, new elites should enter to better represent citizens who, either in their views or in the salience that they attach to an issue, are relatively unheard. A further core aim of the book then is to provide an explanation of the mechanisms through which nonrepresentative elites may continue to take positions at odds with citizens.

The reasoning here is in line with theorizing about cleavages, as Simon Bornscheir also develops in chapter 5. Political cleavages produce a variety of structuring factors that help sustain existing lines of elite political division, even if these divisions are only weakly connected with citizens' preferences. These factors arise from both intra-elite socialization and recruitment, whereby new elite members are chosen based on their affinity with existing elite divisions.

As Shim argues in chapter 4:

> With respect to the persistence of the mass–elite gap beyond the critical juncture, global examples from this volume demonstrate three key path dependency reinforcing mechanisms: (1) established elites marginalizing opponents who can mirror mass preferences, (2) established elites self-selecting those who already share similar views regarding politicization/depoliticization of a specific political dimension, and (3) elite-level socializing through which elites with different views can converge and become more homogeneous.

By placing the explanation for existing mass–elite representation gaps on historical moments that persist, in a sense the book is highlighting a somewhat different set of critical junctures than those that Lipset and Rokkan (1967) famously defined and indeed is advancing their approach. For Lipset and Rokkan, the defining lines of political competition emerged (and then froze) based on the most salient and mobilized political division at the point at which democratic party systems emerged. Some of the critical junctures highlighted in this book are coincident with that approach, when elite interests at the democratizing moment map with those of the mass. But the core argument presented by Shim and Bornschier is that it is elites' interests that are primary, and thus their concerns at the democratizing moment only contingently overlap with those of the mass and thus what is presented by elites to citizens may well diverge considerably. Moreover, it is at least implicit in the argument of the book that critical junctures may emerge largely within elite interests that can reshape the character of political competition, even in the absence of other powerful changes in the nature of mass preferences. In these circumstances, the mass–elite gap may diminish, or it may even broaden in nature, or it may change in its content.

To be sure, the authors make clear that there are constraints on how far elites can stray from representing citizens. As Shim, in support of Bornschier, argues in chapter 1,

> elites tend to have more leeway in politicizing or depoliticizing political dimensions when (1) multiple cleavages cross-cut each other, (2) mobilization from below is weak, (3) repressive capacity is stronger, or (4) there exist frequent authoritarian turns.

In short, the first condition allows elites to make choices about which political dimensions to make most active because they have opportunities to form various coalitions with other elites; the second condition means that elites are less concerned about mass participation, including for example by strong party bases, and so are more willing to stake out issues that matter for their own interests; and the third and fourth conditions may be thought of as different routes to the second, again that elites may choose to ignore public preferences—and in fact the desire among elites to avoid representation may be a strong stimulus to their repressive actions. As the authors make clear, therefore, the mass–elite gap is likely to be more common in new democracies.

This does not mean that incentives for weak congruence are absent in established democracies. For example, the cleavage literature is consistent in observing multidimensionality in party competition in Western Europe, as do many chapters in this book. This allows elites to make some choices about which dimensions to emphasize or to position themselves on. Importantly, when elites also have consensus interests to avoid competing on particular issues, a representation gap is highly likely. The strongest case in point here, referenced by Bornschier in chapter 5, concerns the convergence of mainstream Western European parties on economic programs, from the fall of communism to at least the financial crisis of 2008. This shift was not entirely disassociated from broader societal shifts, in particular the reduction in the size of the industrial working class. It may also have been the result of broader elite consensus on the possible forms of economic management. But as elites converged, large numbers of voters were left relatively unrepresented on the economic dimension, while elite polarization widened over sociocultural issues. This latter development again highlights the importance of the multidimensional approach to the representation gap that the book foregrounds. We need to know which dimension—or even which policy area, as Mahmoud Farag in chapter 6 makes clear—elites focus on to properly understand the gap and its political consequences.

While Western Europe may be characterized by multidimensional political competition and shifting salience attached to a given dimension, our own research (Rohrschneider and Whitefield 2012) pointed to an interesting and surprisingly counterintuitive finding that is very compatible with the constraints outlined above. Namely, levels of mass–elite congruence in postcommunist Eastern Europe appeared to be at almost identical levels to those found in the West. This was due, we argued, to offsetting factors. On the one hand, Western European parties were much more socially and organizationally embedded (the first condition above) compared to the highly volatile "floating parties" in the East that were frequently vehicles for elite advancement, which voters were unable to punish electorally. This assisted in reducing the potential gap in the West. On the other hand, Eastern European political competition was essentially uni- not multidimensional. This was the result, plausibly, of another vital critical juncture, namely how coalitions of opposition that formed against the communist system (as well as in support of it) became embedded in both mass and elite political culture and so remained relatively frozen for many years after the transition. This unidimensionality, however, made it much easier for parties and voters to align themselves and reduced the capacity of elites to choose alternative dimensions on which to compete in their own interests. These various factors appeared to be offsetting between East and West, hence what we labeled the "paradox of equal congruence."

A second illustration of the complexity produced by multidimensionality is engaged with by Andrea Pareschi, Gianfranco Baldini, and Matteo Giglioli in their chapter 3 on stances on Europe, including the very interesting analysis of the often country-idiosyncratic connections of policies to the issue of European integration. Again, much prior research discussed above has pointed to the relative orthogonality of European integration to other dimensions of party competition—in the West but not in the East, at least until recently. At the same time, as further research by us (Rohrschneider and Whitefield 2016) shows, mainstream parties barely shifted their positions on European integration, despite a significant availability of Eurosceptical voters, leaving these voters to the attention of challenger parties. Why should mainstream parties have failed to move? Some of this was, of course, because of the constraints on such parties from their social bases and core constituents. Parties cannot easily be in all places at once, particularly when they have strong policy reputations as in Western Europe, and when movement may only enhance the reputations of competitors who have established issue ownership of a new policy area. But, as Meguid (2005) has very persuasively argued, mainstream parties also have choices to make about how to compete against challengers in which the optimal strategy may often be to deliberately avoid competition on a new dimension, even if it is salient. The same may apply to challenger parties also, as Rovny (2012) has argued by pointing to the blurring strategies of right-wing, populist parties that obfuscate their position on the economy while using directional signals by taking extreme positions and giving strong salience to the issues they wish to compete over, such as immigration.

The theoretical arguments of this book, therefore, might again be briefly summarized to highlight the centrality of elite choices, especially at critical junctures, that give rise to a range of possible but not necessary mass–elite gaps, which once established may be maintained despite democratic competition by elite socialization or by the effective use of competitive strategies by elites either in the democratic marketplace or, in some contexts, by more repressive means. With that in mind, the country studies in the empirical chapters each make a strong case in support of the theory. Indeed, the clear linkage between theory and empirics is one of the most impressive aspects of the book, particularly a multiauthored one such as this.

The first case study by Mahmoud Farag in chapter 6 focuses on Tunisia and analyzes the mass–elite gap on the religious–secular dimension, which strongly divided mass opinion but over which elites chose largely not to compete. This case therefore typifies the mass polarization–elite centrist gap discussed above. In line with the theoretical reasoning underpinning the book, elites made this choice in the Tunisian context at the critical juncture of the revolutionary transformation at the fall of the old regime and this meant that they chose not to polarize on the religious dimension in line with the divisions that existed in society as a whole. Rightly, the author points to some important conditions for this choice, in particular prior consensus-building elite socialization that helped enable cooperation. But the trigger for choice lay in the levels of risk that various elite elements felt in the revolutionary setting. "To successfully navigate the transition to democracy, Ennahda's leadership knew they had to make concessions to their secular counterparts. They also had to bring their party members on board. Counterfactually, Ennahda could have chosen to enforce their religious views in the constitution. *It chose, however, not to because it was uncertain about what the secularists would do*" (italics added). The argument here mirrors that made more theoretically by Przeworski (1991), who suggested that levels of uncertainty about the balance of competing forces in revolutionary transitions might make even ideological opponents choose pathways and institutions that would moderate the possibilities of conflict, if they thought that there was a significant chance of severe political defeat. Moreover, they might make the choice to avoid conflict over issues that significantly divided society and led to a clear gap in their representation of citizens. By contrast, the chapter argues, political elites in Egypt made different choices to activate the religious–secular dimension because at least one elite faction had a belief that it would be able to win the transition outright for the religious pole of the cleavage. We should note here two important substantive and normative implications advanced by the authors. First, as Farag claims, "Egypt did not choose the politics of pragmatism. It polarized the religious–secular divide and subsequently failed to transition into a democracy." Second, the existence of a representation gap as in Tunisia, particularly when elites pact to avoid conflict, may be preferable from a democratic perspective to one in which elites choose to represent citizens, when that conflict may further drive claims that exceed the tolerances of democratic institutions.

Chapter 7 by Andreas Ufen, the second empirical chapter, focuses on the case of Indonesia, where the author provides a dynamic account of shifts in the character of mass–elite gaps over time. Again, the explanation for these shifts highlights specific historical moments when elites had choices to make about how to compete with one another. As in Tunisia and Egypt, religion was a salient divide in public opinion, but it operated alongside other divisions over class and the economy. Importantly, at least immediately after Indonesian independence, parties were also relatively strongly socially rooted. In this initial period of Indonesian democracy, mass–elite divides were low precisely because the main parties "directly translated traditionalist and modernist ideas and sentiments into the party systems." Divisions, in other words, were present in both elite and societal opinion that broadly mapped in representational terms. However, a growing rift between devout and nondevout Muslims and non-Muslims in the late 1950s led to conflict over the role of Islam in the constitution, which resulted in military rule that effectively and brutally suppressed not only religious but also class representation. It is of a broader comparative interest to consider whether authoritarian turns have the general effect of increasing the mass–elite gap. Certainly, the chapter provides a strong argument for that expectation, although we might also note that at least some electoral authoritarian regimes have incentives to build social coalitions that might have a more positive effect on congruence (Chaisty and Whitefield 2023). The final turn in recent Indonesian politics resulted from redemocratization, after which political elites chose not to stress exclusivism on the religious dimension, providing another example of a gap based on elite convergence and mass polarization on the issue. Elite choices were again shaped by the pacted nature of the redemocratization process, which largely excluded social mobilization. This choice was then entrenched via the mechanisms described above by Shim, supported particularly by the institutional design of the New Order. Moreover, while divisions continued in society, the societal roots of parties were undermined, because politics increasingly has been based on clientelistic linkages not programmatic differences. All combined, this leaves an incipient Islamism-based divide in society that is not well represented.

The third case study by Kenneth McElwain in chapter 8 involves consideration of the foreign policy dimension in Japan. It should be noted that political scientists generally expect that foreign policy issues are poorly structured at the mass level, when compared to the elite level, because it is distant from the assumed central issue of the economy (Converse 1964). In that sense, the foreign-policy political dimension example in Japan is illuminating, as it is focused around the role of Japan as an international military force. Stances on this issue were strongly shaped of course by defeat in World War II and subsequent Occupation, and the enforcement of a nonmilitaristic constitution that strongly entrenched structured views among the mass public. Again, critical juncture theory is central to the argument: first, in the aftermath of World War II; then at the end of the Cold War and during the economic slowdown. The second critical juncture offered a window of opportunity for conservative elites to politicize the issue of constitutional revision; when the necessary seat share required for constitutional revision was secured, they actively politicized the constitutional revision issue. However, they faced constraints that came in large part from resistance by the masses who have long been socialized to prefer the status-quo of a nonmilitaristic constitution.

The final empirical case study by Petar Bankov and Sergiu Gherghina in chapter 9 pertains to the issue of European integration in Bulgaria. As much of the literature attests, there was a broad consensus to "return to Europe" at both mass and elite levels across almost all postcommunist Central and Eastern Europe. This consensus persisted at least until the successful accession of these states in 2007 (Vachudova 2005). It is worth noting in this context the concerns that many observers had about the democratic deficits that arose from the accession process where elite and citizens were essentially required to agree to the EU *acquis*. Since accession, however, many countries have witnessed growing Euroscepticism, especially at the elite level. So, while there remains overwhelming mass support in the Central and Eastern European states of the EU for membership, criticisms of aspects of the EU have acquired considerable salience in the appeals and even the policies of elites. Hungary under Viktor Orbán and Poland under the Law and Justice Party are the clearest examples of this phenomenon. The explanation offered by Peter Bankov and Sergiu Gherghina in their chapter highlights the strategic decisions of Bulgarian elites about how to compete against one another for their own advantages and as a means of deflecting from other failures.

Where Might Mass–Elite Congruence Research Go from Here?

As the summary above makes clear, the book offers a rich set of propositions and evidence for the existence, persistence, and variety of mass–elite gaps. In what follows, we briefly consider four aspects of congruence gaps that warrant further theoretical and empirical investigation: the importance of the direction of mass–elite gaps; congruence and democratic commitment; nonprogrammatic congruence; and nondemocratic congruence. We highlight these questions precisely because of the book's central and initial concern that congruence is vital to the long-term stability of democratic systems.[1]

We first suggest that it is important also to consider two distinct aspects of the potential gaps between elites and citizens. The first is more commonly studied, namely, the examination of the *substantive congruence* between citizen and elite stances on a given issue. For example, do parties and voters evaluate politically salient issues in similarly positive or negative ways, or are they split in their views, in which case mass–elite gaps appear? By contrast, *relative congruence* then captures whether elites adopt more pronounced stances, either in a positive or negative direction, relative to their voters.

We can illustrate this distinction by reference to the second issue that we argue needs further development in the congruence literature, namely the extent and the nature of the mass–elite gap that might exist in the evaluation of democracy, and indeed in the levels of commitment to democracy more broadly. While, as the book has convincingly pointed out (see chapter 2), research on gaps has moved expansively to include left–right ideological placement, dimensional placements on economics, culture, and foreign relations, as yet the literature on stances on the democracy dimension remains limited. This lacuna is all the more important to fill given the widespread agreement that democracy is both negatively evaluated in practice by many citizens and parties—even when, as "critical citizens," they remain committed to democracy in principle (Norris 2011)—but also because increasingly many parties and citizens even in established democracies have come to reject representative democracy in favor of populist or illiberal alternatives. So, when do mass–elite gaps on the various aspects of democracy emerge and what might their political consequences be? We illustrate these two sides to congruence gaps—substantive and relative—over democratic performance in figure 10.1.

Substantive representation. Substantively, the top right quadrant captures conditions where parties and voters agree that a democracy performs well. This contrasts with a situation in the lower left quadrant where both parties and voters agree that the performance of a national democracy is poor. Crucially, in both cases, we observe substantive agreement among parties and their voters. We label a substantive linkage in the upper right-hand cell "virtuous" and call the substantive party-voter linkage in the lower left

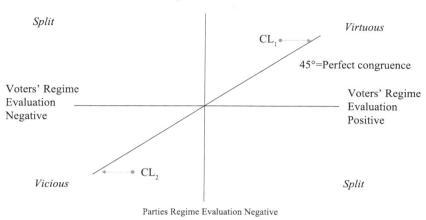

Fig. 10.1. Substantive and Relative Congruence

cell a "vicious" linkage. We also see the possibility for a "split" verdict in which parties and voters disagree directionally.

Relative congruence. Additionally, we can also consider examining whether parties, which may agree with voters that institutions perform positively or negatively, are *more or less extreme* in their evaluations of national institutions than voters are. Accordingly, in the negative quadrant, parties may be more critical than their voters; in the positive quadrant, they may be more positive than their supporters (CL1 and CL2 in fig. 10.1). Our key point is that the pattern that emerges regarding the performance of democracies may have profound implications for the dynamics of political conflict over democratic institutions. For example, if parties in the negative and positive quadrants adopt more marked positions than their voters, not only is cooperation among elites over institutional reform less likely but voters, especially partisan supporters, may be dragged by their party attachments to take more extreme positions (Anderson and Just 2013). In short, relative congruence complements the concept of substantive congruence by examining whether parties adopt more pronounced positions, either in a more unfavorable direction in the negative quadrant or in a more favorable direction in the positive quadrant. In sum, the implications of party–voter agreement about the performance of national democracies likely depend on the directions of the agreement (substantive) and the extent of relative agreement between parties and voters.

The suggestion to focus on substantive and relative congruence does not, of course, contradict the approach of the book, which is to seek to explain the existence of gaps by reference to elite choices during critical junctures. However, substantive and relative congruence add a dimension that is of considerable contemporary significance. Are elites systematically more likely to be more supportive or more negative about democracy than their supporters? Much research suggests that elites and political parties often adopt clearer positions than voters do (Putnam 1976; Dalton, Farrell, and McAllister 2011), in part because elites have more systematically formed views because they may have thought more about issues than mass publics (Converse 1964; Zaller 1992); in part, this is because parties have incentives to lead on those dimensions that they deem important (Rovny 2012). At the same time, as some chapters in this book have argued, in certain conditions—for example, over religious differences in Tunisia and at times in Indonesia—elites have made choices to take stances that are clearly less polarized than their supporters. So, various configurations on democracy gaps are possible. On the one hand, citizens may, under some circumstances, hold more critical views than elites and so provide the demand side for critical parties. On the other hand, political elites, wishing to avoid dealing with intractable policy issues, as chapter 9 has suggested, may have incentives to politicize the democracy dimension for their own interests. What these possibilities point toward then is the application of the book's approach to a further set of cases in which elites have made choices to politicize democratic conflict or to downplay it.

The third additional aspect of mass–elite gaps that we argue calls out for further study relates to nonprogrammatic representation. This is distinct from the primary focus of the book on the relationship between masses and elites on issue dimensions of various sorts, ideological stances, and policy positions. Indeed, these areas have been the central focus of congruence research to date. At the same time, considerable extant research has paid attention to issue salience congruence—whether parties and voters share understandings of the main issues facing the country—and also to valence issues such as corruption: we assume corruption is nondimensional in character as no party is likely to offer overt programmatic support for the practice, but some parties are considered better by voters at fighting it than others (Chaisty and Whitefield 2022).

However, nonprogrammatic representation has a broader scope than salience or valence. In particular, voters and parties may connect on an emotional dimension (Kosmidis et al. 2019), and voters may feel emotionally represented or neglected. Some of this element may also pertain to the question of symbolic representation, in which parties link to voters because they offer "people like us" as their candidates (Heath 2013). When such symbolic representation is absent, voters may feel a politically significant gap even if the same party manages to offer programmatic stances that adequately reflect those of their supporters. The presumption in the literature may be that programmatic representation may be most important for voter linkages; but it is at least worth considering whether the achievement of that is as important as symbolic representation is to at least some political outcomes, from voter turnout to commitment to democracy more generally.

The question of emotional representation has an even broader scope that can be detected in the seemingly increasingly inflammatory language used by political elites to connect to voters, often via nontraditional media. Here, the issue is not that such political rhetoric has a programmatic content, but that its policy content may be secondary to its emotional valence. Politicians may seek to tap into the anger or disgust or cynicism of voters, just as they may alternatively seek to project a positive "morning in America" vision. Moreover, voters—at least some voters in some circumstances—may judge the representation gap by reference to the emotional linkage that they have with elites, parties, and candidates. The nature and extent of emotional mass–elite gaps, however, remain only poorly understood, despite an intuition—held by these authors—that they are of increasing importance, perhaps particularly to the appeals of elites and supporters of parties that are strongly critical of democracies in practice, but without offering clear institutional programs for their reform and improvement.[2]

Again, there is no incompatibility between research on nonprogrammatic mass–elite gaps and the theoretical thrust of this book. Rather, the approach advocated here would suggest focusing again on when elites have incentives to politicize particular emotional appeals, including when they would seek to take emotional stances that are more or less extreme than the stances of their supporters, as was pointed out above in the discussion of relative and substantive congruence. Both relative positions are clearly possible, as was made clear in the cases where elites chose not to polarize over issues. But empirically these relationships have yet to be established. It is also unclear what the political consequences are of representational failures over emotions, particularly if mainstream parties fail not only to adapt their positions on issues—such as European integration—but also fail to find emotional linkages of their own that may be effective in countering the politics of anger and disgust.

The final element of mass–elite gaps that might fruitfully be developed pertains to representation in nondemocratic contexts. Clearly, the study of this raises a range of empirical challenges, including data reliability when citizens may feel unable to express their true policy and other preferences. However, there is also ample evidence that nondemocratic regimes seek and can succeed in building social support, both for specific policies and for the regime itself, and that substantial representational gaps can also emerge that may be politically highly consequential for regime stability. The discussion above in this chapter and the insights of this book generally also raise broader theoretical questions that need to be considered. Indeed, a number of the empirical chapters in this book have pointed to the variety of gaps that nondemocratic politics have opened. In the Tunisian case, elites chose consensus over religion, thus opening a mass–elite gap on the issue as they pacted for democracy; in Egypt, the decision by the Muslim Brotherhood to politicize a form of Islamism intensified its salience and led to a political crisis, to the detriment of democracy in the country. In Indonesia, the nondemocratic turn led to the suppression of religious and class cleavages. To what extent, though, are these cases typical of nondemocratic mass–elite gaps? At least part of the answer may lie in a better understanding of the salient issue divide in nondemocratic states. Research shows that nondemocratic elites have incentives to build social support (Chaisty and Whitefield 2023). They also have nondemocratic mechanisms for obtaining information about citizens' preferences, through controlled "civil society" organizations, state surveillance, and the technologies of polling and social research as developed in democratic states. Feedback may be limited but it is not necessarily absent. At the same time, such regimes will alienate large groups of citizens, both those who are outside of the targeted economic support and those who object to the regime type and who feel deeply unrepresented not only in policy terms but also by the system of (non)representation.

The question then concerns the most relevant dimension on which to judge mass–elite gaps in such polities. Is it a gap in policy across a range of dimensions? Or a gap over system-level issues? If the former, there is no a priori reason to believe that gaps must be systematically higher in nondemocratic states than others. If the latter, then elites in such regimes may also have advantages and strategies to position themselves directionally in a more moderate position on the regime structure than societal forces that may be more polarized on the question—between even more radical hardliners and revolutionary democrats. As the shifting strategies of the Vladimir Putin regime in Russia indicate, a gap in which the regime is between two politically, economically, and socially destabilizing poles in society may well be an effective strategy for regime stability (Chaisty and Whitefield 2013), and the danger to the regime may well appear most powerful when its elites choose to align with one extreme over the other.

By highlighting each of these areas for further research our intent is not to focus on what this excellent book misses. Its theoretical and empirical scope are already ambitiously broad and deep. Rather, it is to emphasize the framework that the book elaborates and how it may be applied to a set of issues that are of substantive importance to the stability of representative systems.

Notes

1. We note also that there are central areas of congruence research that are only marginally considered in the book and over which a great deal of ink has already been spilled, in particular on the question of the role that institutions, especially electoral systems, play in fostering or reducing mass–elite gaps. See Golder and Stramski 2010; Ezrow et al. 2011. This literature is often empirically inconclusive. From the perspective of this book, however, institutions themselves may be the result of elite choices during critical junctures, as for example in the case study of Indonesia's presidential system.

2. Stephen Whitefield is currently embarked on a collaborative project that is analyzing political texts and their reception for emotional content to determine the extent to which elites and citizens align in this respect, and how emotional appeals may link to broader political programs. See "Neoauthoritarianisms in Europe and the Liberal Democratic Response." Horizon/UKRI funded project, www.authlib.eu

References

Anderson, Christopher J., and Aida Just. 2013. "Legitimacy from Above: The Partisan Foundations of Support for the Political System in Democracies." *European Political Science Review* 5 (3): 335–62.

Capoccia, G. 2016. "Critical Junctures." In *The Oxford Handbook of Historical Institutionalism*, edited by Orfeo Fioretos, Tulia G. Falleti, and Adam Sheingate, 89–112. Oxford: Oxford University Press.

Chaisty, P., and S. Whitefield. 2023. "Building Voting Coalitions in Electoral Authoritarian Regimes: A Case Study of the 2020 Constitutional Reform in Russia." *Post-Soviet Affairs* 39 (4): 273–90. https://doi.org/10.1080/1060586X.2023.2172945

Chaisty, P., and S. Whitefield. 2022. "How Challenger Parties Can Win Big with Frozen Cleavages: Explaining the Landslide Victory of the Servant of the People Party in the 2019 Ukrainian Parliamentary Elections." *Party Politics* 28 (1): 115–26. https://doi.org/10.1177/13540688209654

Chaisty, P., and S. Whitefield. 2013. "Forward to Democracy or Back to Authoritarianism? The Attitudinal Bases of Mass Support for the Russian Election Protests of 2011–12." *Post-Soviet Affairs* 29 (5): 387–403.

Converse, P. E. 1964. "The Nature of Belief Systems in Mass Publics." In *Ideology and Its Discontents*, edited by D. E. Apter, 206–61. New York: Free Press of Glencoe.

Dalton, R., D. Farrell, and I. McAllister. 2011. *Political Parties and Democratic Linkage: How Parties Organise Democracy.* Oxford: Oxford University Press.

Ezrow, L., C. De Vries, M. Steenbergen, and E. Edwards. 2011. "Mean Voter Representation and Partisan Constituency Representation: Do Parties Respond to the Mean Voter Position or to Their Supporters?" *Party Politics* 17 (3): 275–301. https://doi.org/10.1177/1354068810372100

Golder, M., and J. Stramski. 2010. "Ideological Congruence and Electoral Institutions." *American Journal of Political Science* 54 (1): 90–106.

Heath, O. 2013. "Policy Representation, Social Representation and Class Voting in Britain." *British Journal of Political Science* 45 (1): 173–93.

Kosmidis, S., S. Hobolt, E. Molloy, and S. Whitefield. 2019. "Party Competition and Emotive Rhetoric." *Comparative Political Studies* 52 (6): 811–37.

Lipset, S. M., and S. Rokkan, eds. 1967. *Party Systems and Voter Alignments: Cross-National Perspectives.* New York: Free Press.

Meguid, B. M. 2005. "Competition between Unequals: The Role of Mainstream Party Competition in Niche Party Success." *American Political Science Review* 99 (3): 327–46.

Norris, P. 2011. *Democratic Deficit: Critical Citizens Revisited.* Cambridge: Cambridge University Press.

Putnam, R. D. 1976. *The Comparative Study of Political Elites.* Englewood Cliffs, NJ: Prentice-Hall.

Przeworksi, A. 1991. *Democracy and the Market.* Cambridge: Cambridge University Press.

Rohrschneider, R., and S. Whitefield. 2012. *The Strain of Representation: How Parties Represent Diverse Voters in Western and Eastern Europe.* Oxford: Oxford University Press.

Rohrschneider, R., and S. Whitefield. 2016. "Responding to Growing EU-Skepticism? The Stances of Political Parties towards European Integration in Western and Eastern Europe Following the Financial Crisis." *European Union Politics* 17 (1): 138–61.

Rovny, J. 2012. "Who Emphasizes and Who Blurs? Party Strategies in Multidimensional Competition." *European Union Politics* 13 (2): 269–92.

Vachudova, M. 2005. *Europe Undivided: Democracy, Leverage and Integration after Communism.* Oxford: Oxford University Press.

Zaller, John. 1992. *The Nature and Origins of Mass Opinion.* Cambridge: Cambridge University Press.

Contributors

Gianfranco Baldini is Associate Professor of Political Science at the University of Bologna. His research focuses on comparative politics in Europe. His latest book is *The Brexit Effect: What Leaving the EU Means for British Politics* (2023). He is currently working on a book on the Brothers of Italy.

Petar Bankov is a lecturer in comparative politics at the University of Glasgow. His work explores the relationship between political parties and local communities with a particular focus on Central and Eastern Europe. Beyond party politics and political geography, he also focuses on political participation and elections.

Simon Bornschier directs the Research Area Political Sociology at the Institute for Political Science at the University of Zurich. His research focuses on the formation and transformation of cleavages and party systems in Western Europe and Latin America. Personal homepage: www.simon-bornschier.eu

Mahmoud Farag is a postdoctoral fellow at the Department of Political Science, Goethe University, Frankfurt, Germany. His research interests include democratization, authoritarianism, cleavage politics, and Middle Eastern politics. His research has appeared in *Government & Opposition*, *European Political Science*, *Mediterranean Politics*, and *PS: Political Science & Politics*, among others.

Sergiu Gherghina is Associate Professor in Comparative Politics at the Department of Politics and International Relations, University of Glasgow. His research interests lie in party politics, legislative and voting behavior, democratization, and the use of direct democracy.

Matteo Giglioli has taught political science at various universities in the United States and Italy, most recently the University of Bologna. He has published on legitimacy, Italian politics, and populism, and has translated Ernest Renan's political works into English. His current research focus is technology policy, especially surveillance, privacy, and disinformation.

Kenneth Mori McElwain is Professor of Comparative Politics at the Institute of Social Science, University of Tokyo. His research focuses on comparative political institutions, most recently on constitutional design and change in Japan. He also serves as Editor-in-Chief of *Social Science Japan Journal*, published by Oxford University Press.

Andrea Pareschi works at Emilia-Romagna Region's Delegation to the EU and holds a PhD in Political Science and European Politics. He is currently affiliated with the University of Bologna and the Ca' Foscari University of Venice. His research interests include European politics, Euroscepticism, populism, mass-elite congruence, and British politics.

Robert Rohrschneider is the Sir Robert Worcester Distinguished Professor in Political Science at the University of Kansas. He has recently coedited, with Jacques Thomassen, the *Oxford Handbook of Political Representation* (2020), and has a very long list of other publications on parties, European politics, and political culture.

Jaemin Shim is Assistant Professor at the Department of Government and International Studies at the Hong Kong Baptist University. His primary research interests lie in democratic representation, comparative welfare states, gender, and legislative politics. He is currently leading the Global Mass-Elite Discrepancy Project (GMED) and Gender and Policy-Vote Trade-Offs Project.

Andreas Ufen is a Senior Research Fellow at the German Institute for Global and Area Studies, Hamburg, and Adjunct Professor for Political Science at the University of Hamburg. His main research interests are political parties, democratization, and digital repression in Southeast Asia, especially in Indonesia and Malaysia.

Stephen Whitefield is Professor of Politics in the Department of Politics and International Relations, and Fellow in Politics, Pembroke College, University of Oxford. He and Robert Rohrschneider have many joint publications, including *The Strain of Representation* (2012).

Index

actor-centered approach, 116
Allied Occupation, 30, 197, 200, 206, 217n3
annexation of Crimea, 236
anticommunism, 103, 123, 125, 129–30
Arab Spring, 148, 161
Argentina, politics, 131–32
Article, 9, constitution, 197, 201, 203, 206–7, 212, 213–15, 216. *See also* constitutional revision
authoritarian turn, 123–25, 177–78, 234, 254

Borisov, Boyko, 233
Bornschier, Simon, 96, 98, 119, 124, 149
broad coalitions, 122, 131, 183–85

Capoccia, Giovanni, 4, 99, 110n3, 248
cartel politics, 179, 182–85
Central and Eastern Europe, 225
charisma-based politics, 131–32
clientelism, 124, 129, 190
Cold War, politics, 33, 124–25, 198
Colombia, politics, 127–30
commercialization of politics, 188
common frameworks, 248, 261. *See also* theoretical framework
comparative analysis, 2, 135
constitutional drafting, 156, 160

constitutional revision, 29–30, 197–99, 206–9, 211, 213, 216
content analysis, 230
counterfactuals, 103, 160–61, 185
critical junctures, 4–5, 10, 26, 80, 98–108, 115–16, 120–21, 126, 148–49, 157–58, 161, 176, 182, 185, 200, 203–4, 229, 235–36, 248–50, 253, 255, 261n1
Czechia, politics, 74

data gathering, 228–29
data reliability, 260
datasets, primary examples
    Arab Barometer survey, 150, 152–53, 164–65
    Comparative Study of Electoral System (CSES), 28
    election manifestos, 151, 155
    EU Engage survey, 64–65, 81–83
    Eurobarometer, 62, 225, 229
    The University of Tokyo–*Asahi* Survey (UTAS), 207–9, 217n5, 218n6
data triangulation, 148, 156
dealignment, 123, 176, 188, 190
democracies, new, 1, 27, 31–32, 33, 93, 98, 100, 107–8, 116, 119–25, 149, 162, 222, 228, 251
democracies, old, 12n1, 33, 97, 107–9
democracies, representative, 1, 18, 64, 103, 106